AF653029

# Tribal Women in India

# Tribal Women in India

V.M. Rao

ABD PUBLISHERS
Jaipur ■ New Delhi

**ABD PUBLISHERS**

**Regd. Off.** "Bony Residency", Gate No. 2
Opp. Tilak Public School, Vishweswariya Nagar,
Gopalpura Road, Jaipur - 302018, India
Ph: 0141 - 2761280, Telefax: 2761381
Email: abdpublishersjpr@gmail.com

**Delhi Office:** 102, 1st Floor, Satyam House,
4327/3, Ansari Road, Darya Ganj,
New Delhi - 110002, India
Ph: 011-45652440

visit us: www.oxfordbookcompany.com

Published in India, 2023

© All Rights Reserved

ISBN : 978-8183760228

Price : ₹ 1625/-

All Rights Reserved. Neither this publication nor any part thereof may be reproduced, stored in a retrieval system, or transmitted, in any form or by any means, electronic, mechanical, photocopying, recording, scanning or otherwise, without the prior written permission of the copyright owner.

Typeset by Shivangi Computer, Jaipur

Printed and bound in India by Thomson Press Ltd.,
New Delhi

# Acknowledgments

My association with tribals started in 1995 with a research project on revitalisation of cooperatives in a viable manner in Tripura. Subsequently, I had the privilege of preparing 'integrated development project for Arunachal Pradesh', and 'socio-economic status of tribal women in Arunachal Pradesh'. The latter was bought out as a book by a Delhi based publisher. Since then, I have been impressed by these innocent, simple living, colourful and light heated people. During this period, I had come across literature on GCC which tempted me to take up the present project. It is funded by Department of Personnel and Training, Ministry of Personnel, Public Grievances, and Pensions, Government of India, New Delhi. I am extremely thankful to the Ministry for the support as also putting up with the delay.

I am also thankful to Shri Bhagwati Prasad, Director, VMNICM for providing necessary administrative support in conducting the study.

My heart felt thanks are due to Shri A. Vidyasagar, IAS, Vice Chairman, and Managing Director of GCC, Visakhapatnam. It would have been impossible to collect primary data covering 105 women members spread over 21 societies drawn from four divisions that too in naxal-prone areas. Shri Vidyasagar also extended help in collecting secondary data from headquarters, divisional offices, as also provided possible logistics during field visits.

I am grateful to four divisional managers (Shri. V. Apparao, Shri. S. Adinarayana, Shri. K. Rajeswar Rao, and Shri. R.P. Singh) for the support extended during field visits. I am indebted to managers of all 21 GPCMSs, and host of employees associated with these societies. It would not have been possible to complete the book without their cooperation. They also educated me on minute details in functioning of these societies, and peculiar problems being faced.

Special thanks are due to 105 respondents for providing necessary information as also some of their husbands who created congenial environment for interviews. Help extended by Dr. R. Ramakrishna, Associate Professor, Department of Cooperation and Applied Economics, Andhra University, Waltair in getting literature on developmental programmes for tribals in Andhra Pradesh is also acknowledged.

Thanks are also due to Mrs. Priyanka P. Lakade, and Mrs. Laxmi R. Koshatwar who typed the manuscript, and inserted necessary corrections. Finally, all observations and inferences are my own, and I will be responsible for defects, if any, in the manuscript.

**V.M. Rao**

# Preface

Tribal population in India is spread over various states with wide variations in their cultures and socio-economic status. Due tc seclusion from general population in the country, they remained backward in many respects. Initial thinking about tribal development was that these people should develop along the lines of their own genius without any impositions, their rights on land and forests he protected, they should be trained for administration and development and their cultures and rites should not be interfered with. During last 58 years a number of development programmes were introduced to bring them closer to the modern world. Statutory provision, education and communication facilities helped them in getting employment, contracts, entering business and politics and adopting improved means of farming.

Tribal women are an integral part of the society and have equal status with their men. In addition to attending the domestic chores, they also perform various activities like tending animals, collection of MFP, fetching water, fuel wood collection, farming and construction. Bride price is universal among tribes and divorce and remarriage are permitted. In addition to provision in the constitution, government has endeavouring and promoting schemes for all-round amelioration and development of socio-economic conditions of tribal women. Towards this aim cooperative societies and self-help groups have done a great lot by providing alternate means of income generation to these tribal women and thereby bringing general well-being of these women and their families. Moreover, these organisations make tribal women aware about various government schemes launched for their benefit, provide literacy, mobility, access to information and health care.

The present book makes an in-depth research into status and role of tribal women, role of cooperative movement and self-help groups in the development and amelioration of these women, effect and outcomes of activities and help of these organisations and recommendations and suggestions for further improvement. All the facts are supported through data in numerous tables.

**V.M. Rao**

# Contents

# Contents

# 1

# Introduction

## Tribal life

Tribals are the fortunate once who shunned the bustle of war-infested plains and made the blessed hills and forests their home. Their simple life is their profound message. To them, every hill, dale, river, forest, and field is blessed by the Mother's presence. They have forged a symbiotic relationship with forest. Their houses, set in sylvan surroundings, are built of locally available materials. Their possessions are a bear minimum essential for life. Tribal economy revolves around subsistence and self-sufficiency. Agriculture is largely to meet domestic demand while collection, and sale of forest produce helps meet cash expenditure. Value-time is devoted to festivals, dancing, and celebration, and thus rightly been described as light-hearted (Ram, 2004). They are reputed for their honesty. Tribals follow no scripture. Since they are away from mainstream for millions of years, we consider them as 'uncivilised' and 'underdeveloped'.

## Tribals of Andhra Pradesh

Andhra Pradesh is the traditional home of 33 recognised scheduled tribes[1] (STs). Areas inhabited by STs account for nearly 11% of the total geographical area of the state, and constitute 7%

of the total population. They are concentrated in Srikakulam, Vizianagaram, Visakhapatnam, East Godavari, West Godavari, Khammam, Warangal, Adilabad, and Mahaboobnagar districts. Lumbada, Koya, Konda Reddi, Gond, Bhagata, Kotia, Konda Dora, Nooka Dora, Khond, Porja, Gadaba, Mali, Goudu, Kammara, Valmiki, Chenchu, Savara, etc. are some of the tribal groups. Except tribes living in plains (Yerukula, Yandi, and Sugali), they live in the hilly and forest tracts of the coastal districts and Telangana region whose habitat is contiguous to the tribal areas of Orissa, Madhya Pradesh and Maharashtra. Some of the major tribal groups like Koya, Gond, Kola, Lambada, Saara, Khond, Gadaba, Porja, Bagata, Konda Dora etc. are found living on either side of the state boundary. Some of the tribes like Konda Reddi and Chenchu confined to Andhra Pradesh only.

Their economy are predominantly agro-forest based, and earn precarious livelihood from innumerable small fragments of settled and podu lands. As tribal agriculture is characterised by small holdings and low yields, income is inadequate and unpredictable. Since these earnings cannot sustain tribals throughout the year, they fall back on forests for sustenance by collecting various minor forest produce to supplement their meager incomes.

## Developmental programs for tribals

Tribal perspectives on forests, and government policies affecting forests have followed different trajectories. State policies driven by industrial demands were in direct conflict with customary use of forest tribals. Colonial state, and post-independence forest policies since 1984 have characterised tribals as indiscriminate users of forests and therefore sought to protect forests from the tribals, and thus were not allowed to collect produce from forests.

With a view to mitigate hardships of these people, governments (both centre and state) have been extending help through various schemes/programs. Initially, multipurpose co-operative societies were organised for overall development of these groups which were replaced by Andhra Pradesh STs Finance and Development Corporation in 1955. Later, it was renamed as Andhra Pradesh Scheduled Tribes Cooperative

Finance and Development Corporation (APSTCFDC) in 1956 which was again renamed as Girijan Cooperative Corporation (GCC) Limited in 1970.[2]

Major objectives of the GCC are (a) to purchase minor forest produce and agricultural produce outright at remunerative prices from tribals, (b) to maintain daily requirement depots in the tribal areas to cater to the daily needs of locals, and (c) to provide credit facilities to tribals for agricultural purpose.[3] GCC has been paying royalty to department of forestry on befalf of tribals so as to enable them to collect forest based products without any difficulty. Presence of GCC in the tribal areas is expected to get higher prices to MFP, greater inflow of money, and gradual stabilisation of prices of MFP in the market. GCC encourages formation of Girijan Primary Cooperative Marketing Societies (GPCMSs) by enrolling members at the village level. GCC has 9 divisions and 43 GPCMSs. Division-wise distribution of GPCMSs are provided in Appendix 1. These primaries have been facing many problems in procurement due to steady decline in area under forest and the resultant decrease in MFP, and unscrupulous competition from private traders. Further, problem is compounded by heavy loan outstanding.

## Status of tribal women

It is a universal truth that status of tribal women is better compared to their counterparts in plains. They are an integral part of the society and have equal status with their men. Women attend variety of activities including household chores, podu, raising animals, collection of minor forest produce, fetching water, fuel wood, and construction works. Tribal household is oval around women who is considered as an asset for the parents, and bride price is universal. Variety of marriages (negotiations, service, capture, intrusion, mutual love and elopement, and exchange) are in practice. Levirate, sororate, and polygamy are sanctioned by tradition among these tribes. Divorce and widow remarriages are permitted and association of customary prescriptions is common (Rio, undated).

The government has realised the importance of women in tribal communities and has been aiming at enrolling them as members. GCC has been encouraging women to form self help groups and providing finance. An attempt is made in this study to observe involvement of women in business operations, management of GPCMSs, and would suggest interventions, if necessary, for enhancing their participation.

## Objectives

The study aims at evaluating performance of GCC and enhancing participations of women in organisation and management of GPMCSs. Specific objectives of the study are

a. to provide an overview of various governmental programs for emancipation of tribals,
b. to analyse the performance of Girijan Cooperative Corporation in terms of procurement of MFP and agricultural produce, supply of essential commodities, and provision of credit,
c. to evaluate progress of selected divisions and GPCMSs,
d. to observe socio-economic background of tribal women and their involvement in SHGs,
e. to understand participation of women in procurement and marketing of MFPs, and
f. to suggest measures enhancing participation of women in GPCMSs which intern help increasing the business, and socio-economic status of women.

## Methodology

Girijan Cooperative Corporation (Andhra Pradesh) is selected for the study mainly because of its long standing and variety of services being extended to tribals in remote and far flung areas of the state. Secondary data for the period 1992–2003 were collected to evaluate performance of GCC. Based on membership, turnover, and facilities extended, a moderate sample of 21 GPCMSs (49% of total GPCMSs) from 4 divisions (Bhadrachalam, Chintapalli, Paderu, and Srisailam) (30% of total divisions) representing 3 regions of Andhra Pradesh were selected. Five women members from each selected society were interviewed (Table 1) using a pre-tested questionnaire to understand their socio-economic background and levels of participation the activities of GPCMSs. Discussions with village elders, officials, and non-officials were also conducted to know the role of women in the working of GPCMSs. Data were collected during October 2003 to February 2004.

**Table 1 Coverage of sample GPCMSs, and respondents**

| *Sr. No.* | *Division* | *GPCMSs* | *Sample respondents* |
|---|---|---|---|
| 1. | Bhadrachalam | 8 | 40 |
| 2. | Chintapalli | 4 | 20 |
| 3. | Paderu | 6 | 30 |
| 4. | Srisailam | 3 | 15 |
| | Total | 21 | 105 |

*Source*: Field visits

## Organisation of report

The report is presented in nine chapters. Chapter 1 is devoted to tribal Andhra Pradesh, developmental programs, status of tribal women, objectives, methodology, and chapterisation. A review of few developmental programs aimed at tribals is contained in Chapter 2. Profile of GCC is provided in Chapter 3, and progress of selected divisions of GCC contained in Chapter 4. Performance of selected GPCMSs is discussed in Chapter 5. Socio-economic analysis of women respondents is covered in Chapter 6. Involvement of women in SHGs also formed part of Chapter 6. Procurement and marketing of MFP by women is given in Chapter 7, and selected case histories formed part of Chapter 8. Summary and policy prescriptions are included in Chapter 9.

---

*Notes*:

1. Scheduled Tribes are those, which are notified by the President of India under Article 342 of the Constitution. The first notification was issued in 1950. The President considers characteristics like the tribes' primitive traits, distinctive culture, shyness with the public at large, geographical isolation, and social

and economic backwardness before notifying them as a Scheduled Tribe. Seventy-five of the 698 Scheduled Tribes are identified as Primitive Tribal Groups considering they are more backward than Scheduled Tribes. For a detailed discussion on the term tribe, see Rao (2003).

2. Though these areas are widely known for most of non-timber forest produce or minor forest produce (MFP), open market forces are playing havoc with tribal economy and thus, GCC's responsibility is to procure a major quantity of MFP at reasonable price brought by tribals.
3. More details on GCC are provided in Chapter 3.

# 2

# Policy Initiatives for Tribal Development

An attempt is made in this chapter to provide a succinct review of policy interventions made by the Government of India for tribal development.

## Tribals in British India

British administrators made serious efforts for gaining full control over tribal areas by extending laws made for the general population of the Madras province. British India witnessed a series of widespread disturbances (Kol Mutiny of 1831, Santal rebellion of 1885, Birsa movement, and Rampa rebellion, and Alluri Sitaram Raju's[1] uprising). These tribal revolts point out imposition of laws made for general public of the state, and any amount of force or coercion would not succeed. Therefore, Britishers took several conciliatory measures in this regard. As a result Ganjam-Vizagapatam Act of 1839 was enacted to exclude tribal areas in the then Ganjam and Vizagapatam districts of the then Madras presidency. Scheduled District Act[2] was extended to tribal areas in 1874 to remove them from the operation of general laws. Under the scheduled district act, tribal areas (scheduled areas) were designated as scheduled districts.

After the Kol Mutiny, Britishers realized that general laws and regulations intended for general population of Bengal and Bihar were not suitable for tribal areas and hence the Regulation 13 of Bengal as promulgated. Captain T. Wilkinson, an agent of governor general, framed special rules called Wilkinson Rules for administration of Civil justice in tribal areas (Rao, undated). These rules stressed the need for active involvement of traditional institutions and traditional functionaries of local tribes. Subsequently, agency courts were constituted and agency rules were issued for administration of civil and criminal justice. Under these agency rules, executive magistrates working in the tribal areas were empowered with necessary powers to administer justice. The special status accorded to scheduled areas under Scheduled Districts Act of 1874 was continued under the Government of India Act, 1935 under which the tribal areas were called partially excluded areas.

## Policies in the independent India

Constitution of India faithfully incorporated comprehensive provisions to safeguard interests of scheduled tribes. Article 46 of the constitution places special responsibility on the state not only for promotion with special care for educational and economic interests of scheduled tribes, among others, but also for protection of the scheduled thibes from social injustice and all forms of exploitation. Articles 15, 16, 17, and 19 make exceptions in favour of scheduled tribes to pursue the noble directives. The special provisions are embodied in the fifth schedule under which a governor may by notification direct that any particular act of parliament or the legislature of the state shall not apply to the scheduled areas or any part thereof. These provisions enable the governor to pursue special legal frame to the scheduled areas analogous to the one in the sixth schedule areas applicable to the north-east. Though the association of cooperatives with tribal areas of India has started with few Christian missionaries, it was only after 1974 that the role of local self government agencies, and cooperatives came to be substantially expanded.

## Bawa Committee

In the 1970's increased concern with small farmers and difficulties of extending green revolution to tribal areas led to fresh interest in these issues. The Bawa Committee (1971)[3] was set up for tribal areas and recommended the Large-sized Agricultural Multi-purpose Cooperative Societies (LAMPs) as a part of tribal sub-plan areas. Similar recommendations were also proposed by Datey Committee (1974). LAMPs were basically a modification of FSS and were thought of as possible organisations both at the taluka level as well as for smaller areas covering group of villages. LAMPs had a larger government representation, more emphasis on local leadership and even greater emphasis on covering all aspects of economic development. The strategy was one of a controlled modernisation and a channelised commercialisation rather than the open commercialisation thought of as tribal areas. They were intended to provide production (short, medium, and long term) as well as consumption credit (a) to undertake marketing and agricultural minor forest produce, (b) to supply fertilisers and other agricultural production requisites, and (c) distribution of consumer goods so that tribals get all their requirements from a single agency.

Greater attention on tribals was focused during Fifth Five Year Plan. The plan envisaged, among others, (a) narrowing down the gap between the level of development in tribal and other areas, (b) improving the quality of life of tribals, (c) bringing about social and cultural integration, and (d) prevention of their exploitation. Keeping this in view, areas having 50% or more of tribal population were delineated and sub-plans envisaged (Rao, 1990). Tribal sub-plan (TSP) is being used to allot funds and planned development. Every central ministry and state government is to draw a sub-plan within the overall plan and allot funds in proportion to the percentage of tribal population. State level cooperative tribal development federations were also organised to promote marketing of minor forest produce and also for supply of essential consumer goods to the tribals.

## TRIFED

Tribal Cooperative Marketing Development Federation of India Limited (TRIFED) was constituted by Government of India in 1987 under the Multi-state Cooperative Societies Act of 1984. If is an apex level federation of state tribal development cooperative federations, and state forest corporations. TRIFED's specific attention is on to provide marketing requirements of forest and agriculture produce of tribal people and to ensure remunerative prices. Specific objectives of TRIFED are (a) to secure higher earnings and generate employment opportunities for the tribal people, (b) to create awareness of the interplay of market forces among tribals, (c) to provide assured markets and remunerative prices for tribal produce and also to undertake price support operations wherever required, (d) to provide marketing and financial support to state-level tribal cooperatives and forest corporations, and (e) to provide full range of services, including organisation and collection of MFP.

### Recent initiatives

Due to enforcement of the provisions of the Panchayats (Extension to the Scheduled Areas), Act 1996 (PESA Act), STs have got political empowerment in the nine major states. In all, 2.44 lakhs seats were reserved for the STs in the three panchayati raj institutions. Government of India constituted Ministry of Tribal Affairs in October 1999 to give more focused attention to the development of STs. Further, a National Commission for Scheduled Areas and Scheduled Tribes (NCSAST) was set up under Article 339(1) of the constitution aimed at reporting on administration of scheduled areas and welfare of STs (Anonymous, 2004).

Government also established Scheduled Tribes Finance and Development Corporation (NSTFDC) with an authorised share capital of Rs. 500 crores was set up in 2001 for financing economically viable projects. As a part of NSTFDC Adivasi Mahila Sashaktikaran Yojana was started for extending financial assistance up to Rs. 50,000 to the eligible scheduled tribe women at subsidised rates of interest. During 2002, the parliament passed SCs and STs Order (Amendment) Act, 2002. This Act provides for inclusion/exclusion/modification of 270 communities in the lists of STs. A separate National Commission for STs is being set up with five members. The bill has already been passed by the parliament.

## National policy on tribals

The policy seeks to bring Scheduled Tribes into mainstream of society through a multi-pronged approach for their all-round development without disturbing their distinct culture. The draft policy focuses its attention on education, health, preservation of culture, and traditional knowledge. National policy recognises that a majority of Scheduled Tribes continue to live below the poverty line, have poor literacy rates, suffer from malnutrition and disease and are vulnerable to displacement.

As regards literacy, draft policy proposes inclusion of tribals in national program of education for all (Sarva Shiksha Abhiyan) run by the Ministry of Human Resource Development. The document also mentioned special incentives like financial assistance, pocket allowance, free distribution of textbooks and school uniforms to tribal children are provided. The policy will link literacy program with supplementary nutrition to overcome nutritional problems. Emphasis was laid on properly documenting and preserving invaluable traditional knowledge. Efforts also would be made to establish centres to train tribal youth in areas of traditional wisdom. National Policy seeks to promote the modern health care system and also a synthesis of the Indian systems of medicine like ayurved and siddha with the tribal system. It is also envisaged to (a) expand number of hospitals in tune with tribal population, (b) to promote cultivation of medicinal plants related value addition strategies through imparting training to youth, and (c) to encourage qualified doctors from tribal communities to serve tribal areas.

As regards resettlement, each scheduled tribe family having land in the earlier settlement shall be given land against land. Also preservation benefits enjoyed at the original settlement shall be continued at the resettlement area and the national policy suggested that any forceful displacement should be avoided. Policy also touched upon important issues like shifting cultivation, land alienation, intellectual property rights, tribal languages, primitive tribes,[4] scheduled tribes and scheduled areas, etc.

## Summary

The special status accorded to scheduled areas under Scheduled Districts Act of 1874 was continued under the Government of India Act, 1935 under which tribal areas were called partially excluded areas. Article 46 of the constitution places special responsibility on the state. Articles 15, 16, 17, and 19 make exception in favour of scheduled tribes to pursue noble directives. The Bawa Committee (1971) recommended large sized agricultural multipurpose cooperative societies as a part of tribal sub-plan areas. Greater attention on tribals was focused during Fifth Five Year Plan. Tribal sub-plan is being used to allot funds and planned development. State level cooperative tribal development federations were also organised to promote marketing of minor forest produce and also supply of essential consumer goods. Further, Trifed was constituted in 1987 with a view to provide marketing requirements of forest and agriculture produce of forest people and to ensure remunerative prices.

Government of India constituted Ministry of Tribal Affairs in October 1999 to give more focused attention of the development of STs. Further, a National Commission for Scheduled Areas and Scheduled Tribes was set up to report on administration of the scheduled areas and welfare of STs followed by a National Policy on tribals which seeks to bring STs into mainstream. The draft policy focuses its attention on education, health, preservation of culture, and traditional knowledge.

---

*Notes:*

1. For more details on Alluri Sitarama Raju, see Appendix 2 (Rao and Rao, 1982).
2. For more details on scheduled areas regulation, see Rao (2003).
3. Shri K.S. Bawa was a joint secretary in the Department of Cooperation, Government of India

4. Primitive Tribal Groups (PTGs) are Scheduled Tribes known for their declining or stagnant population, low levels of literacy, re-agricultural technology, and primarily belonging to hunting and gathering stage, and extreme backwardness, they were considered as a special category for support in 1979. There are 75 such PTGs spread over 15 states and UTs. The 25 lakhs PTGs population constitutes nearly 3.6% of the tribal population and 0.3% of the country's population.

# 3

# Performance of GCC

This chapter is aimed at reviewing various activities of GCC during last 20 years. Performance is studied in terms of procurement of MFP, agriculture produce, supply of daily requirements, and credit operations.

## Mandate of GCC

As mentioned in Chapter 1, GCC has changed its name thrice during the last 50 years. It was registered as a cooperative society in 1970 under the Andhra Pradesh Cooperative Societies Act of 1964. As per bye-laws, its operations shall extend to scheduled areas of the state as also non-scheduled areas where Girijans live in substantial numbers. However, its operations in the non-scheduled (tribal) areas should have the prior approval of the board of directors.

## Objectives

Bye-laws provided, in all, 14 objectives, and some of them are (GCC, 1999):

(a) to purchase MFP and agriculture produce brought by scheduled tribes through affiliated primary marketing societies, and market it to the best advantage of the members,

(b) to undertake processing and grading of MFP and other produce for the benefit of the corporation, affiliated societies, and members,
(c) to supply daily requirements of the members through affiliated societies by making bulk purchases,
(d) to sanction consumption and term loans to GPCMSs for provision to their members, and
(e) to encourage self help, thrift, and cooperation among the affiliated societies and their members.

The management of the corporation shall vest in a board of directors consisting of not more than 18 members of whom 5 non-official directors shall be elected by the general body representing 2 from Telangana region and 3 from Andhra region. Two members to be nominated by the Ministry of Welfare (Ministry of Tribal Affairs), Government of India while the remaining 11 directors including chairman, vice-chairman and managing director shall be nominated by the Government of Andhra Pradesh. The board of directors shall hold office for a period of 3 years from the date of assumption of charge by the chairman.

Over the years, GCC has appointed number of employees which currently stood at over 1500, and most of them are tribals. Since initial years, employment was provided as a social objective and business operations were not given due attention. As a result, unqualified and under-qualified personnel were employed without adequate training. Same procedure is being followed in procurement of MFP and agriculture produce and supply of essential commodities and credit. Organisational chart of GCC is provided in Chart 1. Initially, GCC opened branches to undertake various activities of its interest. Over the period, these branches were registered as Girijan Primary Cooperative Marketing Societies (GPCMSs). Though GPCMSs were registered as independent cooperative institutions in 1994, none of them have a single employee of their own. All the employees of the GPCMSs are deputed from GCC. Till 1999, GCC received 100% aid from the Government of Andhra Pradesh and in the process lost viability. Due to policy decisions taken by the then Chief Minister, GCC was one among the sick

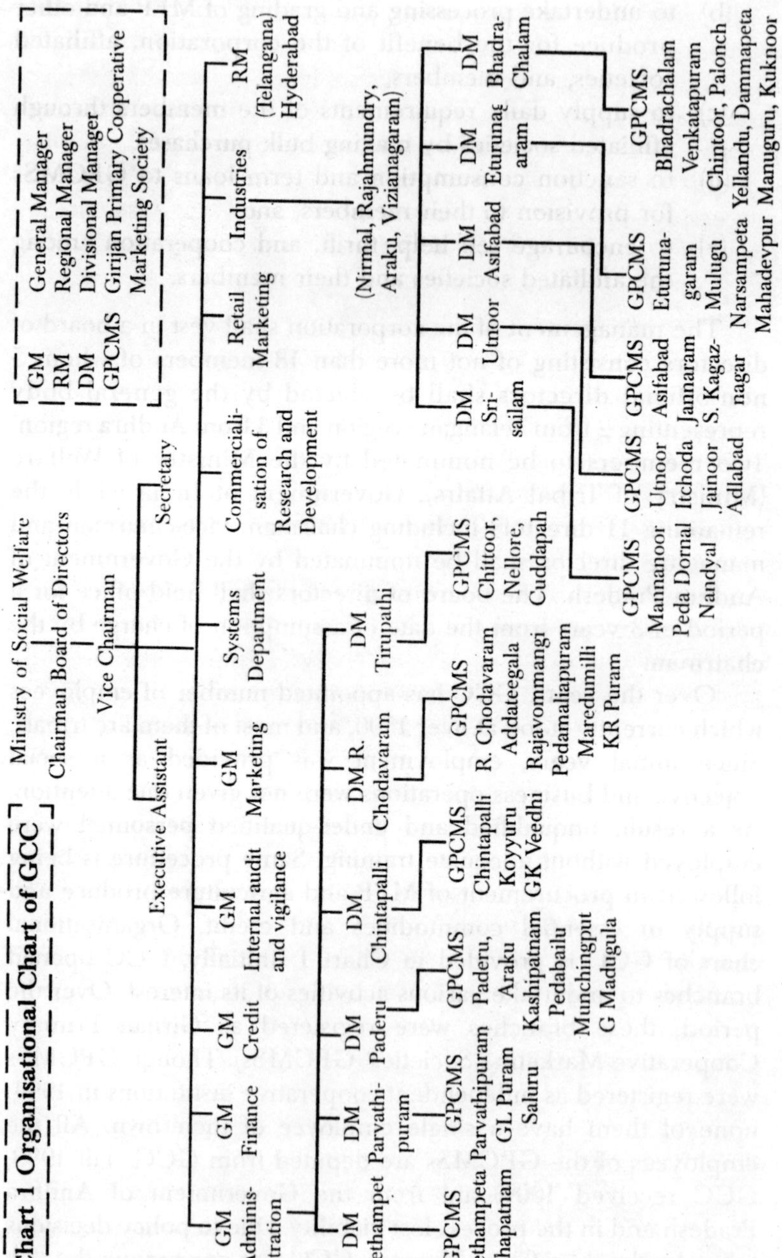


**Chart 1 Organisational Chart of GCC**

units considered to be closed.[1] At this cincture, a dynamic managing director was posted who initiated number of changes and introduced concept of self sufficiency in organisation. Strength of employees was reduced through voluntary retirement scheme. Regular meetings were conduced to percolate the idea of self sufficiency. New markets were explored and number of processing units established. Further, number of disciplinary cases were reduced from 850 in 1999 to 50 in 2003. Brief description about various activities of GCC is provided in the following paragraphs.

## Procurement of MFP and agriculture produce[2]

Procurement is one of the basic functions of GCC. GCC procures MFP and agricultural produce through GPCMSs by giving them a fair price. GCC has monopoly rights on procurement of selected MFPs (Appendix 3). However, such rights are absent in case of agricultural produce.

Procurement is normally done through shandies[2] (weekly markets) by credit-cum-procurement assistants (CCPAs) of GPCMSs. Procurement is also undertaken through various procurement points.[3] This may also take place in the daily requirement depots (DR depots). With a view to cover interior tribal villages and to avoid trekking of long distances by tribals with their produce, GCC has launched focal points. Besides, purchases are also made at the door steps of the tribals. Procurement period varies for MFP to MFP (Appendix 4), and depends on rainfall, humidity, pests, procurement techniques and tools, age of the plant, etc. List of medicinal herbs available in forest areas of Andhra Pradesh along with their uses and availability are provided in Appendix 5. Printed purchase bills are issued to sellers after proper weightment of the stocks and spot payments are made.

Based on past performance, crop prospects and expected market prices, purchase prices are fixed in the beginning of a season. Further, to assess market demand *vis-à-vis* expected rate of a commodity, GCC has been going for disposal of stocks on forward sale basis, whenever feasible.

A separate retail marketing division (RMD) was established

to reach the end consumers directly. The growth in RMD activities has been spectacular. During the last 3–4 years department achieved 30% turnover and the management would like to achieve Rs. 70 crores by the end of 2005. Establishment of processing units was taken up to plough back remunerative prices as also employment generation to tribals. Processing of raw MFP included removal of fiber, seed and foreign matter and packing them in attractive and convenient consumer packs. A list of processing units are provided in Appendix 6. In all, there are 5 processing units under the direct control of GCC. GCC has been manufacturing honey, soaps, processed tamarind, sheekakai powder, soap nut powder, amla powder, french beans, dry chilies etc. A list of various consumers products are provided in Appendix 7.

## Channelising branded products through distribution network

A two tier net work (distributors and retailers) was established to reach out to the end consumers through about 80 distributors and 2 super distributors for Telangana and Rayalaseema regions. Conscious efforts for building brand image through advertisement are also being made. All the products of GCC are sold under the brand name of 'Girijan'. It was contemplated to build awareness about these natural products through rationalised publicity campaign.

## Supply of daily requirements

It is a sales point through which GPCMSs supply essential commodities like rice, kerosene, sugar, wheat, palm oil, etc. under public distribution system (PDS), and also other daily requirements like dhals, soaps, oils, etc. at fair and reasonable prices. Depending upon the concentration of tribals and area of operation, a GPCMS may have depots attached to it. Consequent on the introduction of central scheme for supply of subsidised rice in integrated tribal development project areas, the GPCMSs have been arranging fine and common rice to card holders in the tribal areas. According to the guidelines given earlier by the Government of Andhra

Pradesh, a DR depot was to be opened for total tribal population of 2000.

Besides running retail outlets, GPCMSs have also taken up mandal level stockiest business for distribution of essential commodities on behalf of the Andhra Pradesh essential commodities corporation and Andhra Pradesh Civil Supplies Corporation. Thus, all GPCMSs are presently acting as mandal level stockiests. Transport of essential commodities from the mandal points to the retail outlets has also been taken up by the GPCMSs. After taking over the mandal level stockiest-ship, distribution of essential commodities to the retail outlets has been streamlined.

## Credit activity

Inadequacies and ineffectiveness of the procedures followed by formal credit institutions have proved to be major deterrent for tribal loanees to avail credit facilities. GCC provide loans to the tribal farmers for seasonal agricultural activities at a nominal rate of interest through GPCMSs. The loans are advanced on the basis of area of cultivation, and type of crops raised. The repayment has to be effected soon after harvesting before becoming eligible for loans. Thus, GPCMSs have moved into interior and remote locations and placed their services for the convenience of tribal loanees. GPCMSs takes care of preparation of credit limits, documentation and disbursement of loans at focal points. Further, formation of elders committees from among the loanees and utilising their services for effective execution of loaning operations is part of the GCC's credit policy. The procedure is based on community oriented approach for ensuring coverage of all eligible tribals. Efforts are also made for providing agriculture extension network to improve productivity in these far flung areas. An attempt is made in the following sections to review progress achieved in the above activities. As mentioned in Chapter 1, time series data are used for analysing trends.

## Financial status of GCC

Financial status is studied in the form of membership, share capital, turnover, and net profit/loss, and data for 1981–02 are used (Table 1). GCC has 33 branch offices during 1980–81 which were registered as GPCMSs due to policy change during 1994–95, and since then there was a gradual increase in the GPCMSs which were stabilised at 50. In the reorganisation plan of GCC followed in 2001–02, efforts are being made to reduce the number by merging with nearby GPCMSs. This strategy is being followed with a view to make them vibrant and self-sufficient. As a result, there are 45 such GPCMSs as on today.

Share capital is contributed by both GPCMSs as also Government of Andhra Pradesh. An observation of the composition of share capital reveals that 96% of it comes from Government of Andhra Pradesh while a minuscule percentage is contributed by GPCMSs. This is mainly because majority of GPCMSs are un-viable organisations, and the initial policy was aimed at social service rather than efficient financial management. Over-time, these societies were over-staffed with unqualified personnel. As a result, neither the clientele (tribals) nor employees are happy with the organisation. Share capital increased from Rs. 1.32 crores in 1980–81 to Rs. 20.58 crores in 2001–02. Similarly, turnover increased by 13.42 times during the same period. The federation recorded profits in ten out of the 22 years considered.

## Trends in procurement of MFP

As mentioned elsewhere, procurement has been one of the main functions of GCC. Added to it, GCC has monopoly rights to procure certain MFP from tribal areas. As many as 150 such MFPs are available in the forests of Andhra Pradesh. However, the following analysis covers major MFPs only. Relative shares of various MFPs in the total value of procurement of GCC for selected years are provided in Table 2. Value of procurement was Rs. 40.58 lakhs in 1972–73 which jumped to Rs. 265.58 lakhs by 1982–83, and stood at Rs. 1644.31 lakhs in 2002–03. Thus, there has been a substantial increase in the procurement of MFP during 1973–03. Based on the volume and value of procurement, in all 22 items are identified. However, there are substantial changes in the relative contribution of these commodities over the study period. For example, gum constituted

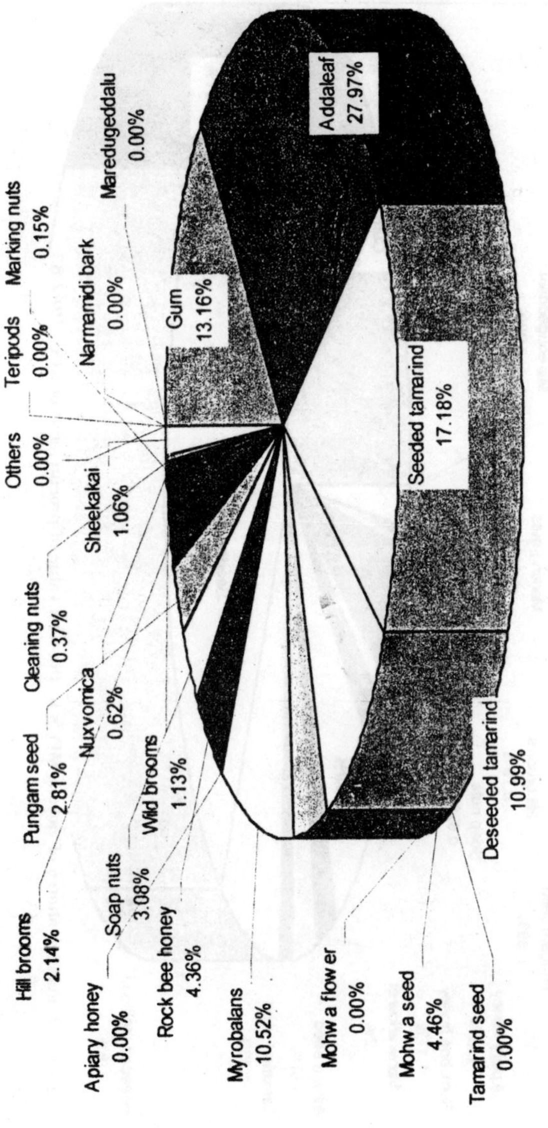


Diagram 1: Relative shares of MFPs in the total value of procurement of GCC, 1972-73

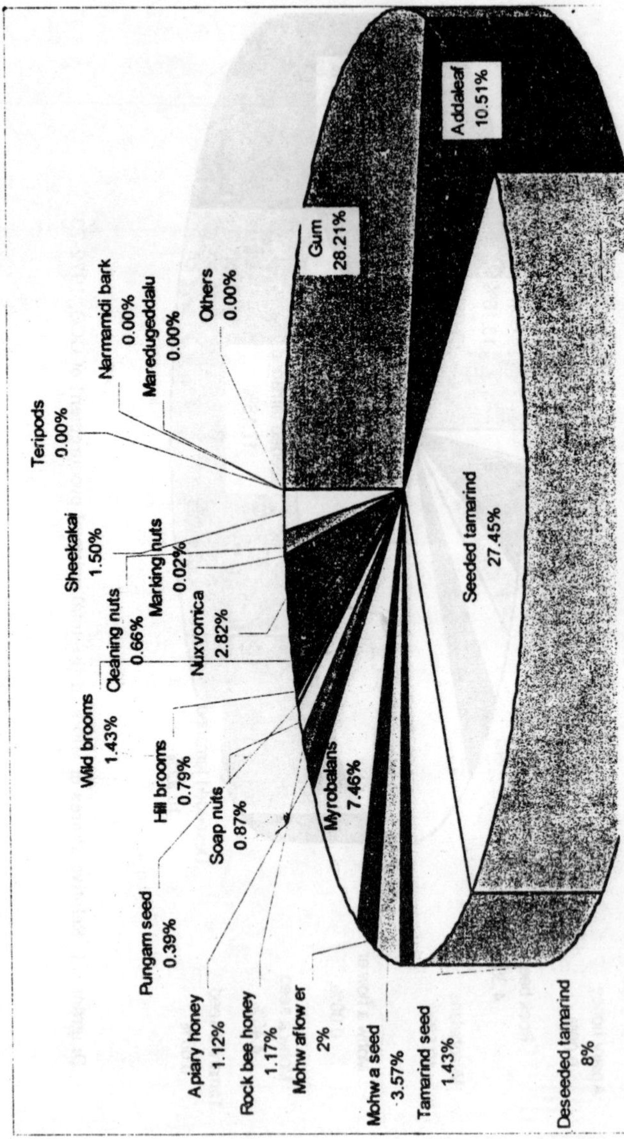


Diagram 2: Relative shares of various MFP's in the total value of procurement of GCC, 1982-83

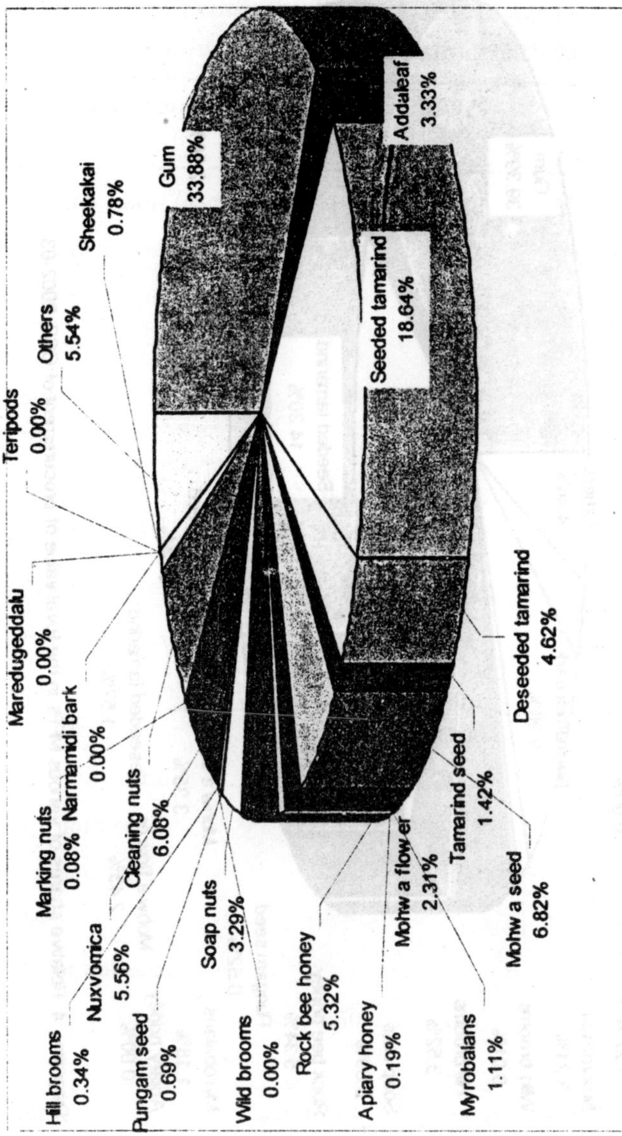


**Diagram 3: Relative shares of MFPs in the total value of procurement of GCC, 1992-93**

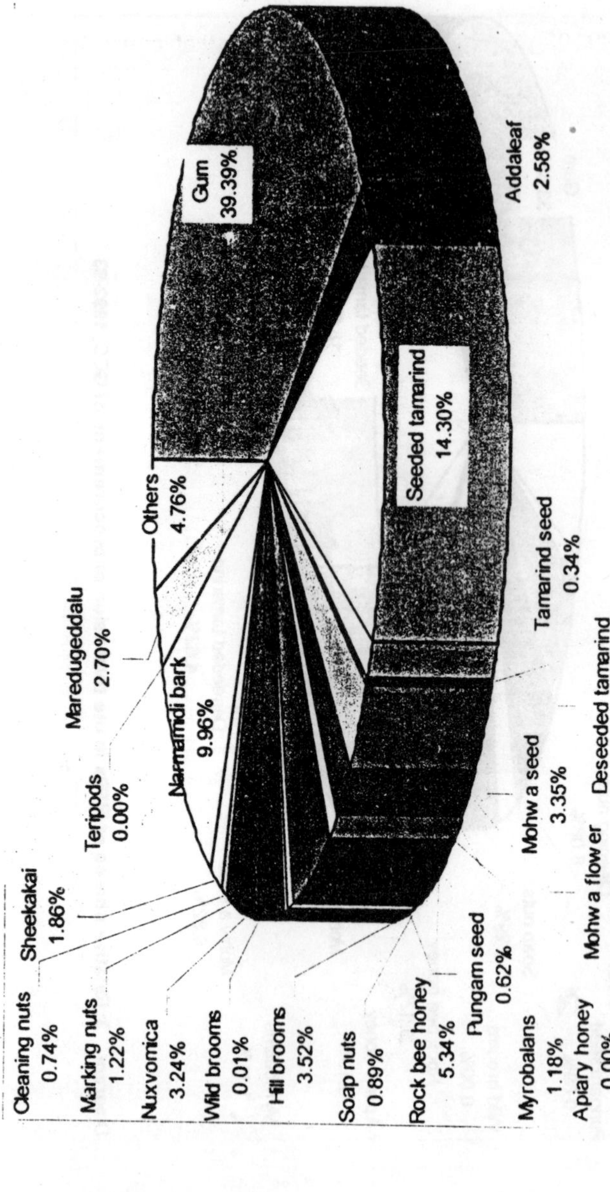


Diagram 4: Relative shares of various MFPs in the toval value of procurement of GCC, 2002-03

13.2% of the total MFP procurement in 1972–73 which increased to 39% by 2002–03. On the other hand, addaleaf contributed 28% in 1972–73 which drastically decreased to 3% in 2002–03. There are ups and downs in the contribution of seeded tamarind whose share is 14% in 2002–03, while deseeded tamarind declined substantially during 1973–03. Other items worth mentioning are rock bee honey, hill brooms, narmamidi bark, mohwa seed, etc. Relative shares of various MFPs in the total value of procurement for 1972–73, 1982–83, 1992–93, and 2002–03 are also provided in Diagrams 1 to 4. Data on quantities procured, value, and price of various MFPs for the period 1973–03 are provided through Appendices 8 to 18. Instability in quantities, value, and prices of these commodities are calculated and provided in Table 3. Coefficient of Variation (CV) has been widely used as indicator instability. It is the ratio of standard deviation to arithmetic mean which is expressed in percentage terms. Among the quantities of various MFPs procured, CV is the highest or wild brooms, followed by Apiary honey, mohwa flower, and pungam seed. On the other hand, myrobalans had the lowest CV. As regards values, hill brooms recorded the highest CV and addaleaf noticed the lowest. Other commodities experienced high CVs are sheekakai, rock bee honey, nuxvomica, and seeded tamarind. As of prices, wild brooms, once again, recorded highest CV and the mohwa seed the lowest. As mentioned earlier, quantities procured are based on number of factors beyond the control of GCC and so is the case with prices which are determined by market forces. Thus, high CVs are understandable.

## Trend analysis

Trend analysis of quantities of various MFPs procured by GCC is carried out and provided in Table 4. All three most commonly used forms (linear, semilog, and double-log) are tried as they provide some readymade explanation to the trend coefficients. In the linear equation, coefficient indicates change by constant amount from year to year, while in the semilog function, it happened to be exponential growth rate (depicts constant ratio of change over the data period). The coefficient in the double-log form is a ready estimate of growth elasticity which is assumed to be constant over the data period. However, this has no economic interpretation as such.

Trend equations are estimated for 18 commodities of which 12 are significant at various level. $R^{-2}$ ranged between as low as 0.02 to as high as 0.80 across commodities and same is true with F-values. A comparison of trends in qualities of various MFPs is provided in Table 5. Procurement of gum decreased by 55.09 quintals/annum over the study period, while mohwa seed, mohwa flower, pungam seed, marking nuts, and seeded tamarind experienced positive and significant annual constant changes during 1973–03. As regards exponential growth rates, mohwa flower (18.9%), tamarind seed (17.6%), and marking nuts (16.3%) experienced increasing annual growth rates. Other results are self explanatory.

Trends in value of MFPs for the period 1973–03 are provided in Table 6. All the 18 items considered are significant either at 5% level or at 1% level thereby showing significant results during 1973–03. $R^{-2}$ ranged between 16% to 90% thereby explaining a maximum variation in the dependant variable by the time. Almost all the F-values are also significant. A comparison of trends in values of various MFPs are provided in Table 7. A perusal of Table indicates that maximum increase was noticed in gum, while the maximum decrease in apiary honey. Maximum exponential growth rate as recorded by marking nuts (28.7%/ annum), followed by mohwa flower (21.1%/annum).

Trends in prices of various MFPs procured are provided in Table 8. Almost all the prices of various commodities studied noticed positive and significant results. Adjusted coefficient of multiple determination along with F-values were also significant at 5% and 1% levels. A comparison of trends of these prices are also provided in Table 9 which are self explanatory.

## Procurement of agricultural produce

Procurement of various agricultural produces (quintals) for 1991–03 is provided in Table 10. Commodities included are cotton, niger, maize, red gram, french beans, groundnuts, paddy, cashewnutes, etc. However, there has been a steady decline in

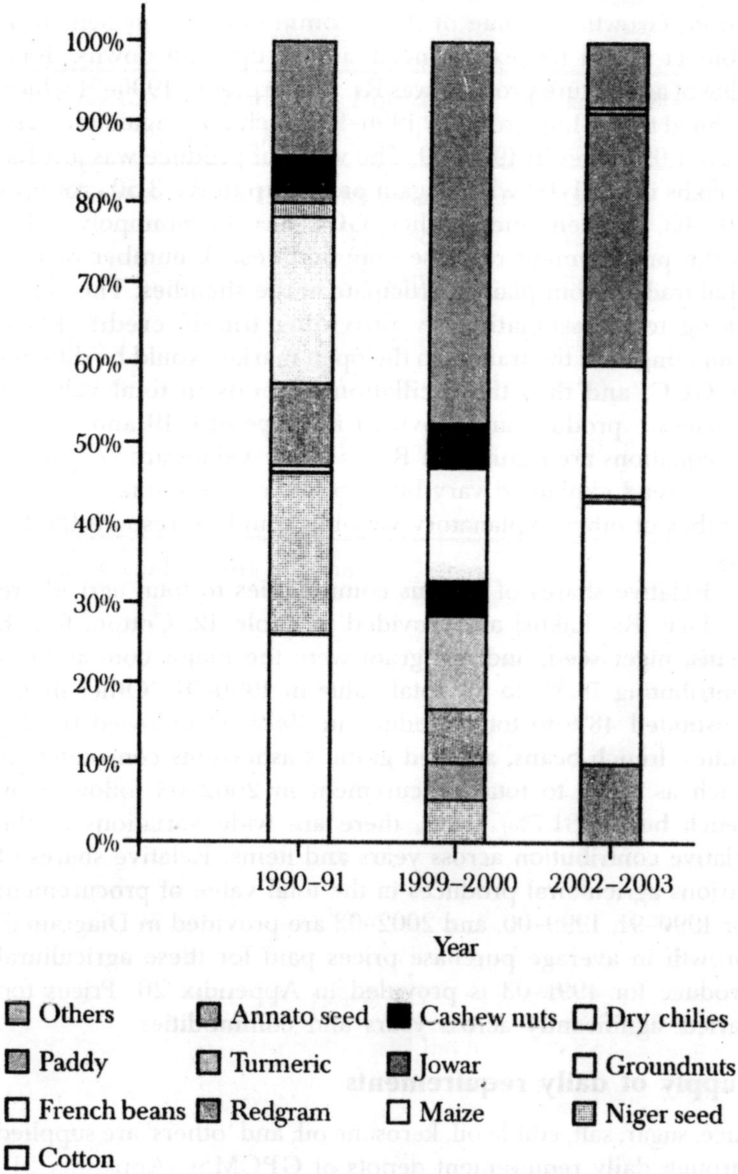


***Diagram 5. Relative shares of various agricultural produces to the total value of procurement of GCC, for selected years***

the quantities procured across commodities over the study period. Growth in value of these commodities is presented in Table 11 which too experienced similar ups and downs. Total value of agriculture produce was Rs. 5.84 crores in 1990–91 which declined to Rs. 1.06 crores in 1996–97 which once again increase to Rs. 4.09 crores in 1998–99. The value of produce was just Rs. 40 lakhs in 2001–02 which again picked up to Rs. 3.50 crores in 2002–03. As mentioned earlier, GCC has no monopoly rights on the procurement of these commodities. A number of non tribal traders from plains participate in the shandies. They have a long term association by providing timely credit. Thus, competing with the traders in the open market would be difficult for GCC, and thus the oscillations. Trends in total value of agriculture produce are provided in Appendix 19 and non of the equations are significant. $R^{-2}$ as also F-values are very poor. Thus, trend explained vary little variation in the total value. A number of other explanatory variable could be responsible for this.

Relative shares of various commodities to total agriculture produce (Rs. Lakhs) are provided in Table 12. Cotton, french beans, niger seed, and red gram were the major commodities contributing 78.5% to the total value in 1990–91. 'Other items' constituted 48% to total produce in 1999–00 followed by dry chilies, french beans, and red gram. Cashewnuts constituted as much as 1/3rd to total procurement in 2002–03 followed by french beans (31.7%). Thus, there are wide variations in the relative contribution across years and items. Relative shares of various agricultural produces in the total value of procurement for 1990–91, 1999–00, and 2002–03 are provided in Diagram 5. Growth in average purchase prices paid for these agricultural produce for 1991–03 is provided in Appendix 20. Prices too varied significantly across years and commodities.

## Supply of daily requirements

Rice, sugar, salt, edible oil, kerosene oil, and 'others' are supplied through daily requirement depots of GPCMSs (Appendix 21). Total value of these commodities increased from Rs. 4.91 crores in 1980–81 to Rs. 80.05 crores in 2002–03. However, commodity-wise data are available from 1986–87. Rice constituted 42% of the total value of domestic requirement supplied in 2002–03. As mentioned earlier, GPCMS have the monopoly rights to supply various categories of card holders in the agency areas. Same is true with sugar, salt, edible oil, and kerosene oil. Other items constituted 1/3rd of the total supplies. Trend analysis of these commodities indicated that all three types of equations for rice, sugar, salt, kerosene oil, 'others', and 'total' are significant at 1% level of significance. In the case of rice, $R^{-2}$ explained 82% to 88% of the total variation, and same is the case with 'others'. As of total supplies, $R^{-2}$ ranged between 92–96%, and all of them are positive and significant.

## Credit operations

GCC provides short, and medium term, and consumption loans. Off late, it has also started providing loans to SHGs. As of short term loans, they are basically meant for crop cultivation. Borrowers, amount disbursed, loan amount/ borrower, and recovery are provided in Table 14. A tribal farmer is required to be a member to be eligible for borrowing from GCC. Next criteria for availing loan is to have titles of the land, and he/she should not be a defaulter. Thus, borrowers column indicates the number of loanees in a particular year. This membership has no other incentives/benefits. In other words non-member can also sell MFP and agricultural produce at the GPCMSs as also can purchase daily requirements from the DR depots.

Huge amounts of loans were provided during 1992–93, 1993–94, and 1994–95. According to discussions with field officials, viability of the project and genuineness of the borrower were over-looked, and loans were provided to meet huge and unrealistic targets. International fund for agricultural development and the Government of The Netherlands provided funds for this purpose for an overall socio-economic develop-ment of tribals. Loan amount/borrower has shown no trend which nevertheless increased from Rs. 2017 to Rs. 3575 during study period. Recovery was less than satisfactory during 1991–96, and 1999–2000. As on today, GCC has to recover Rs. 8 crores from previous borrowers. Present management of GCC has worked out a one time payment scheme with waiver of interest component, and the results are encouraging (Table 14). For example recovery was 180% in 2001–02. Trend equations estimated for these variables were satisfactory, in that borrowers and loan amount/borrower were significant (Appendix 22).

Trends in demand, collection, and balance of short-term loans are provided in Appendix 23 which nevertheless explains the above phenomena. The picture is very sad during the last 6 years. Loans disbursed for medium term, consumption purpose, SHGs, and 'others' are provided in Appendix 24. Loaning activity depends on the quantum of amount available with the GCC in a particular crop year. There is hardly any finance under these activities for the last 6 years.

## Swot analysis

Based on the above discussion, a modest attempt is made to identify strengths, weaknesses, opportunities, and threats to the organisation under discussion.

### *Strengths*

Organic forest produce
Environment friendly products
Highly nutritious and rare products
Farm fresh products
Have medicinal value
Naturally grown forest cover
Huge domestic and international market
Easy processing and value addition
Scope for abundant income and employment generation
Huge network of GCC with over 50 years of experience
Hard working tribals
Government support

### *Weakness*

Continuous denudation of forest cover
Steady decline in yield due to age of the plants, adverse climate, rainfall, temperature, humidity, etc.

Unorganised sector
Lack of standardisation and packaging
Little quality consciousness
Lack of proper storage, processing, and transport
Orthodox mentality of stake holders (ITDA, Department of forests, various other government departments, GCC, NGOs, tribals, etc.)
Lack of government control

Lack of perspective planning
Locational disadvantage (poor infrastructure, far flung and hilly areas with inhospitable terrain)
Exploitation by middle men from tribal and non-tribal areas
Unskilled and easy going tribals
Lack of tools and technologies in harvesting MFPs
Lack of knowledge about preservation and conservation of various species of MFPs
Lack of advertising for forest produce
Lack of sufficient financial support
Contradicting interests of department of foresty, GCC, tribals, and naxalites

***Opportunities***

Increasing domestic and export demand
Increase in health and quality consciousness
Commitment by tribals and their traditional skills
Scope for variety of by-products, co-products, and joint products
Easy value addition
Huge network of GCC
Government support

***Threats***

Synthetic substitutes
Decline in area under forest cover
Decline in production of MFP
Aberrations in prices of MFPs
Quality deterioration during storage
Unethical exploitation by middlemen
Staying away from forest areas by tribal youth

Low status attributed to collection of MFP among tribal youth
Unrest due to naxalites
Adverse government policy

## Summary

GCC was registered as a cooperative society in 1970. Management of GCC shall vest in a board of directors consisting on not more than 18 members. Over the years, GCC appointed number of employees which currently stood at over 1500, and most of them are tribals. Initially, GCC opened branches to undertake various activities (procurement MFP and agricultural produce, supply of daily requirements, and credit). Over the period, these branches were registered as Girijan Primary Cooperative Marketing Societies (GPCMSs). GCC has monopoly rights on procurement of selected MFPs. Procurement is normally done through shandies (weekly markets) by credit-cum-procurement assistants (CCPAs) of GPCMSs. Establishment of processing units, and a separate retail marketing division (RMD) were started to plough back remunerative prices to tribals and quality products to consumers. Conscious efforts for building brand image through advertisement are also being made, and products of GCC are sold under the brand name of 'Girijan'.

GCC has 33 branch offices during 1980–81 which were registered as GPCMSs during 1994–95, and currently 45 such GPCMSs are functional. Composition of share capital revealed that 96% of it comes from Government of Andhra Pradesh. The federation recorded procurement was Rs. 40.58 lakhs in 1972–73 which increased to Rs. 16.44 crores by 2002–03. There are substantial changes in the relative contribution of various MFPs over the study period. Trend equations estimated for 18 commodities shown significant results for 12. $R^{-2}$ ranged between as low as 0.02 to as high as 0.80 across commodities and same is true with F-values. A comparison of trends in values of various MFPs indicated maximum increase in gum, while maximum decrease in apiary honey. Trends in prices of various MFPs noticed positive and significant results.

Total value of agriculture produce procured was Rs. 5.84 crores in 1990–91 and has an erratic trend, it was just Rs. 40

**Table 1 Growth in membership, share capital, and turnover (Rs. lakhs), 1981–2002**

| *Sr. No.* | *Year* | *Membership* | *Share capital** | *Trunover* | *Net Profit/loss* |
|---|---|---|---|---|---|
| 1 | 1980–81 | 33 | 132.05 | 590.29 | -24.86 |
| 2 | 1981–82 | 33 | 131.69 | 977.20 | -47.24 |
| 3 | 1982–83 | 33 | 108.62 | 1282.83 | 4.44 |
| 4 | 1983–84 | 33 | 143.26 | 1284.80 | -60.35 |
| 5 | 1984–85 | 33 | 142.90 | 1837.16 | 5.81 |
| 6 | 1985–86 | 33 | 142.18 | 1805.76 | -36.25 |
| 7 | 1986–87 | 33 | 141.81 | 1937.73 | -43.95 |
| 8 | 1987–88 | 33 | 138.95 | 2618.91 | 53.50 |
| 9 | 1988–89 | 33 | 129.14 | 4186.74 | 266.72 |
| 10 | 1989–90 | 33 | 129.14 | 4374.61 | 266.43 |
| 11 | 1990–91 | 34 | 129.14 | 5271.14 | -295.46 |
| 12 | 1991–92 | 34 | 418.42 | 5729.06 | -24.23 |
| 13 | 1992–93 | 36 | 696.22 | 5571.58 | -240.97 |
| 14 | 1993–94 | 47 | 1175.98 | 6016.24 | -667.20 |
| 15 | 1994–95 | 49 | 1195.16 | 5527.52 | -103.52 |
| 16 | 1995–96 | 49 | 1223.96 | 5170.32 | 252.61 |
| 17 | 1996–97 | 50 | 1779.96 | 6048.22 | 465.30 |
| 18 | 1997–98 | 50 | 1832.16 | 6881.09 | 234.36 |
| 19 | 1998–99 | 50 | 1958.17 | 7695.56 | 250.44 |
| 20 | 1999–00 | 50 | 1958.17 | 8643.72 | 19.60 |
| 21 | 2000–01 | 50 | 1958.17 | 10285.88 | -276.68 |
| 22 | 2001–02 | 50 | 2058.17 | 8514.58 | -300.53 |

* Out of Rs. 2058.17 lakhs, state government contributed Rs. 975.63 lakhs.

*Source*: Records of GCC

lakhs in 2001–02. Cotton, french beans, niger seed, and red gram were the major commodities contributing 78.5% to the total value in 1990–91. Cashewnuts constituted as much as 1/3rd to total procurement in 2002–03 followed by french beans (31.7%). Thus, there are wide variations in the relative contribution across years and items.

Total value of domestic requirements (rice, sugar, salt, edible oil, kerosene oil, etc.) supplied increased from Rs. 4.91 crores in

**Table 2 Relative shares of various MFPs in the total value (Rs. lakhs) or procurement of GCC, selected years**

| *S.No.* | *Commodity* | *1972–73* | *1982–83* | *1992–93* | *2002–03* |
|---|---|---|---|---|---|
| 1 | Gum | 5.34 (13.2) | 74.92 (28.2) | 267.21 (33.9) | 647.68 (39.0) |
| 2 | Addaleaf | 11.35 (28.0) | 27.91 (10.5) | 26.26 (3.3) | 42.50 (3.0) |
| 3 | Seeded tamarind | 6.97 (17.2) | 72.91 (27.5) | 147.03 (18.6) | 235.17 (14.0) |
| 4 | Deseeded tamarind | 4.46 (11.0) | 21.50 (8.1) | 36.47 (4.6) | 25.86 (2.0) |
| 5 | Tamarind seed | 0 (0.0) | 3.81 (1.4) | 11.18 (1.4) | 5.53 (0.3) |
| 6 | Mohwa seed | 1.81 (4.5) | 9.49 (3.6) | 53.79 (6.8) | 55.07 (3.3) |
| 7 | Mohwaflower | 0 (0.0) | 6.61 (2.5) | 18.22 (2.3) | 40.02 (2.4) |
| 8 | Myrobalans | 4.27 (10.5) | 19.81 (7.5) | 8.75 (1.1) | 19.45 (1.2) |
| 9 | Apiary honey | 0 (0.0) | 2.98 (1.1) | 1.50 (0.2) | 0 (0.0) |
| 10 | Rock bee honey | 1.77 (4.4) | 3.10 (1.2) | 41.93 (5.3) | 87.74 (5.3) |
| 11 | Soap nuts | 1.25 (3.1) | 2.32 (0.9) | 25.92 (3.3) | 14.62 (0.9) |
| 12 | Punga m seed | 1.14 (2.8) | 1.04 (0.4) | 5.45 (0.7) | 10.17 (0.6) |
| 13 | Hill brooms | 0.87 (2.1) | 2.10 (0.8) | 2.72 (0.3) | 57.82 (3.5) |
| 14 | Wild brooms | 0.46 (1.1) | 3.80 (1.4) | 0 (0.0) | 0.12 (0.0) |
| 15 | Nuxvomica | 0.25 (0.6) | 7.48 (2.8) | 43.84 (5.6) | 53.35 (3.2) |
| 16 | Marking nuts | 0.06 (0.1) | 0.06 (0.0) | 0.63 (0.1) | 20.05 (1.2) |
| 17 | Cleaning nuts | 0.15 (0.4) | 1.76 (0.7) | 47.94 (6.1) | 12.12 (0.7) |
| 18 | Sheekakai | 0.43 (1.1) | 3.98 (1.5) | 6.13 (0.8) | 30.58 (1.9) |
| 19 | Narmamidi bark | 0 (0.0) | 0 (0.0) | 0 (0.0) | 163.81 (10.0) |
| 20 | Teripods | 0 (0.0) | 0 (0.0) | 0 (0.0) | 0 (0.0) |
| 21 | Maredugeddalu | 0 (0.0) | 0 (0.0) | 0 (0.0) | 44.34 (2.7) |
| 22 | Others | 0 (0.0) | 0 (0.0) | 43.70 (5.5) | 78.31 (4.8) |
| 23 | Total | 40.58 (100.0) | 265.58 (100.0) | 788.67 (100.0) | 1644.31 (100.0) |

*Source*: Records of GCC

1980–81 to Rs. 80.05 crores in 2002–03. Rice constituted 42% of the total value of domestic requirements supplied in 2002–03. As of credit operations, huge amounts of loans were provided during 1992–93, 1993–94, and 1994–95. Loan amount/borrower has shown no trend which, nevertheless, increased from Rs. 2017 to Rs. 3575 during study period. Recovery was less than satisfactory during 1991–96, and 1999–00. As on today, GCC has to recover Rs. 8 crores from previous borrowers. Trend equations for borrowers, and amount disbursed were satisfactory, in that borrowers and loan amount/borrower, and recovery were significant. Loans disbursed for medium term, consumption purpose, SHGs, and 'others' are insignificant.

**Table 3 Coefficient of variation (%) in quantity, value, and price of MFPs procured by GCC, 1973–2003**

| *S.No.* | *MFP* | *Quantity* | *Value* | *Price* |
|---|---|---|---|---|
| 1 | Gum | 0.61 | 0.84 | 0.95 |
| 2 | Addaleaf | 0.47 | 0.57 | 0.88 |
| 3 | Seeded tamarind | 0.48 | 1.08 | 0.73 |
| 4 | Deseeded tamarind | 0.49 | 0.97 | 0.72 |
| 5 | Tamarind seed | 0.58 | 1.02 | 0.95 |
| 6 | Mohwa seed | 0.61 | 0.99 | 0.59 |
| 7 | Mohwa flower | 0.91 | 1.06 | 0.70 |
| 8 | Myrobalans | 0.35 | 1.21 | 1.04 |
| 9 | Apiary honey | 1.21 | 0.84 | 0.48 |
| 10 | Rock bee honey | 0.84 | 1.32 | 0.74 |
| 11 | Soap nuts | 0.56 | 0.97 | 0.78 |
| 12 | Pungam seed | 0.91 | 1.29 | 0.61 |
| 13 | Hill brooms | 0.74 | 1.36 | 0.93 |
| 14 | Wild brooms | 1.22 | 1.14 | 1.62 |
| 15 | Nuxvomica | 0.59 | 1.34 | 0.84 |
| 16 | Sheekakai | 0.56 | 1.23 | 0.86 |

*Source*: Calculated from Appendices 3.6 to 3.14

**Table 4 Trends in quantities of MFPs produced by GCC, 1973–2003**

| S. No. | MFP | Intercept | Ceofficient | t-value | $\overline{R}^2$ | F-value |
|---|---|---|---|---|---|---|
| 1 | 1 | 2 | 3 | 4 | 5 | 6 |
| 1 | Gum | | | | | |
| | Linear | 13107.26 | –55.0871 | 0.36 | 0.03 | 0.13 |
| | Semilog | 9.27 | –0.0012 | 0.12 | 0.03 | 0.01 |
| | Double-log | 8.88 | 0.1481 | 1.24 | 0.02 | 1.53 |
| 2 | Addaleaf | | | | | |
| | Linear | 40183.57 | –1021.13** | 7.74 | 0.66 | 59.88 |
| | Semilog | 10.78 | –0.0530** | 6.82 | 0.60 | 46.54 |
| | Double-log | 11.14 | –0.4769** | 4.76 | 0.42 | 22.69 |
| 3 | Seeded tamarind | | | | | |
| | Linear | 19289.26 | 1418.08** | 4.50 | 0.39 | 20.24 |
| | Semilog | 9.90 | 0.0384** | 4.65 | 0.41 | 21.65 |
| | Double-log | 9.54 | 0.3889** | 4.27 | 0.37 | 18.23 |
| 4 | Deseeded tamarind | | | | | |
| | Linear | 6517.54 | 38.4601 | 0.54 | 0.02 | 0.29 |
| | Semilog | 8.5112 | 0.0122 | 0.86 | 0.09 | 0.75 |
| | Double-log | 8.5063 | 0.0792 | 0.52 | 0.02 | 0.27 |
| 5 | Tamarind seed | | | | | |
| | Linear | 5069.22 | 163.1516@ | 1.85 | 0.08 | 3.43 |
| | Semilog | 5.1503 | 0.1758** | 2.84 | 0.19 | 8.07 |
| | Double-log | 0.70 | 2.8811** | 5.55 | 0.50 | 30.81 |
| 6 | Mohwa seed | | | | | |
| | Linear | 1955.7935 | 211.2165** | 3.85 | 0.34 | 14.84 |
| | Semilog | 7.71 | 0.0425** | 4.13 | 0.35 | 17.08 |
| | Double-log | 7.31 | 0.4317** | 3.84 | 0.31 | 14.71 |
| 7 | Mohwa flower | | | | | |
| | Linear | 1212.37 | 324.41** | 3.16 | 0.23 | 9.98 |
| | Semilog | 4.49 | 0.1888** | 3.97 | 0.33 | 15.74 |
| | Double-log | 0.76 | 2.68** | 6.95 | 0.61 | 48.24 |
| 8 | Myrobalans | | | | | |
| | Linear | 12751.26 | 37.4915 | 0.39 | 0.03 | 0.15 |
| | Semilog | 9.40 | 0.00255 | 0.34 | 0.03 | 0.12 |
| | Double-log | 9.38 | 0.0237 | 0.30 | 0.03 | 0.09 |
| 9 | Apiary honey | | | | | |
| | Linear | 454.40 | –16.30** | 3.74 | 0.41 | 13.97 |
| | Semilog | 7.95 | –0.1937** | 4.63 | 0.52 | 21.46 |
| | Double-log | 14.93 | –3.68** | 4.48 | 0.50 | 20.08 |

*Contd.*

| 1 | 2 | 3 | 4 | 5 | 6 | 7 |
|---|---|---|---|---|---|---|
| 10 | Rock bee honey | | | | | |
| | Linear | -106.47 | 52.43** | 6.61 | 0.59 | 43.71 |
| | Semilog | 5.07 | 0.0738** | 6.56 | 0.58 | 42.97 |
| | Double-log | 4.65 | 0.63** | 4.30 | 0.37 | 18.48 |
| 11 | Soap nuts | | | | | |
| | Linear | 891.96 | 52.2887** | 3.05 | 0.22 | 9.28 |
| | Semilog | 6.71 | 0.03616** | 3.35 | 0.25 | 11.23 |
| | Double-log | 6.38 | 0.36123** | 3.07 | 0.22 | 9.43 |
| 12 | Pungam seed | | | | | |
| | Linear | 369.52 | 104.6593** | 3.22 | 0.24 | 10.39 |
| | Semilog | 6.50 | 0.04702** | 2.90 | 0.20 | 8.43 |
| | Double-log | 6.56 | 0.2767@ | 1.46 | 0.04 | 2.14 |
| 13 | Hill brooms | | | | | |
| | Linear | 4.34 | -0.0788@ | 1.77 | 0.07 | 3.13 |
| | Semilog | 1.36 | -0.0296 * | 2.15 | 0.11 | 4.61 |
| | Double-log | 1.65 | -0.3046 * | 2.06 | 0.10 | 4.24 |
| 14 | Wild brooms | | | | | |
| | Linear | 26.94 | -1.0482** | 6.50 | 0.58 | 42.28 |
| | Semilog | 5.32 | -0.3478** | 10.99 | 0.80 | 120.69 |
| | Double-log | 7.40 | -3.0362** | 5.85 | 0.53 | 34.18 |
| 15 | Nuxvomica | | | | | |
| | Linear | 2922.65 | 5.7113** | 0.16 | 0.03 | 0.02 |
| | Semilog | 7.79 | 0.0020** | 0.16 | 0.03 | 0.02 |
| | Double-log | 7.52 | 0.1213** | 0.88 | 0.01 | 0.78 |
| 16 | Marking nuts | | | | | |
| | Linear | -1678.3 | 244.65** | 6.54 | 0.58 | 42.86 |
| | Semilog | 3.05 | 0.1629 * | 2.29 | 0.12 | 5.26 |
| | Double-log | 3.25 | 0.9589 | 1.19 | 0.01 | 1.42 |
| 17 | Cleaning nuts | | | | | |
| | Linear | 370.83 | 58.0835 | 1.13 | 0.01 | 1.28 |
| | Semilog | 4.22 | 0.0696 | 0.98 | 0.001 | 0.97 |
| | Double-log | 4.46 | 0.3434 | 0.45 | 0.03 | 0.20 |
| 18 | Sheekakai | | | | | |
| | Linear | 1096.2 | 14.8887 | 0.10 | 0.0003 | 0.99 |
| | Semilog | 6.72 | 0.0172 | 1.25 | 0.02 | 1.56 |
| | Double-log | 6.68 | 0.1265 | 0.85 | 0.01 | 0.71 |

@ Significant at 10% level of significance
* Significant at 5% level of significance
** Significant at 1% level of significance

*Source:* Estimated

**Table 5 A comparison of trends in quantities of various MFPs procured by GCC, 1973–2003**

| *S. No.* | *MFP* | *Annual constant change (quintals/ annum)* | *Exponential growth rate (%/annum)* |
|---|---|---|---|
| 1 | Gum | –55.09 | –0.12 |
| 2 | Addaleaf | –1021.13** | –5.30** |
| 3 | Seeded tamarind | 1418.08** | 3.84** |
| 4 | Deseeded tamarind | 38.46 | 1.22 |
| 5 | Tamarind seed | 163.15@ | 17.58** |
| 6 | Mohwa seed | 211.22** | 4.25** |
| 7 | Mohwa flower | 324.41** | 18.88** |
| 8 | Myrobalans | 37.49 | 0.26 |
| 9 | Apiary honey | –16.30** | –19.37** |
| 10 | Rock bee honey | 52.43** | 7.38** |
| 11 | Soap nuts | 52.29** | 3.62** |
| 12 | Pungam seed | 104.66** | 4.70** |
| 13 | Hill brooms | –0.08@ | –2.96* |
| 14 | Wild brooms | –1.05** | –34.78** |
| 15 | Nuxvomica | 5.71 | 0.20 |
| 16 | Marking nuts | 244.65** | 16.29* |
| 17 | Cleaning nuts | 58.08 | 6.96 |
| 18 | Sheekakai | 14.89 | 1.72 |

@ Significant at 10% level of significance

* Significant at 5% level of significance

** Significant at 1% level of significance

*Source:* Calculated from Table 4

**Table 6 Trends in value of MFPs procured by GCC, 1973–2003**

| *S. No.* | *MFP* | *Intercept* | *Ceofficient* | *t-value* | *$R^{-2}$* | *F-value* |
|---|---|---|---|---|---|---|
| *1* | *2* | *3* | *4* | *5* | *6* | *7* |
| 1 | Gum | | | | | |
| | Linear | –55.11 | 20.3195** | 7.58 | 0.65 | 57.46 |
| | Semilog | 2.94 | 0.1287** | 9.66 | 0.75 | 93.36 |
| | Double-log | 1.40 | 1.4283** | 11.79 | 0.82 | 139.01 |
| 2 | Addaleaf | | | | | |
| | Linear | 6.62 | 0.9809** | 5.24 | 0.47 | 27.46 |
| | Semilog | 2.18 | 0.0471** | 5.30 | 0.47 | 28.10 |
| | Double-log | 1.71 | 0.4872** | 5.02 | 0.45 | 25.17 |
| 3 | Seeded tamarind | | | | | |
| | Linear | –73.06 | 12.8084** | 7.69 | 0.66 | 59.09 |
| | Semilog | 2.28 | 0.1254** | 16.27 | 0.90 | 264.67 |
| | Double-log | 1.11 | 1.2589** | 10.75 | 0.79 | 115.56 |
| 4 | Deseeded tamarind | | | | | |
| | Linear | –9.83 | 2.98** | 5.91 | 0.53 | 34.94 |
| | Semilog | 1.68 | 0.0928** | 6.52 | 0.58 | 42.57 |
| | Double-log | 0.93 | 0.8866** | 5.16 | 0.46 | 26.59 |
| 5 | Tamarind seed | | | | | |
| | Linear | –3.74 | 0.6497** | 6.56 | 0.60 | 43.09 |
| | Semilog | –0.66 | 0.1222** | 7.77 | 0.68 | 60.41 |
| | Double-log | –2.90 | 1.6179** | 7.70 | 0.68 | 59.29 |
| 6 | Mohwa seed | | | | | |
| | Linear | –9.59 | 2.4550** | 6.02 | 0.54 | 36.21 |
| | Semilog | 0.90 | 0.1184** | 9.83 | 0.76 | 96.59 |
| | Double-log | –0.29 | 1.2238** | 8.73 | 0.71 | 76.13 |
| 7 | Mohwa flower | | | | | |
| | Linear | –5.31 | 1.2550** | 5.13 | 0.47 | 26.27 |
| | Semilog | –2.06 | 0.2106** | 5.98 | 0.55 | 35.79 |
| | Double-log | –5.88 | 2.8032** | 7.64 | 0.66 | 58.34 |
| 8 | Myrobalans | | | | | |
| | Linear | –11.16 | 2.2874** | 4.93 | 0.44 | 24.29 |
| | Semilog | 0.75 | 0.1147** | 9.10 | 0.73 | 82.75 |
| | Double-log | –0.33 | 1.1573** | 7.56 | 0.65 | 57.15 |
| 9 | Apiary honey | | | | | |
| | Linear | 5.07 | –0.1404 * | 2.16 | 0.16 | 4.65 |
| | Semilog | 2.48 | –0.1059 * | 2.43 | 0.21 | 5.92 |
| | Double-log | 6.12 | –1.9507 * | 2.29 | 0.18 | 5.24 |

*Contd.*

| 1 | 2 | 3 | 4 | 5 | 6 | 7 |
|---|---|---|---|---|---|---|
| 10 | Rock bee honey | | | | | |
| | Linear | –18.43 | 2.4823** | 7.26 | 0.63 | 52.69 |
| | Semilog | –0.59 | 0.1609** | 12.09 | 0.83 | 146.08 |
| | Double-log | –1.78 | 1.4962** | 7.11 | 0.63 | 50.60 |
| 11 | Soap nuts | | | | | |
| | Linear | –3.29 | 0.7598** | 7.27 | 0.63 | 52.82 |
| | Semilog | –0.45 | 0.1249** | 9.71 | 0.76 | 94.20 |
| | Double-log | –1.51 | 1.2119** | 7.09 | 0.62 | 50.22 |
| 12 | Pungam seed | | | | | |
| | Linear | –3.63 | 0.6356** | 5.06 | 0.45 | 25.63 |
| | Semilog | –0.90 | 0.1200** | 6.89 | 0.61 | 47.45 |
| | Double-log | –1.49 | 0.9955** | 4.18 | 0.35 | 17.50 |
| 13 | Hill brooms | | | | | |
| | Linear | –5.55 | 0.8799** | 5.13 | 0.46 | 26.33 |
| | Semilog | –0.34 | 0.1142** | 10.60 | 0.79 | 112.33 |
| | Double-log | –1.32 | 1.1127** | 7.58 | 0.65 | 57.41 |
| 14 | Wild brooms | | | | | |
| | Linear | 4.58 | –0.1465** | 3.32 | 0.25 | 11.00 |
| | Semilog | 2.24 | –0.1753** | 5.16 | 0.46 | 26.64 |
| | Double-log | 2.92 | –1.3850** | 3.22 | 0.24 | 10.36 |
| 15 | Nuxvomica | | | | | |
| | Linear | –0.30 | 0.6869 * | 2.60 | 0.16 | 6.78 |
| | Semilog | 0.34 | 0.0836** | 4.14 | 0.35 | 17.13 |
| | Double-log | –0.81 | 0.9846** | 4.90 | 0.43 | 24.03 |
| 16 | Marking nuts | | | | | |
| | Linear | –5.53 | 0.6579** | 5.06 | 0.45 | 25.61 |
| | Semilog | –5.68 | 0.2868** | 9.44 | 0.75 | 89.03 |
| | Double-log | –7.32 | 2.4730** | 5.32 | 0.48 | 28.29 |
| 17 | Cleaning nuts | | | | | |
| | Linear | –5.48 | 4.7426 | 1.61 | 0.05 | 2.59 |
| | Semilog | –3.09 | 0.1708** | 4.25 | 0.36 | 18.04 |
| | Double-log | –4.55 | 1.6634** | 3.70 | 0.30 | 13.68 |
| 18 | Sheekakai | | | | | |
| | Linear | –3.41 | 0.6276** | 5.32 | 0.48 | 28.28 |
| | Semilog | –0.70 | 0.1169** | 7.59 | 0.65 | 57.67 |
| | Double-log | –1.60 | 1.1031** | 5.63 | 0.51 | 31.66 |

* Significant at 5% level of significance

** Significant at 1% level of significance

*Source:* Estimated

**Table 7 A comparison of trends in values of various MFPs procured by GCC, 1973–2003**

| *S. No.* | *MFP* | *Annual constant change (Rs. lakhs)* | *Exponential growth rate (%/annum)* |
|---|---|---|---|
| *1* | *2* | *3* | *4* |
| 1 | Gum | 20.32 ** | 12.87 ** |
| 2 | Addaleaf | 0.98 ** | 4.71 ** |
| 3 | Seeded tamarind | 12.81 ** | 12.54 ** |
| 4 | Deseeded tamarind | 2.98 ** | 9.28 ** |
| 5 | Tamarind seed | 0.65 ** | 12.22 ** |
| 6 | Mohwa seed | 2.46 ** | 11.84 ** |
| 7 | Mohwa flower | 1.26 ** | 21.06 ** |
| 8 | Myrobalans | 2.29 ** | 11.47 ** |
| 9 | Apiary honey | -0.14 * | -10.59 * |
| 10 | Rock bee honey | 2.48 ** | 16.09 ** |
| 11 | Soap nuts | 0.76 ** | 12.49 ** |
| 12 | Pungam seed | 0.64 ** | 12.00 ** |
| 13 | Hill brooms | 0.88 ** | 11.42 ** |
| 14 | Wild brooms | -0.15 ** | -17.53 ** |
| 15 | Nuxvomica | 0.69 * | 8.36 ** |
| 16 | Marking nuts | 0.66 ** | 28.68 ** |
| 17 | Cleaning nuts | 4.74 | 17.08 ** |
| 18 | Sheekakai | 0.63 ** | 11.69 ** |

* Significant at 5% level of significance

** Significant at 1% level of significance

*Source:* Calculated from Table 6

**Table 8 Trends in price of MFPs procured by GCC, 1973–2003**

| *S. No.* | *MFP* | *Intercept* | *Coefficient* | *t-value* | $R^{-2}$ | *F-value* |
|---|---|---|---|---|---|---|
| *1* | *2* | *3* | *4* | *5* | *6* | *7* |
| 1 | Gum | | | | | |
| | Linear | –1422.4 | 249.0714 ** | 14.08 | 0.87 | 198.36 |
| | Semilog | 5.18 | 0.1300 ** | 29.77 | 0.97 | 886.45 |
| | Double-log | 4.04 | 1.2804 ** | 11.80 | 0.82 | 139.29 |
| 2 | Addaleaf | | | | | |
| | Linear | –55.90 | 11.9456 ** | 11.87 | 0.82 | 140.88 |
| | Semilog | 2.87 | 0.1020 ** | 26.95 | 0.96 | 726.31 |
| | Double-log | 2.05 | 0.9737 ** | 9.91 | 0.76 | 98.14 |
| 3 | Seeded tamarind | | | | | |
| | Linear | –49.94 | 19.4984 ** | 13.14 | 0.85 | 172.76 |
| | Semilog | 3.88 | 0.0872 ** | 21.65 | 0.94 | 468.91 |
| | Double-log | 3.08 | 0.8708 ** | 11.79 | 0.82 | 139.03 |
| 4 | Deseeded tamarind | | | | | |
| | Linear | –306.41 | 325.7757 ** | 6.09 | 0.55 | 37.05 |
| | Semilog | 4.68 | 0.0807 ** | 15.60 | 0.89 | 243.35 |
| | Double-log | 3.94 | 0.8082 ** | 10.44 | 0.78 | 108.98 |
| 5 | Tamarind seed | | | | | |
| | Linear | –54.28 | 11.2581 ** | 6.44 | 0.59 | 41.47 |
| | Semilog | 2.37 | 0.1178 ** | 9.26 | 0.75 | 85.71 |
| | Double-log | 0.37 | 1.5004 ** | 7.93 | 0.69 | 62.91 |
| 6 | Mohwa seed | | | | | |
| | Linear | –17.02 | 29.3113 ** | 14.20 | 0.88 | 201.66 |
| | Semilog | 4.77 | 0.719 ** | 16.09 | 0.90 | 258.91 |
| | Double-log | 3.46 | 0.9503 ** | 15.31 | 0.89 | 234.54 |

| 1 | 2 | 3 | 4 | 5 | 6 | 7 |
|---|---|---|---|---|---|---|
| 7 | Mohwa flower | | | | | |
| | Linear | –25.04 | 13.5502 ** | 10.84 | 0.80 | 117.46 |
| | Semilog | –2.06 | 0.2106 ** | 5.98 | 0.55 | 35.79 |
| | Double-log | –5.88 | 2.8032 ** | 7.64 | 0.66 | 58.34 |
| 8 | Myrobalans | | | | | |
| | Linear | –112.99 | 24.5600 ** | 6.43 | 0.57 | 41.37 |
| | Semilog | 2.79 | 0.1320 ** | 11.17 | 0.80 | 124.82 |
| | Double-log | 1.54 | 1.3361 ** | 8.89 | 0.72 | 79.04 |
| 9 | Apiary honey | | | | | |
| | Linear | –1491.23 | 215.2233 ** | 9.47 | 0.82 | 89.76 |
| | Semilog | 6.04 | 0.0880 ** | 10.01 | 0.84 | 100.22 |
| | Double-log | 2.68 | 1.73 ** | 11.71 | 0.88 | 137.20 |
| 10 | Rock bee honey | | | | | |
| | Linear | –399.46 | 142.36 ** | 13.81 | 0.86 | 190.76 |
| | Semilog | 5.83 | 0.0876 ** | 21.08 | 0.94 | 444.48 |
| | Double-log | 5.07 | 0.8603 ** | 10.67 | 0.79 | 113.91 |
| 11 | Soap nuts | | | | | |
| | Linear | –316.38 | 301.9232 ** | 5.91 | 0.53 | 34.98 |
| | Semilog | 4.35 | 0.0888 ** | 16.43 | 0.90 | 270.10 |
| | Double-log | 3.63 | 0.8508 ** | 8.87 | 0.72 | 78.72 |
| 12 | Pungam seed | | | | | |
| | Linear | –7.47 | 15.5738 ** | 17.35 | 0.91 | 301.17 |
| | Semilog | 4.11 | 0.0729 ** | 21.42 | 0.94 | 458.74 |
| | Double-log | 3.47 | 0.7181 ** | 10.88 | 0.80 | 118.46 |

*Contd.*

| 1 | 2 | 3 | 4 | 5 | 6 | 7 |
|---|---|---|---|---|---|---|
| 13 | Hill brooms | | | | | |
| | Linear | -206.07 | 38.6536 ** | 12.63 | 0.84 | 159.39 |
| | Semilog | 2.92 | 0.1475 ** | 15.41 | 0.89 | 237.50 |
| | Double-log | 1.58 | 1.4700 ** | 10.12 | 0.77 | 102.47 |
| 14. | Wild brooms | | | | | |
| | Linear | -260.88 | 32.76 ** | 5.25 | 0.47 | 27.60 |
| | Semilog | 1.66 | 0.0905 ** | 1.32 | 0.02 | 1.73 |
| | Double-log | 1.28 | 0.7233 ** | 0.97 | -0.002 | 0.95 |
| 15 | Nuxvomica | | | | | |
| | Linear | -22.4 | 20.0432 ** | 5.65 | 0.51 | 31.93 |
| | Semilog | 4.06 | 0.0815 ** | 8.83 | 0.72 | 78.05 |
| | Double-log | 3.19 | 0.8614 ** | 8.59 | 0.71 | 73.81 |
| 16 | Marking nuts | | | | | |
| | Linear | -63.99 | 10.4790 ** | 7.71 | 0.66 | 59.39 |
| | Semilog | 0.87 | 0.1460 ** | 2.77 | 0.18 | 7.70 |
| | Double-log | 0.33 | 1.1417 * | 1.92 | 0.08 | 3.69 |
| 17 | Cleaning nuts | | | | | |
| | Linear | -70.23 | 18.7560 ** | 9.35 | 0.74 | 87.47 |
| | Semilog | 3.41 | 0.1187 ** | 14.30 | 0.88 | 204.39 |
| | Double-log | 2.37 | 1.1413 ** | 12.90 | 0.86 | 166.29 |
| 18 | Sheekakai | | | | | |
| | Linear | -109.26 | 36.3001 ** | 7.51 | 0.65 | 56.40 |
| | Semilog | 4.11 | 0.1011 ** | 12.68 | 0.84 | 160.85 |
| | Double-log | 3.21 | 1.0016 ** | 8.90 | 0.72 | 79.17 |

* Significant at 5% level of significance

** Significant at 1% level of significance

*Source:* Estimated

**Table 9**

**A comparison of trends in values of various MFPs procured by GCC, 1973–2003**

| *S. No.* | *MFP* | *Annual constant change (Rs./quintal)* | *Exponential growth rate (%/annum)* |
|---|---|---|---|
| 1 | Gum | 249.07** | 13.00** |
| 2 | Addaleaf | 11.95** | 10.20** |
| 3 | Seeded tamarind | 19.50** | 8.72** |
| 4 | Deseeded tamarind | 325.78** | 8.07** |
| 5 | Tamarind seed | 11.26** | 11.78** |
| 6 | Mohwa seed | 29.31** | 7.19** |
| 7 | Myrobalans | 13.55** | 21.06** |
| 8 | Mohwa flower | 24.56** | 13.20** |
| 9 | Apiary honey | 215.22** | 8.80** |
| 10 | Rock bee honey | 142.36** | 8.76** |
| 11 | Soap nuts | 301.93** | 8.88** |
| 12 | Pungam seed | 15.57** | 7.29** |
| 13 | Hill brooms | 38.65** | 14.75** |
| 14 | Wild brooms | 32.76** | 9.05** |
| 15 | Nuxvomica | 20.04** | 8.15** |
| 16 | Marking nuts | 10.48** | 14.60** |
| 17 | Cleaning nuts | 18.76** | 11.87** |
| 18 | Sheekakai | 36.30** | 10.11** |

* Significant at 5% level of significance

** Significant at 1% level of significance

*Source:* Calculated from Table 8

**Table 10 Growth in procurement of agriculture product (quintals), 1991–2003**

| S. No. | Commodity | 1990–91 | 1991–92 | 1992–93 | 1993–94 | 1994–95 | 1995–96 | 1996–97 |
|---|---|---|---|---|---|---|---|---|
| 1 | Cotton | 17012 | 19288 | 18234 | 10031 | 4649 | 3485 | 828 |
| 2 | Niger seed | 11089 | 19528 | 16204 | 1911 | 2890 | 14324 | 3387 |
| 3 | Maize | 2471 | 14245 | 8435 | 15391 | 3338 | 10 | – |
| 4 | Redgram | 6813 | 3884 | 476 | 869 | 812 | 344 | 489 |
| 5 | French beans | 14235 | 3361 | 1365 | 918 | 1123 | 637 | 1131 |
| 6 | Groundnuts | 1014 | 1877 | 3929 | 1522 | 4 | – | – |
| 7 | Jowar | 4443 | 3775 | 8799 | 591 | 23 | 28 | 74 |
| 8 | Turmeric | 573 | 879 | 265 | 537 | 104 | 15 | 32 |
| 9 | Paddy | 1108 | 2578 | 4817 | 3821 | 3414 | 1364 | 183 |
| 10 | Dry chilies | 442 | 365 | 148 | 1256 | 633 | 291 | 366 |
| 11 | Cashewnuts | 2497 | 347 | 837 | 184 | 5 | 189 | 33 |
| 12 | Annato seed | 33 | 381 | 5 | – | 2 | 5 | 491 |
| 13 | Others | – | – | – | – | – | – | – |
| 14 | Total | – | – | – | – | – | – | – |

**Table 10 Growth in procurement of agriculture product (quintals), 1991–2003**

| *S. No.* | *Commodity* | *1997–98* | *1998–99* | *1999–00* | *2000–01* | *2001–02* | *2002–03* |
|---|---|---|---|---|---|---|---|
| 1 | Cotton | 820 | 416 | 306 | 1688 | – | 30 |
| 2 | Niger seed | 8898 | 2078 | 1907 | 351 | 246 | 31 |
| 3 | Maize | – | 431 | 8189 | 993 | – | 113 |
| 4 | Redgram | 168 | 8937 | 2833 | 1181 | 1124 | 2863 |
| 5 | French beans | 552 | 750 | 5139 | 2166 | 147 | 5163 |
| 6 | Groundnuts | – | 3 | – | – | – | 44 |
| 7 | Jowar | 60 | 228 | 174 | 145 | 2 | 224 |
| 8 | Turmeric | 18 | 8 | – | 229 | 118 | 128 |
| 9 | Paddy | – | 3946 | 5100 | 78 | 39 | 114 |
| 10 | Dry chilies | 155 | 3043 | 3166 | 3750 | 269 | 1495 |
| 11 | Cashewnuts | – | 299 | 732 | 5020 | – | 3764 |
| 12 | Annato seed | 22 | 48 | 66 | 13 | 176 | 126 |
| 13 | Others | – | – | – | – | – | – |
| 14 | Total | – | – | – | – | – | – |

*Source*: Records of GCC

**Table 11 Growth in procurement of agriculture product (Rs. lakhs), 1991–2003**

| *S. No.* | *Commodity* | *1990–91* | *1991–92* | *1992–93* | *1993–94* | *1994–95* | *1995–96* | *1996–97* |
|---|---|---|---|---|---|---|---|---|
| 1 | Cotton | 157.66 | 256.30 | 191.46 | 121.48 | 102.13 | 75.12 | 14.91 |
| 2 | Niger seed | 115.98 | 224.51 | 153.93 | 16.70 | 34.74 | 168.02 | 39.52 |
| 3 | Maize | 3.85 | 48.26 | 28.14 | 38.08 | 13.06 | 0.03 | – |
| 4 | Redgram | 59.37 | 37.22 | 4.28 | 7.79 | 10.36 | 5.25 | 5.81 |
| 5 | French beans | 124.97 | 20.33 | 14.17 | 10.02 | 15.40 | 7.88 | 15.01 |
| 6 | Groundnuts | 8.59 | 16.33 | 30.39 | 10.43 | 0.05 | – | – |
| 7 | Jowar | 8.10 | 12.34 | 15.62 | 1.42 | 0.08 | 0.21 | 0.33 |
| 8 | Turmeric | 5.65 | 9.62 | 4.01 | 2.50 | 2.04 | 0.24 | 0.51 |
| 9 | Paddy | 2.25 | 7.50 | 13.23 | 14.06 | 9.45 | 5.36 | 0.77 |
| 10 | Dry chilies | 3.94 | 7.09 | 2.67 | 16.16 | 13.89 | 9.22 | 9.99 |
| 11 | Cashewnuts | 32.38 | 6.36 | 21.10 | 2.84 | 0.11 | 4.26 | 0.93 |
| 12 | Annato seed | 0.16 | 2.65 | 0.04 | – | 0.02 | 0.18 | 13.46 |
| 13 | Others | 60.89 | 24.86 | 13.79 | 4.45 | 8.55 | 2.89 | 4.78 |
| 14 | Total | 583.79 | 673.38 | 492.83 | 245.93 | 209.88 | 278.66 | 106.02 |

**Table 11 Growth in procurement of agriculture product (Rs. lakhs), 1991–03**

| S. No. | Commodity | 1997–98 | 1998–99 | 1999–00 | 2000–01 | 2001–02 | 2002–03 |
|---|---|---|---|---|---|---|---|
| 1 | Cotton | 15.08 | 7.82 | 5.57 | 37.64 | – | 0.50 |
| 2 | Niger seed | 105.74 | 25.91 | 30.55 | 5.56 | 2.95 | 0.46 |
| 3 | Maize | – | 1.70 | 35.18 | 3.64 | – | 0.51 |
| 4 | Redgram | 2.06 | 98.37 | 48.57 | 13.74 | 15.53 | 37.28 |
| 5 | French beans | 8.74 | 15.52 | 77.53 | 32.24 | 2.25 | 110.95 |
| 6 | Groundnuts | – | 0.03 | – | – | – | 0.99 |
| 7 | Jowar | 0.25 | 1.04 | 1.06 | 0.63 | 0.01 | 1.12 |
| 8 | Turmeric | 0.30 | 0.23 | – | 4.81 | 4.03 | 3.86 |
| 9 | Paddy | – | 19.74 | 29.76 | 0.38 | 0.24 | 8.22 |
| 10 | Dry chilies | 3.05 | 90.11 | 82.93 | 99.49 | 6.42 | 46.59 |
| 11 | Cashewnuts | – | 0.09 | 29.78 | 193.57 | – | 115.95 |
| 12 | Annato seed | 0.21 | 0.56 | 0.72 | 0.17 | 5.19 | 2.36 |
| 13 | Others | 13.59 | 148.47 | 317.01 | 7.61 | 3.18 | 21.40 |
| 14 | Total | 149.02 | 409.47 | 658.66 | 399.49 | 39.80 | 350.19 |

*Source*: Records of GCC

**Table 12**

**Relative shares of various commodities to total agriculture produce (Rs. lakhs), selected years**

| *S. No.* | *Commodity* | *1990–91* | *1999–00* | *2002–03* |
|---|---|---|---|---|
| *1* | *2* | *3* | *4* | *5* |
| 1 | Cotton | 157.66 | 5.57 | 0.50 |
| | | (27.0) | (0.8) | (0.1) |
| 2 | Niger seed | 115.98 | 30.55 | 0.46 |
| | | (19.9) | (4.6) | (0.1) |
| 3 | Maize | 3.85 | 35.18 | 0.51 |
| | | (0.7) | (5.3) | (0.1) |
| 4 | Redgram | 59.37 | 48.57 | 37.28 |
| | | (10.2) | (7.4) | (10.6) |
| 5 | French beans | 124.97 | 77.53 | 110.95 |
| | | (21.4) | (11.8) | (31.7) |
| 6 | Groundnuts | 8.59 | 0 | 0.99 |
| | | (1.5) | (0.0) | (0.3) |
| 7 | Jowar | 8.10 | 1.06 | 1.12 |
| | | (1.4) | (0.2) | (0.3) |
| 8 | Turmeric | 5.65 | 0 | 3.86 |
| | | (1.0) | (0.0) | (1.1) |

*Contd.*

| *1* | *2* | *3* | *4* | *5* |
|---|---|---|---|---|
| 9 | Paddy | 2.25 | 29.76 | 8.22 |
| | | (0.4) | (4.5) | (2.3) |
| 10 | Dry chilies | 3.94 | 82.93 | 46.59 |
| | | (0.7) | (12.6) | (13.3) |
| 11 | Cashewnuts | 32.38 | 29.78 | 115.95 |
| | | (5.5) | (4.5) | (33.1) |
| 12 | Annato seed | 0.16 | 0.72 | 2.36 |
| | | (0.0) | (0.1) | (0.7) |
| 13 | Others | 60.89 | 317.01 | 21.40 |
| | | (10.4) | (48.1) | (6.1) |
| 14 | Total | 583.79 | 658.66 | 350.19 |
| | | (100.0) | (100.0) | (100.0) |

*Source:* Records of GCC

**Table 13 Trends in sale of daily requirement items by GCC, 1987–03**

| *S. No.* | *Daily requirement* | *Intercept* | *Ceofficient* | *t-value* | *$R^{-2}$* | *F-value* |
|---|---|---|---|---|---|---|
| 1 | Rice | | | | | |
| | Linear | 254.17 | 151.7795 ** | 9.79 | 0.86 | 95.92 |
| | Semilog | 6.79 | 0.0661 ** | 8.73 | 0.82 | 76.13 |
| | Double-log | 5.28 | 0.9416 ** | 11.13 | 0.88 | 123.85 |
| 2 | Sugar | | | | | |
| | Linear | 0.46 | 30.9736 ** | 5.15 | 0.61 | 26.48 |
| | Semilog | 4.87 | 0.0783 ** | 5.54 | 0.65 | 30.66 |
| | Double-log | 2.97 | 1.1595 ** | 7.20 | 0.76 | 51.84 |
| 3 | Salt | | | | | |
| | Linear | –12.30 | 2.2403 ** | 7.50 | 0.78 | 56.26 |
| | Semilog | 1.20 | 0.1123 ** | 8.53 | 0.82 | 72.78 |
| | Double-log | –1.15 | 1.5234 ** | 7.83 | 0.79 | 61.29 |
| 4 | Edible oil | | | | | |
| | Linear | 121.18 | 6.4038 | 1.71 | 0.11 | 2.91 |
| | Semilog | 4.87 | 0.0297 | 1.73 | 0.11 | 2.99 |
| | Double-log | 4.44 | 0.3332 | 1.36 | 0.05 | 1.86 |
| 5 | Kerosene oil | | | | | |
| | Linear | –387.90 | 52.0122 ** | 5.78 | 0.67 | 33.36 |
| | Semilog | 3.81 | 0.1282 ** | 11.52 | 0.89 | 132.69 |
| | Double-log | 1.17 | 1.7243 ** | 9.42 | 0.85 | 88.80 |
| 6 | Others | | | | | |
| | Linear | –660.37 | 116.7513 ** | 10.39 | 0.87 | 107.98 |
| | Semilog | 4.80 | 0.1326 ** | 8.84 | 0.83 | 78.22 |
| | Double-log | 1.77 | 1.8975 ** | 11.88 | 0.90 | 141.24 |
| 7 | Total | | | | | |
| | Linear | –386.36 | 341.4820 ** | 23.70 | 0.96 | 561.60 |
| | Semilog | 6.49 | 0.1206 ** | 15.49 | 0.92 | 240.03 |
| | Double-log | 5.69 | 1.0043 ** | 19.49 | 0.95 | 380.01 |

** Significant at 1% level of significance

*Source:* Estimated

**Table 14 Short-term loans (Rs. lakhs) disbursed by GCC, 1991–03**

| *S. No.* | *Year* | *Borrowers* | *Amount disbursed* | *Loan amount/ borrower (Rupees)* | *Recovery* | *%* |
|---|---|---|---|---|---|---|
| 1 | 1990–91 | 8064 | 162.64 | 2017 | 73.26 | 45 |
| 2 | 1991–92 | 40132 | 659.28 | 1643 | 311.90 | 47 |
| 3 | 1992–93 | 84819 | 1363.38 | 1607 | 586.38 | 43 |
| 4 | 1993–94 | 39522 | 969.49 | 2453 | 706.72 | 73 |
| 5 | 1994–95 | 24777 | 600.89 | 2425 | 363.88 | 61 |
| 6 | 1995–96 | 16687 | 491.32 | 2944 | 315.40 | 63 |
| 7 | 1996–97 | 9245 | 229.63 | 2484 | 201.30 | 88 |
| 8 | 1997–98 | 8928 | 287.13 | 3216 | 396.78 | 138 |
| 9 | 1998–99 | 15390 | 292.92 | 1903 | 249.83 | 85 |
| 10 | 1999–00 | 11314 | 493.93 | 4366 | 190.93 | 39 |
| 11 | 2000–01 | 12181 | 502.45 | 4125 | 340.30 | 68 |
| 12 | 2001–02 | 6919 | 206.75 | 2988 | 371.79 | 180 |
| 13 | 2002–03 | 7860 | 281.00 | 3575 | 264.89 | 94 |

*Source:* Records of GCC

*Notes*:

1. Since 1999, GCC has been receiving Rs. 11 crores/annum out of Rs. 21 crores required towards cost of establishment. The balance amount is met through internal sources.
2. This section is heavily benefited from Roy (1997), and Vidyasagar (2003).

3. Shandies are places where the tribals gather on a particular day in a week with their produce and weekly collections. Shandy provided a forum for sale and purchase of any type of commodity where both tribal and non-tribal merchants participate. Tribals sell their MFP and agriculture produce and purchase daily requirements from these shandies. It is a merry making day after seven hard working days. Thus, shandies are part and parcel of tribal life. Tribal life without shandies is dry and life-less.
4. It is a place where the CCPA would procure MFP from tribals on a particular day in a week.

# 4

# Progress of Selected Divisions of GCC

Progress in various functions (procurement of MFPs agriculture produce, supply of daily requirements, and credit operations) of selected divisions[1] contained in this chapter. Attempt is also made to compare performance of selected divisions and prescriptions provided for revitalization of GPCMSs. Divisions are arranged in alphabetical order.

## An overview of divisions

As mentioned earlier, there are 10 divisions with 45 GPCMSs. Maximum number of GPCMSs are located in Bhadrachalam[2] division followed by Utnoor (Table 1). As of membership, Bhadrachalam division, once again, stood first followed by Pravatipuram and Rampachodavaram. In all, GCC has 3.72 lakhs membership. All GPCMSs together contributed Rs. 82.44 lakhs to the share capital of GCC. Bhadrachalam, once again outperformed other divisions followed by Eturnagaram and Utnoor. Division-wise performance of short term, medium term consumption, and loans provided to self help groups are provided in Tables 2 to 5.[3] A perusal of these tables indicate recovery is less than satisfactory across divisions. From among divisions, Bhadrachalam did satisfactorily compared to others

The status of consumption loans is still worse with zero recovery, and same is true with loans provided to SHGs. Across GPCMSs, performance of short term loans is provided in Table 6. Utnoor has the higest (Rs. 2.76 crores) outstanding, and Shirpurkagaz-nagar has the lowest (Rs. 3.88 lakhs). An attempt is made in the following sections to describe various activities of selected divisions.

## Bhadrachalam division

This division is inhabited by Koya, Konda Reddy, Lambada, Yerukula, and Yanadi tribes. It has 1.09 lakhs tribal household, with a total population of 4.51 lakhs (2001). There are about 700 women MFP collectors in the division. With a view to help local tribals, GCC started a division way back in 1957. Division has 8 GPCMSs and the relevant data are provided in Table 7. Bhadrachalam and Palwancha societies are 14 decades old while Manuguru and Kukunoor have just completed 10 years. The division has over 73,000 membership with Rs. 21.56 lakhs share capital. These societies have 266 employees of which 123 are tribals, and 20% of the total employers are women. Society-wise sanctioned, and existing posts are provided in Appendix 25. They have been running four mandal level stockiest points.

### Procurement of MFPs and agriculture produce

As mentioned elsewhere in the report, shandies are lifeline of tribals and there is no day without shandy in a week (Table 8), and GCC undertakes procurement of MFPs in these shandies. Various MFPs available in the area are provided in Table 9. Gum karaya, mohwa seed, myrobalans, and nuxvomica are the major MFPs in the area. Of the four mentioned above, gum karaya contributed 2/3rds to the total MFP procured (Table 10). However, it's contribution varied between 90–95% during 1991–95. Procurement of MFPs depends not only on availability but also on prevailing prices in neighbouring states (Orissa), and presence of private traders in the market. Though, GCC has monopoly rights in procurement of these commodities certain amount of smuggling/pilferage is unavoidable. According to the local officials, as much as 20% of the produce is sold to outside agencies. Progress in procurement of agriculture produce is presented in Table 11. Chilies is the single major item among this category. Off-late, it's contribution is as much as 90–95% of the total agriculture produce.

## Supply of daily requirements on credit

Society-wise availability of ration cards, and relevant particulars are provided in Table 12. In all , the division covers 30 revenue mandals and has 66,232 ration cards. Yellandu has maximum (16,773) number of ration cards with 150 daily requirement depots of which 4 are run by SHGs. DR depot at Munuguru also involved in distribution of LPG. As of supply of demestic requirements (Table 13), increased from Rs. 6.60 crores in 1990–91 to Rs. 13.71 crores in 2002–03 registering more than 100% growth during the last 13 years. As expected, rest constituted as much as 40–45% of the total domestic supplies. Performance of the division in terms of providing short term loans is satisfactory (Table 14). Though there is no trend in the amount disbursed, recovery has been over 80% during the study period. Other loans provided in the division are furnished in Table 15, and medium term loans constituted major chunk in this category. Targets and achievements in credit disbursement across GPCMSs are provided in Table 16, and all of them performed well during the period under consideration.

# Chintapalli division

Chintapalli division was carved out of Paderu in November 1990, and functioned during 1990–01. It was re-opened from July 1, 03. Jurisdiction of the division is limited to the areas covered by GPCMSs of Chintapalli, Gudem Kotha Veedhi, and Koyyuru. These three GPCMSs cover five revenue mandals (Chintapalli, Gudem Kotha Veedhi, Koyyuru, Part of Goludonda, and Nathavaram) with five forest ranges. The division has 683 revenue villages of which 255 are located in Chintapalli, 218 in Gudem Kotha Veedhi, and 210 in Koyyuru. Total tribal population of the area is 1.40 lakhs. Bhagata, Konda Dora, Nooka Dora, Pedda Dora, Valmiki, and Kodu are major tribes in this division. Gum, honey, sheekakai, myrobalans, addaleaf, cleaning nuts, marking nuts, pungam seed, RS roots, nuxvomica, narmamidi bark, hill brooms, seeded tamarind, deseeded tamarind, tamarind seed, dry amla, etc. are the MFPs. available in the division. Niger seed, french beans (red and white), cuttings, redgram, maize, jowar, turmeric, annato seed, dola seed (nepalam seed), etc. are the agriculture produce of the area.

In all,16 shandies are there in the division (Table 17). Data on membership, share capital, and turnover of the division are provided in Table 18. The share capital of all three GPCMSs is Rs. 3.66 lakhs with total turnover of Rs. 14.86 crores. Membership, share capital, and turnover steadily increased during 1991–03.

## Procurement of MFPs and agricultural produce

Gum karaya, tamarind, and myrobalans are three major MFPs procured. Total value of MFPs procured declined steadily during the period under observation (Table 19). There are wide fluctuations in the relative contribution of various MFPs to total procurement. Procurement in gum karaya has shown no trend, while tamarind has increased its share substantially during 1991–03. For example, value of tamarind constituted 0.7% of the total MFP procurement in 1990–91 which increased to 47% by 2002–03. On the other hand, gum karaya contributed around 40% in 1990–91, and declined to 24% by 2002–03. French beans, and niger seed are two important agriculture produce procured in the division. Once again, total value of agriculture produce procured has shown no trend at all during 1991–03 (Table 20). It never increased Rs. 50 lakhs during the 13 years for which data are available, and touched a low of Rs. 8.15 lakhs in 1997–98. Of the total procurement in 2002–03, french beans accounted for 93%.

### *Supply of essential commodities, and credit*

The division has 77 DR depots of which 3 are managed by SHGs. Maximum number of DR deports are located in Koyyuru. All the three GPCMSs put together have 37,981 ration cards of which 7.4% are pink. Supply of domestic requirements steadily increased from Rs. 1.67 crores in 1990–91 to Rs. 5.40 crores in 2001–03 (Table 21). Across various commodities, rice constituted 62.5% of the total supplies while, 'others' contributed 25%. Sugar and kerosene each accounted for approximately 4–5% of the total supplies. There is a scope for coverage in the 'others'.

The division has started loaning operations from 1990–91 onwards under crop loans, and consumption loans. As indicated earlier, maximum loaning operations were carried out during 1992–95, and as much as Rs. 2.62 crores were disbursed during this period (Table 22). Loan disbursed/member has shown steady increase and stood at Rs. 6067 in 2001–02 which dwindled to Rs. 1706 in 2002–03. Reasons for high amount of loan disbursed in 2001–02 are, however, not available. Except during 1998–99, recovery performance has been more than 50%.

### Grain banks

In pursuance of the instructions of Government of Andhra Pradesh, grain banks were established covering 746 families from 16 villages of primitive tribal groups during 2003. Particulars on grain bank scheme are provided in Appendix 26. Each grain bank is being supplied food grains (regi/sama) @ a quintal/ family (one time supply) which is to be rotated among the family in 3 spells in a year. The quantity so borrowed shall be returned in kind along with nominal rate of interest in the form of grains only. The cost of the scheme is Rs. 4.40 lakhs, and in progress.

## Paderu division

It is situated at 3500 ft above the mean sea level, and 150 kms away district head quarters, Visakhapatnam. It has a huge forest cover, coffee plantations, etc. Paderu, Araku Valley, Burra caves, and Mastsyagundam[4] are the places of tourist and mythological importance in the area. Bhagata, Vakmiki, Konda Dora, Konda Kammari, Gadaba, Kondulu, Samantha, etc. tribals inhabit Paderu division. There are about 1.20 lakhs tribal families residing in the area. The area is covered by 6 GPCMSs (Paderu, G. Madugula, Pedabayalu, Munchingput, Araku Valley, and Kasipatnam). The division has 119 DR depots with about 73,000 ration cards (Table 23), and Paderu has highest number of depots as also ration cards. Shandies organised in the division are provided in Table 24.

## Procurement of MFPs and agricultural produce

Tamarind, addaleaf, gum, myrobalans, marking nuts, and pungam seed are the major items of MFPs being procured in the division. Progress in procurement of various MFPs during 1992–03 is provided in Table 25. There are wide variations across various MFPs procured during the study period while gum, tamarind, honey, and myrobalans have improved their share. Amla fruit, mohwa-seed, soap nuts, etc. are new arrivals in the market. Progress of various MFPs in value terms is provided in Table 26. It steadily increased from Rs. 66 lahks in 1991–92 to Rs. 360.5 lakhs in 2002–03, while maximum value of procurement was achieved in 2000–01 (Rs. 5.59 crores). As of procurement of agriculture produce french beans, niger seed, redgram, and nipalem seed were the major items during 1992–99, while rajama, redgram, white beans, kashmir beans during 2002–03 (Table 27). The division procured huge quantities of coffee seed during 1998–00. Value of agriculture produce too underwent wide fluctuations (Table 28). It was as low as Rs. 6.62 lakhs in 1993–94 and reached a maximum of Rs. 1.56 crores in 1999–00. As mentioned earlier, this area has lot of potential with irrigated agriculture. However, due to presence of number of private traders from plains, GPCMSs are not in a position to compete with them. Quantities and values procured exhibit the same story.

## Supply of essential commodities, and loans

Particulars on supply of essential commodities and loans provided during 1991–03 are provided in Table 29. DR sales increased from Rs. 4.8 crores in 1990–91 to Rs. 16.35 crores in 2002–03 constituting approximately 3/4ths of the total division's turnover. As expected, loans provided have shown erratic trend, and it's share is declining slowly. Turnover, in terms of procurement of MFP, agriculture produce, supply of essential commodities, and loans issued, is around Rs. 22 crores in 2002–03 of which 17% is contributed by MFP, and 16.75% by agricultural produce. Loans constituted less than 1% of the total turnover of the division.

Activity-wise targets and achievements (2002–03) for the division are provided in Table 30. On the whole, division fall short of 19% of the total targets fixed for the year. Across activities, it lagged behind heavily in recovery of loans (80%), procurement of MFP (37%), and agriculture produce (37%). The division out-performed targets fixed in RMD sales.

## Value additions through processing

Flower tamarind cake making units were established at V. Madugula, and S. Kota godown points in 2001. Subsequently, six more units were established during 2002, and seeded tamarind is processed into consumable packs at these processing centres. The work was entrusted to women self help groups. Besides, supplying to the Civil Supplies Corporation under Griha Mitra Scheme, these packets are being sold in the urban market through RMD network. Similarly, rajama, white beans, and cutting procured in the division are packet into ½ kg packs. Mechanised screening and packing is being done at Paderu.

# Srisailam[5] division

With a view to cater to the requirements of the tribal population of Rayalaseema reion, a division was created in July 1987 with headquarters at Nandyal which was later shifted to Srisailam in 1989. Change was mainly aimed at maintaining close liaison with ITDA (primitive tribal group, Chenchu). This division has three GPCMSs (Mannanur, Pedda Dornal, and Nandyal) with 39,630 chenchus (Table 31). Mannanur is the oldest society while Nandyal is over 13 years. Of the total Chenchu population in the region, 40% are covered by mannanur GPCMSs. Important MFPs available in the division are gum karaya, gum kondagogu, mohwa seed, rock bee honey, nuxvomica, soapnuts, naramamidi bark, maredugeddalu, amla, and myrobalans.

## Procurement of MFPs and agriculture produce

Progress in procurement of various MFPs for the period 1992–03 is provided in Table 32. Data presented in table supports the above findings. There are oscillations in the data on procurement across various MFPs. For example, gum karaya decreased from 220 tonnes in 1991–92 to 43 tonnes in 2002–03, and that of gum kondagogu increased from 34 tonnes in 1993–94 to 90 tonnes by

2002–03. Similarly, wide variations can be noticed in the quantities of other MFPs procured during study period. Growth in value of MFPs procured for the above period is provided in Table 33. As expected, there are wide fluctuations in the value of MFPs procured. Total value of MFPs procured was the lowest (Rs. 65.12 lakhs) in 1998–99, and the highest (Rs. 202.24 lakhs) in 2002–03.

The division undertook meager amount of business in agricultural produce during 1992–03. Major produce available in this category are cotton, chilies, paddy, and sunflower (Table 34). Though number of other crops are also available in the region, GPCMSs failed to procure because of non-availability of cash, competition from private traders, age old linkage between tribal and traders, non-availability of godowns, etc. Growth in value of procurement of these crops is provided in Table 35.

## Supply of essential commodities and credit

There are 40 DR depots of which 11 are run by women self help groups. As many as 25 items are made available in these DR depots. GPCMSs have also been supplying essential commodities and other provisions to the ashram schools of Department of Tribal Welfare and residential schools functioning under ITDA. Growth in sale of domestic requirements for 1996–03 is provided in Table 36. Sales increased from Rs. 95.57 lakhs in 1995–96 to Rs. 3.12 crores in 2002–03 (Table 37). Of the total sales of 2002–03, 62% was contributed by Mannanur GPCMS. As of short term credit operations, division has provided Rs. 83.12 lakhs during 1991–03 of which Rs. 24.89 lakhs was collected (Table 37). Baring 1994–95, 1995–96, 2000–01 and 2002–03, repayment was less than 20%. The division also provided medium term loans to 29 beneficiaries during 1991–92, and 1998–99, an amount of Rs. 1.3 lakhs was provided under this category, and the repayment was hardly Rs. 6000. Apart from short and medium term loans, GPCMSs also provided consumption loans during 1991–94 to 1418 beneficiaries and disbursed an amount of Rs. 7.96 lakhs of which Rs. 5.57 lakhs is outstanding.

### Training

Training on scientific collection of gum karaya, marudugeddalu and naramamidi bark was imparted to 329 MFP collectors during 2002–03. Kovel foundation (Visakhapatnam) provided necessary training in this regard. Society-wise details are given in Table 38.

### Grain banks

To provide sustenance to BPL tribal families during lean season and thereby checking migration and starvation deaths, about 111 grain banks have been established during 1996–97, 1997–98, and 2000–01 (Table 39) in the project area. In addition, 60 grain banks have been sanctioned for 2002–03 covering 1931 BPL families. Village level working committees are formed for all 60 grain banks. However, grain banks could not be grounded due to non-release of rice at Rs. 565/quintal under central sector scheme and efforts are on to get extension of the scheme.

## Comparison of selected divisions

Business activities of a GPCMS depends on a number of factors: operational area, tribal population, forest cover, productivity of forests, type of species, ration cards allotted, hostels in the area, presence of private traders, motivation of GPCMS's employees, funds available with GPCMS, etc. Given their geographical location, socio-economic status of its clientele, it would be difficult to increase business in these far-flung areas. However, a modest attempt is made to evaluate the performance of these societies based on employees, procurement of MFP and agriculture produce, and supply of essential commodities and credit, and turnover/employee (Table 40). Across divisions, essential commodities constituted major chunk of their business followed by procurement of MFP, and agriculture produce. Employees/society is lowest in Srisailam division and the highest in Bhadrachalam, while turnover/employee is the highest in Paderu followed by Srisailam. Paderu is a potential area with irrigated ariculture and large forest cover while Srisailam division has lowest number of employees. Thus, the results are in conformity with above findings.

Division-wise degree of viability of GPCMSs is provided in Table 41. Viability is considered on the basis of grant required as percentage of salaries. Majority of the societies cluster around 51–75% of requirement bracket. As many as 9 out of 21 require upto 50% of salaries.

## Summary

Progress in various functions (procurements of MFPs and agriculture produce, supply of daily requirements, and credit operations) of selected divisions are studied in Chapter 4. There are 10 divisions with 45 GPCMSs, and 3.72 lakhs membership. All GPCMSs together contributed Rs. 82.44 lakhs to the share capital of GCC. Recovery is less than satisfactory across divisions. Utnoor has the highest (Rs. 2.76 crores) outstanding, and Shirpurkagaznagar has the lowest (Rs. 3.88 lakhs).

Bhadrachalam division has 8 GPCMSs with 73,000 membership, and Rs. 21.56 lakhs share capital. Gum karaya, mohwa seed, myrobalans, and nuxvomica are the major MFPs in the area, and gum karaya contributed 2/3rds to the total value of MFP procured. According to local officials, as much as 20% of the produce is sold to outside agencies. Chilies is the single major item in agricultural produce. In all, division covers 30 revenue mandals, and has 66,232 ration cards. Supply of domestic requirements increased from Rs. 6.60 crores in 1990–91 to Rs. 13.71 crores in 2002–03 registering more than 100% growth during the last 13 years. 'Rest' constituted as much as 40–45% of the total domestic supplies. Though there is no trend in the amounts disbursed, recovery has been over 80% during the study period.

Chintapalli division was carved out of Paderu in November 1990, and functioned during 1990-01. The division has 683 revenue villages with a tribal population of 1.40 lakhs. In all, 16 shandies are there in the division. Gum karaya, tamarind, and myrobalans are three major MFPs procured. total value of MFPs procured declined steadily during the period under observation. Procurement in gum karaya has shown no trend, white tamarind has increased its share substantially during 1991–03. Procurement of agriculture produce never increased Rs. 50 lakhs during the

13 years for which data are available, and touched a low of Rs. 8.15 lakhs in 1997–98. Of the total procurement in 2002–03, french beans accounted for 93%. Supply of domestic requirements steadily increased from Rs. 1.67 crores in 1990–91 to Rs. 5.40 crores in 2002–03. Across various commodities, rice constitued 62.5% of the total supplies while 'others' contributed 25%. Maximum loaning operations were carried out during 1992–95, and as much as Rs. 2.62 crores were disbursed. Loan disbursed/member has shown steady increase and stood at Rs. 6067 in 2001–02 which dwindled to Rs. 1706 in 2002–03. Grain banks were established covering 746 families from 16 villages of primitive tribal groups during 2003.

Paderu division has 6 GPCMSs (Paderu, G. Madugula, Pedabayalu, Munchingput, Araku Valley, and Kasipatnam). The division has 119 DR depots with about 73,000 ration cards. Tamarind, addaleaf, gum, myrobalans, marking nuts, and pungam seed are the major items of MFPs in the division. Value of MFPs procured increased steadily from Rs. 66 lakhs in 1991–92 to Rs. 360.5 lakhs in 2002–03, while maximum value of procurement was noticed in 2000–01 (Rs. 5.59 crores). As of procurement of agriculture produce, french beans, niger seed, redgram, and nipalem seed were the major items during 1992–95, while rajama, redgram, white beans, and kashmir beans during 2000–03. Value of agriculture produce too underwent wide fluctuations. DR sales increased from Rs.4.8 crores in 1990–91 to Rs. 16.35 crores in 2002–03 constituting approximately 3/4ths of the total division's turnover. Turnover, in terms of procurement of MFP, agriculture produce, supply of essential commodities, and loans issued, is around Rs. 22 crores in 2002–03 of which 17% is contributed by MFP, and 16.75% by agricultural produce. Division fall short of 19% of the total targets for 2002–03. Flower tamarind cake making units were established at eight places, and seeded tamarind is processed into consumable packs at these processing centres.

Srisailam division has three GPCMSs (Mannanur, Pedda Dornal, and Nandyal) with 39,630 chenchus. Important MFPs available in the division are gum karaya, gum kondagogu, mohwa seed, rock bee honey, nuxvomica, soapnuts, naramamidi bark, marédugeddalu, amla, and myrobalans. Gum karaya decreased from 220 tonnes in 1991–92 to 43 tonnes in 2002–03, and that of gum kondagogu increased from 34 tonnes in 1993–94 to 90 tonnes by 2002–03. Total value of MFPs procured was the lowest (Rs. 65.12 lakhs) in 1998–99, and the highest (Rs. 202.24 lakhs) in 2002–03. Major agricultural produce available in the area are cotton, chillies, paddy, and sunflower. Sales increased from Rs. 95.57 lakhs in 1995–96 to Rs. 3.12 crores in 2002-03. Of the total sales in 2002–03, 62% was contributed by Mannanur GPCMS. As of short term credit operations, divisions has provided Rs. 83.12 lakhs during 1991–03 of which Rs. 24.89 lakhs was collected. Training on scientific collection of MFPs was imparted to 329 MFP collectors during 2002–03. About 111 grain banks have been established during 1996–97, 1997–98, and 2000–01.

Across divisions, essential commodities constituted major chunk of the business followed by MFP, and agriculture produce. Employees/society is the lowest in Srisailam division and the highest in Bhadrachalam, while turnover/employee is the highest in Paderu followed by Srisailam. Majority of the GPCMSs fall short of 51–75% of their salaries which is reimbursed by the GCC.

**Table 1 Division-wise membership and share capital**

| *S. No.* | *Division* | *GPCMSs* | *Membership* | *Share capital (Rs. lakhs)* |
|---|---|---|---|---|
| 1 | Seethampeta | 2 | 27288 | 3.62 |
| 2 | Parvathipuram | 3 | 70622 | 5.87 |
| 3 | Paderu | 6 | 43173 | 5.49 |
| 4 | Chintapalli | 3 | 22659 | 5.39 |
| 5 | Rampachodavaram | 6 | 55274 | 10.63 |
| 6 | Tirupathi | 3 | 3835 | 0.71 |
| 7 | Bhadrachalam | 8 | 73401 | 20.57 |
| 8 | Eturunagaram | 4 | 36901 | 15.56 |
| 9 | Utnoor | 7 | 35485 | 13.01 |
| 10 | Srisailam | 3 | 3726 | 1.59 |
| 11 | Total | 45 | 372364 | 82.44 |

*Source*: Records of GCC

**Table 2 Division-wise demand, collection, and balance of short-term loans (principal and interest), 2003**

| *S. No.* | *Division* | *Demand* | *Recoveries* | | | *Balance* | *Recovery (%)* |
|---|---|---|---|---|---|---|---|
| | | | *Principal* | *Interest* | *Total* | | |
| 1 | Rampacho-davaram | 437.72 | 0.79 | 14.75 | 15.54 | 436.93 | 0.18 |
| 2 | Seethampeta | 197.34 | 0.00 | 11.51 | 11.51 | 197.3 | 0.00 |
| 3 | Parvathipuram | 110.02 | 0.65 | 6.37 | 6.37 | 109.37 | 0.59 |
| 4 | Paderu | 212.75 | 4.19 | 17.32 | 17.32 | 208.56 | 1.97 |
| 5 | Chintapalli | 180.54 | 0.00 | 3.07 | 3.07 | 180.54 | 0.00 |
| 6 | Tirupathi | 36.63 | 0.18 | 1.39 | 1.39 | 36.45 | 0.49 |
| 7 | Bhadrachalam | 296.94 | 24.95 | 48.25 | 48.25 | 271.99 | 8.40 |
| 8 | Paloncha | 443.96 | 13.52 | 50.32 | 50.32 | 430.44 | 3.05 |
| 9 | Utnoor | 504.40 | 0.00 | 12.48 | 12.48 | 504.40 | 0.00 |
| 10 | Asifabad | 129.54 | 1.88 | 9.03 | 9.03 | 127.66 | 1.45 |
| 11 | Eturunagaram | 474.62 | 11.46 | 38.29 | 28.29 | 463.16 | 2.41 |
| 12 | Srisailam | 99.54 | 0.00 | 2.53 | 2.53 | 99.54 | 0.00 |
| | Total | 3124.00 | 57.62 | 216.10 | 216.10 | 3066.38 | 1.84 |

*Source*: Records of GCC

**Table 3 Division-wise demand, collection, and balance of medium-term loans (principal and interest), 2003**

| *S. No.* | *Division* | *Demand* | *Recoveries* | | | *Balance* | *Recovery (%)* |
|---|---|---|---|---|---|---|---|
| | | | *Principal* | *Interest* | *Total* | | |
| 1 | Rampacho-davaram | 68.37 | 0.00 | 0.38 | 0.38 | 68.37 | 0.00 |
| 2 | Seethampeta | 13.54 | 0.00 | 0.32 | 0.32 | 13.54 | 0.00 |
| 3 | Parvathipuram | 2.58 | 0.00 | 0.01 | 0.01 | 2.58 | 0.00 |
| 4 | Paderu | 5.05 | 0.00 | 0.05 | 0.05 | 5.05 | 0.00 |
| 5 | Chintapalli | 24.39 | 0.75 | 0.78 | 1.53 | 23.64 | 0.00 |
| 6 | Tirupathi | 12.66 | 0.00 | 0.01 | 0.01 | 12.66 | 0.00 |
| 7 | Bhadrachalam | 86.96 | 0.00 | 1.30 | 1.30 | 86.96 | 0.00 |
| 8 | Paloncha | 52.51 | 2.96 | 28.89 | 31.85 | 49.55 | 0.00 |
| 9 | Utnoor | 9.79 | 0.00 | 0.00 | 0.00 | 9.79 | 5.64 |
| 10 | Asifabad | 2.35 | 0.00 | 0.00 | 0.00 | 2.35 | 0.00 |
| 11 | Eturunagaram | 11.75 | 0.00 | 0.00 | 0.00 | 11.75 | 0.00 |
| 12 | Srisailam | 0.75 | 0.00 | 0.00 | 0.01 | 0.78 | 0.00 |
| | Total | 290.73 | 3.71 | 31.75 | 35.46 | 287.02 | 1.28 |

*Source*: Records of GCC

**Table 4 Division-wise demand, collection, and balance of consumption loans (principal and interest), 2003**

| S. No. | Division | Demand | Recoveries | | | Balance | Recovery (%) |
|---|---|---|---|---|---|---|---|
| | | | Principal | Interest | Total | | |
| 1 | Rampacho-davaram | 7.48 | 0.00 | 0.01 | 0.01 | 7.48 | 0.00 |
| 2 | Seethampeta | 2.83 | 0.00 | 0.00 | 0.00 | 2.83 | 0.00 |
| 3 | Parvathipuram | 6.58 | 0.00 | 0.03 | 0.03 | 6.58 | 0.00 |
| 4 | Paderu | 16.58 | 0.00 | 0.02 | 0.02 | 16.58 | 0.00 |
| 5 | Chintapalli | 7.34 | 0.03 | 0.01 | 0.04 | 7.31 | 0.00 |
| 6 | Tirupathi | 3.25 | 0.00 | 0.02 | 0.02 | 3.25 | 0.00 |
| 7 | Bhadrachalam | 7.91 | 0.00 | 0.00 | 0.00 | 7.91 | 0.00 |
| 8 | Paloncha | 6.01 | 0.00 | 0.00 | 0.00 | 6.01 | 0.00 |
| 9 | Utnoor | 1.02 | 0.00 | 0.00 | 0.00 | 1.02 | 0.00 |
| 10 | Asifabad | 1.65 | 0.00 | 0.00 | 0.00 | 1.65 | 0.00 |
| 11 | Eturunagaram | 3.50 | 0.00 | 0.00 | 0.00 | 3.50 | 0.00 |
| 12 | Srisailam | 7.54 | 0.00 | 0.02 | 0.02 | 7.54 | 0.00 |
| | Total | 71.69 | 0.03 | 0.11 | 0.14 | 71.66 | 0.04 |

*Source*: Records of GCC

**Table 5 Division-wise demand, collection, and balance of self help groups (principal and interest), 2003**

| S. No. | Division | Demand | Recoveries | | | Balance | Recovery (%) |
|---|---|---|---|---|---|---|---|
| | | | Principal | Interest | Total | | |
| 1 | Rampacho-davaram | 6.17 | 0.00 | 0.00 | 0.00 | 6.17 | 0.00 |
| 2 | Seethampeta | 9.53 | 0.00 | 1.08 | 1.08 | 9.53 | 0.00 |
| 3 | Parvathipuram | 0.05 | 0.00 | 0.00 | 0.00 | 0.05 | 0.00 |
| 4 | Paderu | 3.76 | 0.00 | 0.03 | 0.03 | 3.76 | 0.00 |
| 5 | Chintapalli | 6.08 | 0.00 | 0.02 | 0.03 | 6.07 | 0.00 |
| 6 | Tirupathi | 0.00 | 0.01 | 0.00 | 0.00 | 0.00 | 0.01 |
| 7 | Bhadrachalam | 0.00 | 0.00 | 0.00 | 0.00 | 0.00 | 0.00 |
| 8 | Paloncha | 14.78 | 0.00 | 0.00 | 0.00 | 14.78 | 0.00 |
| 9 | Utnoor | 0.00 | 0.00 | 0.00 | 0.00 | 0.00 | 0.00 |
| 10 | Asifabad | 0.00 | 0.00 | 0.00 | 0.00 | 0.00 | 0.00 |
| 11 | Eturunagaram | 0.00 | 0.00 | 0.00 | 0.00 | 0.00 | 0.00 |
| 12 | Srisailam | 0.00 | 0.00 | 0.00 | 0.00 | 0.00 | 0.00 |
| | Total | 40.37 | 0.01 | 1.13 | 1.14 | 40.36 | 0.02 |

*Source*: Records of GCC

**Table 6 Demand, collection, and balance of short term loans, 2003 (Rs. lakhs)**

| *S. No.* | *GPCMS* | *Demand* | *Recoveries* | *Balance* | *Recovery (%)* |
|---|---|---|---|---|---|
| *1* | *2* | *3* | *4* | *5* | *6* |
| 1 | Rampachodavaram | 112.75 | – | 112.75 | 0.00 |
| 2 | Addateegala | 139.01 | – | 139.01 | 0.00 |
| 3 | Rajavommangi | 47.64 | – | 47.64 | 0.00 |
| 4 | Pedamallapuram | 15.01 | – | 15.01 | 0.00 |
| 5 | Maredumalli | 7.05 | 2.14 | 4.91 | |
| 6 | K.R. Puram | 96.49 | – | 96.49 | 0.00 |
| 7 | Seethampeta | 70.61 | – | 70.61 | 0.00 |
| 8 | Pathapatnam | 47.29 | – | 47.29 | 0.00 |
| 9 | Parvathipuram | 42.25 | – | 42.25 | 0.00 |
| 10 | G.L. Puram | 36.39 | 0.03 | 36.36 | |
| 11 | Saluru | 26.14 | 0.34 | 25.80 | |
| 12 | Paderu | 84.90 | 0.00 | 84.90 | 0.00 |
| 13 | G. Madugula | 8.79 | 0.31 | 8.48 | |
| 14 | Munchingput | 72.09 | 0.00 | 72.09 | 0.00 |
| 15 | Pedabayalu | 8.62 | 2.71 | 5.91 | |
| 16 | Araku | 45.92 | 0.00 | 45.92 | 0.00 |
| 17 | Kasipatnam | 9.57 | 1.92 | 7.66 | |
| 18 | Chintapalli | 28.62 | 0.00 | 28.62 | 0.00 |
| 19 | G.K. Veedhi | 37.32 | 0.00 | 37.32 | 0.00 |
| 20 | Koyyuru | 109.03 | 0.00 | 109.03 | 0.00 |
| 21 | Chittoor | 27.54 | 0.00 | 27.54 | 0.00 |
| 22 | Nellore | 7.18 | 0.00 | 7.18 | 0.00 |
| 23 | Cuddapah | 4.98 | 0.00 | 4.98 | 0.00 |
| 24 | Bhadrachalam | 120.33 | 7.97 | 112.36 | |
| 25 | Venkatpuram | 123.51 | 17.69 | 105.82 | |
| 26 | Chintoor | 80.98 | 0.00 | 80.98 | 0.00 |
| 27 | Palwancha | 113.26 | 0.00 | 113.26 | 0.00 |
| 28 | Dammapeta | 102.84 | 0.00 | 102.84 | 0.00 |

*Continued*

| 1 | 2 | 3 | 4 | 5 | 6 |
|---|---|---|---|---|---|
| 29 | Yellandu | 105.67 | 9.09 | 96.59 | |
| 30 | Manuguru | 106.94 | 0.00 | 106.94 | 0.00 |
| 31 | Kukunoor | 64.85 | 0.00 | 64.85 | 0.00 |
| 32 | Utnoor | 276.36 | 0.00 | 276.36 | 0.00 |
| 33 | Jainoor | 38.42 | 0.00 | 38.42 | 0.00 |
| 34 | Itchada | 207.20 | 0.00 | 207.20 | 0.00 |
| 35 | Adilabad | 62.70 | 0.00 | 62.70 | 0.00 |
| 36 | Asifabad | 82.35 | 0.00 | 82.35 | 0.00 |
| 37 | Sirpurkagaznagar | 3.88 | 0.00 | 3.88 | 0.00 |
| 38 | Jannaram | 47.70 | 1.19 | 46.51 | |
| 39 | Eturunagaram | 117.12 | 0.00 | 117.12 | 0.00 |
| 40 | Mulugu | 108.00 | 1.83 | 106.17 | |
| 41 | Narasampet | 245.33 | 0.00 | 245.33 | 0.00 |
| 42 | Mahadevpur | 41.43 | 2.05 | 39.38 | |
| 43 | Peda dornal | 30.35 | 0.00 | 30.35 | 0.00 |
| 44 | Mannanoor | 90.08 | 0.00 | 90.08 | 0.00 |
| 45 | Nandyala | 10.41 | 0.00 | 10.41 | 0.00 |

*Source*: Records of GCC

**Table 7 Particulars of various GPCMSs of Bhadrachalam division**

| *S. No.* | *GPCMS* | *Organisation* | *Membership* | *Paid-up share capital (Rs. lakhs)* |
|---|---|---|---|---|
| 1 | Bhadrachalam | 05-08-1964 | 13533 | 2.00 |
| 2 | Venkatapuram | 10-12-1975 | 7913 | 3.25 |
| 3 | Chinthuru | 01-11-1992 | 2744 | 2.30 |
| 4 | Palwancha | 16-04-1964 | 14797 | 2.55 |
| 5 | Dammapeta | 22-03-1972 | 17599 | 3.17 |
| 6 | Yellandu | 02-03-1972 | 14539 | 5.66 |
| 7 | Manuguru | 24-05-1994 | 1370 | 1.55 |
| 8 | Kukunoor | 03-06-1994 | 864 | 1.08 |
| 9 | Total | | 73359 | 21.56 |

*Source*: Records of the division

**Table 8 Weekly shandies of Bhadrachalam division**

| *S. No.* | *Day* | *Place* | |
|---|---|---|---|
| 1 | Monday | (1) Alubaka | (2) V.R. Puram |
| | | (3) Annapureddipalli | (4) Mulakalpalli |
| 2 | Tuesday | (1) Kuturu | (2) Venkatapuram |
| | | (3) Dammapeta | |
| 3 | Wednesday | (1) Chinthuru | (2) Wazeedu |
| | | (3) Aswaraopeta | |
| 4 | Thursday | (1) Maraigudem | (2) Peruru |
| 5 | Friday | (1) China Nallaballi | (2) Edugurallapalli |
| | | (3) Velairpad | |
| 6 | Saturday | (1) Janagandhapuram | |
| 7 | Sunday | (1) Cherla | (2) Peda Midisileru |
| | | (3) Mothugudem | (4) Narayanapuram |

*Source*: Records of the division

**Table 9 Availability of various MFPs in Bhadrachalam**

| *S. No.* | *MFP* | *Season* |
|---|---|---|
| 1 | Gum | Throughout year |
| 2 | Gum tiruman | April to June |
| 3 | Nuxvomica | November to January |
| 4 | Cleaning nuts | December to May |
| 5 | Honey | October to May |
| 6 | Narmamidi bark | Throughout year |
| 7 | Wild brooms | December to February |
| 8 | Mohwa seed | June to August |

*Source*: Records of the division

**Table 10 Growth (Rs. lakhs) in purchase of MFP in Bhadrachalam, 1991–03**

| *S. No.* | *Year* | *Gum* | *Seeded tamarind* | *Deseeded tamarind* | *Myrobalans* | *Mohwa seed* | *Adda-leaf* | *Mohwa flower* | *Nux-vomica* | *Total MFP* |
|---|---|---|---|---|---|---|---|---|---|---|
| 1 | 1990–91 | 166.42 | 0.81 | – | 1.40 | 2.07 | 0.00 | 0.05 | 1.86 | 176.41 |
| 2 | 1991–92 | 87.16 | 0.27 | – | 0.73 | 3.21 | – | 1.42 | 2.98 | 97.52 |
| 3 | 1992–93 | 169.09 | – | – | 0.58 | 9.32 | – | 0.64 | 11.21 | 201.57 |
| 4 | 1993–94 | 68.40 | 0.20 | – | 0.04 | 1.20 | – | 0.22 | 8.93 | 92.12 |
| 5 | 1994–95 | 86.27 | 0.14 | 0.07 | 0.02 | 1.05 | – | – | 1.36 | 90.08 |
| 6 | 1995–96 | 175.52 | 0.05 | – | 0.18 | 1.34 | – | 0.05 | 5.73 | 200.38 |
| 7 | 1996–97 | 177.77 | 0.08 | – | 0.22 | 2.67 | – | – | 1.72 | 179.75 |
| 8 | 1997–98 | 88.34 | – | 0.36 | 0.15 | 13.38 | – | – | 0.14 | 89.94 |
| 9 | 1998–99 | 69.78 | 0.35 | 0.77 | 1.46 | 0.92 | – | – | 0.81 | 77.81 |
| 10 | 1999–00 | 97.68 | – | 0.93 | 6.89 | 25.33 | – | 0.02 | 0.02 | 152.85 |
| 11 | 2000–01 | 132.52 | – | 7.34 | 0.29 | 15.22 | – | 0.02 | 0.16 | 194.93 |
| 12 | 2001–02 | 149.20 | – | 2.91 | 0.14 | 10.50 | – | 0.08 | 2.75 | 194.48 |
| 13 | 2002–03 | 174.64 | 0.15 | 2.74 | 0.07 | 11.86 | – | 6.67 | 18.70 | 265.61 |

**Table 11 Growth (Rs. lakhs) in procurement of agricultural produce in Bhadrachalam division, 1991–03**

| *S. No.* | *Year* | *Niger seed* | *Cotton* | *Annato seed* | *French beans* | *Redgram* | *Chilies* | *Maize* | *Total* |
|---|---|---|---|---|---|---|---|---|---|
| 1 | 1990–91 | – | – | – | – | 2.32 | 0.57 | – | 2.89 |
| 2 | 1991–92 | – | – | – | – | 0.40 | 12.03 | 0.82 | 13.25 |
| 3 | 1992–93 | – | – | – | – | – | 14.88 | – | 14.88 |
| 4 | 1993–94 | – | 1.29 | – | – | – | 11.73 | – | 13.02 |
| 5 | 1994–95 | – | – | – | – | – | 4.72 | – | 4.72 |
| 6 | 1995–96 | – | – | – | – | – | – | 0.40 | 0.58 |
| 7 | 1996–97 | – | – | – | – | – | 0.29 | 0.51 | 1.07 |
| 8 | 1997–98 | – | – | – | – | – | 1.73 | – | 1.73 |
| 9 | 1998–99 | – | – | – | – | 1.65 | 23.17 | – | 24.83 |
| 10 | 1999–00 | – | – | – | – | 0.16 | 31.74 | – | 33.62 |
| 11 | 2000–01 | – | – | – | – | – | 56.60 | – | 58.82 |
| 12 | 2001–02 | – | – | – | – | – | 5.76 | – | 6.44 |
| 13 | 2002–03 | – | – | – | – | 7.96 | 29.91 | 0.50 | 43.23 |

*Source*: Records of the division

**Table 12 Society-wise distribution of DR depots, ration cards, and monthly allotments in Bhadrachalam division**

| *S. No.* | *GPCMS* | *Revenue mandals* | *DR depots* | *Ration cards* | *Allotments/month (quintals)* | | |
|---|---|---|---|---|---|---|---|
| | | | | | *Rice* | *Sugar* | *Kerosence oils (litres)* |
| 1 | Bhadrachalam | 03 | 11 | 4977 | 5200 | 221 | 13378 |
| 2 | Venkatapuram | 03 | 21 | 7507 | 1400 | 194 | 9073 |
| 3 | Chinthuru | 02 | 12 | 4792 | 1705 | 60 | 12150 |
| 4 | Palwancha | 04 | 19 | 8339 | 1313 | 105 | 34534 |
| 5 | Yellandu | 07 | 33 | 16773 | 3730 | 225 | 53808 |
| 6 | Dammapeta | 06 | 29 | 14900 | 3000 | 100 | 23000 |
| 7 | Manuguru | 03 | 12 | 4165 | 1075 | 65 | 3209 |
| 8 | Kukunoor | 02 | 09 | 4779 | 982 | 61 | 13864 |
| 9 | Total | 30 | 146 | 66232 | 18405 | 1031 | 163016 |

*Source*: Records of the division

**Table 13 Growth in supply of domestic requirements in Bhadrachalam division (Rs. lakhs), 1991–03**

| *S. No.* | *Year* | *Rice* | *Sugar* | *Salt* | *Edible oil* | *Kerosene oil* | *Others* | *Total* |
|---|---|---|---|---|---|---|---|---|
| 1 | 1990–91 | 380.24 | 60.57 | 2.21 | 20.50 | 39.42 | 157.48 | 660.42 |
| 2 | 1991–92 | 510.56 | 71.06 | 5.45 | 28.15 | 35.72 | 160.33 | 811.27 |
| 3 | 1992–93 | 421.36 | 109.09 | 1.94 | 54.64 | 47.28 | 325.93 | 960.24 |
| 4 | 1993–94 | 450.19 | 98.34 | 1.75 | 12.71 | 38.29 | 185.12 | 786.40 |
| 5 | 1994–95 | 363.81 | 104.78 | 2.77 | 27.67 | 35.14 | 261.32 | 795.49 |
| 6 | 1995–96 | 366.48 | 108.23 | 8.02 | 23.39 | 42.70 | 102.14 | 650.96 |
| 7 | 1996–97 | 487.06 | 139.02 | 5.57 | 26.45 | 43.83 | 125.28 | 827.21 |
| 8 | 1997–98 | 501.05 | 154.88 | 5.37 | 31.94 | 47.54 | 206.16 | 946.94 |
| 9 | 1998–99 | 526.82 | 135.77 | 5.99 | 49.04 | 53.70 | 306.42 | 1077.74 |
| 10 | 1999–00 | 448.72 | 135.84 | 5.62 | 37.12 | 54.66 | 274.19 | 996.15 |
| 11 | 2000–01 | 609.84 | 160.89 | 5.95 | 47.49 | 100.52 | 300.13 | 1224.82 |
| 12 | 2001–02 | 602.66 | 118.05 | 8.72 | 60.95 | 137.51 | 328.06 | 1255.96 |
| 13 | 2002–03 | 586.49 | 97.003 | 6.507 | 68.23 | 144.815 | 470.66 | 1370.71 |

*Source*: Records of the division

**Table 14 Growth in short term loans provided in Bhadrachalam division (Rs. lakhs), 1991–03**

| *S. No.* | *Year* | *No. of loanees* | *Amount disbursed* | *Recovery* | *Percentage* |
|---|---|---|---|---|---|
| 1 | 1990–91 | 2256 | 32.60 | 18.08 | 55.46 |
| 2 | 1991–92 | 3428 | 44.99 | 29.10 | 64.68 |
| 3 | 1992–93 | 6916 | 154.76 | 63.36 | 40.94 |
| 4 | 1993–94 | 4919 | 165.22 | 139.57 | 84.47 |
| 5 | 1994–95 | 3529 | 118.64 | 120.83 | 101.84 |
| 6 | 1995–96 | 4588 | 119.23 | 100.32 | 84.13 |
| 7 | 1996-97 | 4269 | 122.20 | 115.61 | 94.60 |
| 8 | 1997–98 | 2205 | 102.30 | 82.61 | 80.75 |
| 9 | 1998–99 | 2292 | 113.07 | 110.72 | 97.92 |
| 10 | 1999–00 | 3305 | 168.81 | 131.96 | 78.17 |
| 11 | 2000–01 | 3706 | 183.29 | 154.65 | 84.37 |
| 12 | 2001–02 | 2735 | 122.00 | 101.88 | 83.50 |
| 13 | 2002–03 | 2307 | 94.73 | 72.39 | 76.41 |

*Source*: Records of the division

**Table 15 Other loans issued in Bhadrachalam division**

| *S. No.* | *Year* | *Medium term* | *Consumption* | *SHGs* | *Others* | *Total* |
|---|---|---|---|---|---|---|
| 1 | 1990–91 | – | – | – | – | – |
| 2 | 1991–92 | 2.33 | 4.33 | – | – | 6.66 |
| 3 | 1992–93 | 44.31 | 6.61 | – | – | 50.92 |
| 4 | 1993–94 | 22.62 | 2.52 | – | – | 25.14 |
| 5 | 1994–95 | 38.64 | – | – | – | 38.64 |
| 6 | 1995–96 | – | – | – | – | – |
| 7 | 1996–97 | – | – | – | – | – |
| 8 | 1997–98 | 0.08 | – | 3.00 | – | 3.08 |
| 9 | 1998–99 | 1.05 | – | – | – | 1.05 |
| 10 | 1999–00 | – | – | – | – | – |
| 11 | 2000–01 | – | – | – | – | – |
| 12 | 2001–02 | – | – | – | – | – |
| 13 | 2002–03 | 1.90 | – | – | – | 1.90 |

*Source*: Records of the division

**Table 16 Cumulative performance of various GPCMSs in credit disbursement in Bhadrachalam division (March–November 2003)**

| *S. No.* | *GPCMS* | *Yearly target (Rs. lakhs)* | *Cumulative target (Rs. lakhs)* | *Cumulative achievement (Rs. lakhs)* | *Grade* |
|---|---|---|---|---|---|
| 1 | Bhadrachalam | 17.90 | 15.75 | 15.756 | A |
| 2 | Venkatapuram | 8.31 | 6.05 | 6.050 | A |
| 3 | Chinthuru | 22.28 | 18.62 | 17.938 | A |
| 4 | Palwancha | 9.95 | 6.96 | 6.960 | A |
| 5 | Yellandu | 18.60 | 18.60 | 18.602 | A |
| 6 | Dammapeta | 9.01 | 9.01 | 9.011 | A |
| 7 | Manuguru | 9.99 | 7.50 | 5.980 | A |
| 8 | Kukunoor | 5.37 | 5.37 | 5.376 | A |
| 9 | Total | 101.41 | 87.86 | 85.673 | A |

*Source*: Records of the division

**Table 17 GPCMSs-wise shandy days in Chintapalli division**

| *S. No.* | *GPCMS* | *Place* | *Day* |
|---|---|---|---|
| 1 | Chintapalli | Downuru | Friday |
| | | Lambasingi | Thursday |
| | | Lothugedda Junction | Tuesday |
| | | Chintapalli | Wednesday |
| | | Annavaram | Monday |
| | | Kalyanapulova | Saturday |
| 2 | Koyyuru | K.D. Peta | Monday |
| | | Kakarpadu | Sunday |
| | | Sarabannapalem | Sunday |
| | | Sarugudu | Friday |
| 3 | GK Veedhi | Darakonda | Sunday |
| | | RV Nagar | Monday |
| | | Pedavalasa | Friday |
| | | GK Veedhi | Thursday |
| | | Jarrela | Sunday |
| | | Sapparla | Saturday |

*Source*: Records of the division

**Table 18 Growth in membership, share capital, and turnover in Chintapalli division (Rs. lakhs), 1991–03**

| *S. No.* | *Year* | *Membership* | *Share Capital* | *Turnover* |
|---|---|---|---|---|
| 1 | 1990–91 | 10210 | 0.44 | 173.25 |
| 2 | 1991–92 | 11242 | 0.69 | 540.11 |
| 3 | 1992–93 | 12646 | 0.91 | 602.59 |
| 4 | 1993–94 | 22106 | 2.68 | 619.24 |
| 5 | 1994–95 | 23324 | 2.76 | 696.38 |
| 6 | 1995–96 | 23612 | 2.91 | 754.63 |
| 7 | 1996–97 | 23794 | 2.91 | 885.08 |
| 8 | 1997–98 | 23854 | 3.04 | 971.24 |
| 9 | 1998–99 | 23890 | 3.04 | 1108.16 |
| 10 | 1999–00 | 23910 | 3.05 | 1168.86 |
| 11 | 2000–01 | 23925 | 3.05 | 1281.58 |
| 12 | 2001–02 | 23925 | 3.06 | 1249.01 |
| 13 | 2002–03 | 23946 | 3.66 | 1485.64 |

*Source*: Records of the division

**Table 19 Growth in purchase of MFPs in Chintapalli division (Rs. lakhs), 1991–03**

| *S. No.* | *Year* | *Gum karaya* | *Tamarind* | *Myrobalans* | *Other MFP* | *Total MFP* |
|---|---|---|---|---|---|---|
| 1 | 1990–91 | 22.80 | 0.40 | 3.43 | 31.15 | 57.78 |
| 2 | 1991–92 | 11.46 | 3.78 | 1.11 | 21.06 | 37.41 |
| 3 | 1992–93 | 6.69 | 3.85 | 0.79 | 24.79 | 36.22 |
| 4 | 1993–94 | 10.7 | 6.10 | 1.58 | 31.97 | 50.45 |
| 5 | 1994–95 | 10.66 | 10.36 | 1.4 | 4.94 | 27.38 |
| 6 | 1995–96 | 12.61 | 5.70 | 4.31 | 13.27 | 35.89 |
| 7 | 1996–97 | 16.31 | 8.60 | 0.86 | 4.08 | 29.85 |
| 8 | 1997–98 | 22.03 | 13.19 | 1.73 | 1.46 | 38.41 |
| 9 | 1998–99 | 12.55 | 10.71 | 2.1 | 3.01 | 28.42 |
| 10 | 1999–00 | 13.50 | 13.41 | 8.96 | 8.13 | 50.00 |
| 11 | 2000–01 | 10.24 | 34.23 | 5.96 | 3.6 | 54.03 |
| 12 | 2001–02 | 9.6 | 34.69 | 2.67 | 3.15 | 49.14 |
| 13 | 2002–03 | 10.27 | 20.31 | 0.89 | 11.42 | 42.89 |

*Source*: Records of the division

**Table 20 Growth in procurement of agricultural produce in Chintapalli division (Rs. lakhs), 1991–03**

| *S. No.* | *Year* | *Niger seed* | *Annato seed* | *French beans* | *Redgram* | *Other agicultural produce* | *Total* |
|---|---|---|---|---|---|---|---|
| 1 | 1990–91 | 3.19 | 0.03 | 32.41 | 0.23 | 0.19 | 36.05 |
| 2 | 1991–92 | 35.42 | 0.00 | 8.75 | 0.85 | 1.47 | 46.49 |
| 3 | 1992–93 | 23.87 | 0.24 | 6.77 | 1.06 | 0.00 | 31.94 |
| 4 | 1993–94 | 17.17 | 0.18 | 9.17 | 1.62 | 0.56 | 28.70 |
| 5 | 1994–95 | 3.31 | 0.16 | 6.07 | 0.97 | 0.21 | 10.72 |
| 6 | 1995–96 | 4.09 | 0.36 | 3.77 | 0.29 | 0.00 | 8.51 |
| 7 | 1996–97 | 1.39 | 0.90 | 5.94 | 0.22 | 0.00 | 8.45 |
| 8 | 1997–98 | 4.04 | 0.33 | 3.63 | 0.15 | 0.00 | 8.15 |
| 9 | 1998–99 | 1.72 | 0.27 | 11.42 | 0.50 | 0.00 | 13.91 |
| 10 | 1999–00 | 0.81 | 0.33 | 19.81 | 0.47 | 0.00 | 21.42 |
| 11 | 2000–01 | 0.52 | 0.62 | 16.96 | 0.12 | 0.00 | 18.22 |
| 12 | 2001–02 | 0.29 | 2.89 | 6.03 | 1.40 | 0.00 | 10.65 |
| 13 | 2002–03 | 1.15 | 1.12 | 46.52 | 1.05 | 0.00 | 49.84 |

*Source*: Records of the division

**Table 21 Growth in supply of domestic requirements in Chintapalli division (Rs. lakhs), 1991–03**

| S. No. | Year | Rice | Sugar | Salt | Edible oils | Kerosene | Others | Total |
|---|---|---|---|---|---|---|---|---|
| 1 | 1990–91 | 113.89 | 3.68 | 2.75 | 7.22 | 4.59 | 34.64 | 166.77 |
| 2 | 1991–92 | 183.36 | 14.78 | 2.87 | 7.64 | 13.50 | 42.98 | 265.13 |
| 3 | 1992–93 | 155.50 | 15.20 | 2.78 | 7.67 | 13.43 | 38.65 | 233.23 |
| 4 | 1993–94 | 206.94 | 15.59 | 3.05 | 8.19 | 14.19 | 41.74 | 289.70 |
| 5 | 1994–95 | 218.14 | 15.49 | 2.90 | 7.79 | 13.22 | 37.61 | 295.15 |
| 6 | 1995–96 | 208.96 | 16.22 | 2.56 | 6.97 | 14.08 | 32.60 | 281.39 |
| 7 | 1996–97 | 256.55 | 16.38 | 3.38 | 9.23 | 15.91 | 41.21 | 342.66 |
| 8 | 1997–98 | 283.44 | 18.17 | 4.12 | 10.93 | 17.74 | 60.18 | 394.58 |
| 9 | 1998–99 | 293.77 | 19.43 | 4.60 | 12.11 | 18.85 | 58.52 | 407.28 |
| 10 | 1999–00 | 303.73 | 19.68 | 4.52 | 11.55 | 18.52 | 58.31 | 416.31 |
| 11 | 2000–01 | 346.01 | 22.59 | 6.31 | 16.54 | 23.14 | 89.10 | 503.69 |
| 12 | 2001–02 | 312.82 | 22.06 | 5.25 | 13.68 | 22.28 | 113.53 | 489.62 |
| 13 | 2002–03 | 337.44 | 24.54 | 4.10 | 12.92 | 25.44 | 135.42 | 539.86 |

*Source*: Records of the division

**Table 22 Short term loans in Chintapalli division (Rs. lakhs), 1991–03**

| S. No. | Year | No. of loanees | Amount disbursed | Loan disbursed/ member (rupees) | Recovery | Recovery (%) |
|---|---|---|---|---|---|---|
| 1 | 1990–91 | 462 | 4.36 | 943.72 | 3.53 | 81 |
| 2 | 1991–92 | 5233 | 56.30 | 1075.90 | 49.66 | 88 |
| 3 | 1992–93 | 7653 | 111.27 | 1453.97 | 60.86 | 55 |
| 4 | 1993–94 | 4772 | 57.35 | 1201.74 | 43.15 | 75 |
| 5 | 1994–95 | 2803 | 36.88 | 1315.73 | 28.51 | 77 |
| 6 | 1995–96 | 1244 | 16.53 | 1328.62 | 11.99 | 72 |
| 7 | 1996–97 | 470 | 7.08 | 1505.53 | 5.53 | 78 |
| 8 | 1997–98 | 295 | 4.86 | 1674.46 | 3.15 | 65 |
| 9 | 1998–99 | 162 | 3.40 | 2087.73 | 1.56 | 46 |
| 10 | 1999–00 | 67 | 1.80 | 2686.57 | 1.28 | 71 |
| 11 | 2000–01 | 146 | 2.69 | 1377.39 | 2.01 | 75 |
| 12 | 2001–02 | 15 | 0.91 | 6066.67 | 0.90 | 98 |
| 13 | 2002–03 | 258 | 4.40 | 1706.59 | 3.23 | 73 |

*Source*: Records of the division

**Table 23 GPCMSs-wise DR depots, and ration cards in Paderu division**

| *S. No.* | *GPCMS* | *D.R. depots* | *Ration Cards* |
|---|---|---|---|
| 1 | Paderu | 31 | 23513 |
| 2 | G. Madugula | 12 | 9692 |
| 3 | Araku Valley | 24 | 16517 |
| 4 | Munchingput | 18 | 7219 |
| 5 | Pedabayalu | 16 | 7478 |
| 6 | Kasipatnam | 18 | 9049 |
| 7 | Total | 119 | 73468 |

*Source*: Records of the division

**Table 24 GPCMSs-wise shandy places in Paderu division**

| *S. No.* | *GPCMS* | *Sunday* | *Monday* | *Tuesday* | *Wednesday* |
|---|---|---|---|---|---|
| 1 | G. Madugula | | | G. Madugula | |
| 2 | Paderu | Vantlamamidi | V. Madugula | | Kinchumanda |
| 3 | Pedabayalu | and Minimuluru | Pedabayalu and Rudalota | | |
| 4 | Munchingput | Jolaput | Kumada | | |
| 5 | Araku Valley | Sunkarametta | | | Gorapur |
| 6 | Kasipatnam | | Ananthagiri | Gummakota | Kasipatnam and Damuku |

***Continued Table 24***

| *S. No.* | *GPCMS* | *Thursday* | *Friday* | *Saturday* |
|---|---|---|---|---|
| 1 | G. Madugula | Maddigaruvu | | |
| 2 | Paderu | Guttulaput and Konam | Paderu | Hukumpeta |
| 3 | Pedabayalu | Bondapalli and Pedakodapalli | | |
| 4 | Munchingput | | | Munchingput |
| 5 | Araku Valley | Dumbriguda | Araku | Gannela |

*Source*: Records of the division

## Table 25 Procurement (quintals) of MFP in Paderu division, 1992–03

| *S. No.* | *MFP* | *1991–1992* | *1992–1993* | *1993–1994* | *1994–1995* | *1995–1996* | *1996–1997* |
|---|---|---|---|---|---|---|---|
| 1 | Gum | 111 | 72.41 | 140.89 | 176.37 | 104 | 100.74 |
| 2 | Seeded Tamarind | 1288 | 14114 | 17418 | 15650.14 | 108555 | 18 |
| 3 | Myrobalans | 2154 | 141 | 4738 | 1937.3 | 5986 | 2051 |
| 4 | Hill Brooms (Nos.) | 20206 | 7749 | 42562 | 109215 | 138086 | |
| 5 | Pungam seed | 502 | 202 | 2081 | 1229 | 1579 | 1384 |
| 6 | Marking nuts | 318 | 120 | 66.4 | 1775 | 517 | 1644 |
| 7 | R.B. Honey | 40 | 9.42 | 0.05 | 5.5 | 29 | 25 |
| 8 | Clearing nuts | 26 | 514 | 66 | 10 | 64 | 4.5 |
| 9 | Tamarind seed | 130 | 373 | | 202.45 | 284 | 14 |
| 10 | Addaleaf | 14516 | 13931 | 18044 | 17467.91 | 14181 | 14389 |
| 11 | Naramamidi bark | 1981 | 207 | | 169 | 987 | 1395 |

***Continued Table 25***

| *S. No.* | *MFP* | *1997–1998* | *1998–1999* | *1999–2000* | *2000–2001* | *2001–2002* | *2002–2003* |
|---|---|---|---|---|---|---|---|
| 1 | Gum | 155.73 | 274 | 351 | 377 | 465.03 | 555.10 |
| 2 | Seeded Tamarind | 18088 | 24616 | 16510 | 57383 | 30038.03 | 39646.06 |
| 3 | Myrobalans | 18.02 | 4758 | 6936 | 9474 | 4144.76 | 4310.60 |
| 4 | Hill Brooms (Nos.) | 9767 | 45739 | 21812 | 46611 | 54057 | 75705 |
| 5 | Pungam seed | 2320 | 387 | 1846 | 1053 | 436.89 | 454.31 |
| 6 | Marking nuts | 8.12 | 875 | 2546 | 2443 | 1226.89 | 2285.15 |
| 7 | R.B. Honey | 18.26 | 198 | 226 | 431 | 306.40 | 333.60 |
| 8 | Clearing nuts | 2.19 | 35 | 118 | 36 | 10.16 | 61.38 |
| 9 | Tamarind seed | 0 | 12 | 374 | 190 | | |
| 10 | Addaleaf | 15891 | 8552 | 4651 | 10107 | 3912.07 | 11769.10 |
| 11 | Addaleaf plates | 0 | 30434 | 2186 | 90455 | | 35492 |
| 12 | Flower Tamarind | 0 | 0 | 12 | 649 | | |
| 13 | Naramamidi bark | 0.62 | 644 | 985 | 663 | 277.03 | 2314.63 |
| 14 | Seekakai | 362 | 1142 | 896 | 511 | 1749.65 | 813.37 |
| 15 | Soapnuts | | 4 | 32 | 12 | 18.16 | 186.80 |
| 16 | Addaleaf stemcut | | 3923 | 29 | | | |
| 17 | Deseeded tamarind | 72 | 14 | 39 | 57 | | |
| 18 | Mohawa seed | | | 337 | 24 | | 6.40 |
| 19 | Nuxvomica | 13 | 0 | 6 | | 9.85 | 64.11 |
| 20 | Bee wax | 14 | 1 | 2 | | | 1.05 |
| 21 | Amla fruit | | | 1 | 5 | 5.29 | 6.97 |
| 22 | Amla pulp | | | | 658 | 60.89 | 2264.77 |
| 23 | R.S. roots | | | | 48 | 23.89 | 830.93 |
| 24 | Kusumoil seed | | | | | 14.78 | 2.00 |
| 25 | Tanikayalu | | | | | | 14.06 |

Figures for 2000–03 pertains to Paderu and Chintapalli divisions

*Source*: Records of the division

**Table 26 Procurement (Rs. lakhs) of MFP in Paderu division, 1992–03**

| S. No. | MFP | 1991–1992 | 1992–1993 | 1993–1994 | 1994–1995 | 1995–1996 | 1996–1997 |
|---|---|---|---|---|---|---|---|
| 1 | Gum | 2.81 | 2.11 | 6.92 | 12.73 | 6.5 | 8.24 |
| 2 | Seeded Tamarind | 28.58 | 39.4 | 39.4 | 56.11 | 41.2 | 104.65 |
| 3 | Myrobalans | 2.97 | 0.62 | 9.43 | 5.97 | 17.82 | 6.57 |
| 4 | Hill Brooms (Nos.) | 0.81 | 0.24 | 0 | 2.8 | 7.97 | 8.36 |
| 5 | Pungam seed | 1.96 | 0.81 | 8.16 | 2.78 | 6.32 | 1.93 |
| 6 | Marking nuts | 0.24 | 0.09 | 0.06 | 0.57 | 1.23 | 5.24 |
| 7 | R.B. Honey | 1.2 | 0.25 | 0.01 | 0.17 | 1.1 | 0.29 |
| 8 | Clearing nuts | 0.16 | 4.11 | 0.53 | 0.04 | 0.26 | 0.08 |
| 9 | Tamarind seed | 0.1 | 0.28 | 0 | 0.41 | 0.5 | 0.02 |
| 10 | Addaleaf | 17.35 | 23.93 | 28.41 | 37.16 | 25.8 | 31.97 |
| 11 | Flower tamarind | 9.8 | 0.86 | 0 | 0.91 | 7.67 | 15.1 |
| 12 | Total | 65.98 | 72.7 | 92.92 | 119.65 | 116.37 | 182.45 |

***Continued Table 26***

| *S. No.* | *MFP* | *1997–1998* | *1998–1999* | *1999–2000* | *2000–2001* | *2001–2002* | *2002–2003* |
|---|---|---|---|---|---|---|---|
| 1 | Gum | 12.67 | 21.44 | 30.46 | 32.65 | 40.40 | 47.03 |
| 2 | Seeded Tamarind | 97.51 | 169.35 | 124.32 | 364.89 | 160.03 | 152.37 |
| 3 | Myrobalans | 7.2 | 24.37 | 48.29 | 47.82 | 13.19 | 9.24 |
| 4 | Hill Brooms (Nos.) | 0.65 | 2.29 | 1.29 | 3.70 | 4.92 | 8.12 |
| 5 | Pungam seed | 8.12 | 1.37 | 8.15 | 4.71 | 19.49 | 2.44 |
| 6 | Marking nuts | 1.49 | 2.6 | 6.48 | 5.16 | 3.58 | 5.62 |
| 7 | R.B. Honey | 0.73 | 6.03 | 7.33 | 17.23 | 12.46 | 13.64 |
| 8 | Cleaning nuts | 0.01 | 0.14 | 0.48 | 0.14 | 0.05 | 0.49 |
| 9 | Tamarind seed | 0 | 0.02 | 1.17 | 0.29 | | |
| 10 | Addaleaf | 43.7 | 26.28 | 14.36 | 43.28 | 12.86 | 40.94 |
| 11 | Flower Tamarind | | 7.72 | 0.19 | 9.74 | | |
| 12 | Addaleaf plates | 0 | 3.05 | 0.12 | 7.22 | | 1.85 |
| 13 | Naramamidi bark | 7.49 | 5.66 | 17.22 | 12.60 | 5.54 | 46.29 |
| 14 | Seekakai | 1.54 | 0.05 | 5.16 | 6.19 | 16.77 | 9.36 |
| 15 | Soapnuts | | | 0.25 | 0.09 | 0.18 | 1.00 |
| 16 | Addaleaf stemcut | | 15.73 | 0.10 | | | |
| 17 | Deseeded tamarind | 0.68 | 0.16 | 0.59 | 0.85 | | |
| 18 | Mohawa seed | | | 3.37 | 0.19 | | 0.05 |
| 19 | Nuxvomica | 0.05 | 0 | 0.02 | | 0.06 | 0.64 |
| 20 | Apiary honey | | | 0.08 | | | 0.03 |
| 21 | Bee wax | 0.7 | 0.03 | 0.03 | 0.20 | 0.37 | 0.49 |
| 22 | Amla fruit | | | | 1.32 | 0.42 | 7.32 |
| 23 | Amla pulp | | | | 0.70 | 0.51 | 13.40 |
| 24 | R.S. roots | | | | | 0.88 | 0.12 |
| 25 | Kusumoil seed | | | | | | 0.05 |
| 26 | Tanikayalu | | | | | | 0.01 |
| 27 | Total | 182.54 | 286.29 | 269.46 | 558.97 | 300.71 | 360.5 |

*Source*: Records of the division

**Table 27 Procurement (quintals) of agricultural produce in Paderu division, 1992–03**

| S. No. | Agricultural produce | 1991–1992 | 1992–1993 | 1993–1994 | 1994–1995 |
|---|---|---|---|---|---|
| 1 | French beans (red) | 498.00 | 111.00 | 7.00 | 148.00 |
| 2 | French beans (white) | 330.00 | 61.00 | 8.00 | 43.00 |
| 3 | Rajama (white) | | | | |
| 4 | Rajama (red-big) | | | | |
| 5 | Niger seed | 12209.00 | 8929.00 | 319.00 | 2336.00 |
| 6 | Redgram | 1252.00 | 138.00 | 8.00 | 694.00 |
| 7 | Horsegram | 263.00 | 179.00 | 5.00 | 39.00 |
| 8 | Coffee seed | | | | |
| 9 | Annatto seed | | | | |
| 10 | White beans (rounds) | | | | |
| 11 | Cuttings | | | | |
| 12 | Turmeric | 231.00 | 41.00 | 37.00 | • |
| 13 | Jowar | | | | |
| 14 | Kashmir beans | | | | |
| 15 | Mustard seed | | | | |
| 16 | Black gram | | | | |
| 17 | Cashew nuts | | | | |
| 18 | Peeper | | | | |
| 19 | Silver oak seed | | | | |
| 20 | Nepalem seed | 68.00 | 504.00 | 526.00 | 160.00 |
| 21 | Sunflower seed | 0.00 | 26.00 | 11.00 | 2.85 |

***Continued Table 27***

| *S. No.* | *Agricultural produce* | *1995–1996* | *1996–1997* | *1997–1998* | *1998–1999* |
|---|---|---|---|---|---|
| 1 | French beans (red) | | | | |
| 2 | French beans (white) | 19.00 | 43.00 | 241.00 | 399.00 |
| 3 | Rajama (white) | | | | |
| 4 | Rajama (red-big) | 140.00 | 520.00 | 303.00 | 182.00 |
| 5 | Niger seed | 12059.00 | 2125.00 | 8527.00 | 1640.00 |
| 6 | Redgram | 256.00 | 78.00 | 112.00 | 114.00 |
| 7 | Horsegram | 4.00 | | | |
| 8 | Coffee seed | 5.53 | 0.22 | 226.00 | 1546.00 |
| 9 | Annatto seed | | 441.00 | 15.00 | 45.00 |
| 10 | White beans (rounds) | | | | 1.00 |
| 11 | Cuttings | | | | 5.00 |
| 12 | Turmeric | | | | 5.00 |
| 13 | Jowar | | | | 146.00 |
| 14 | Kashmir beans | | | | 1.00 |
| 15 | Mustard seed | | | | |
| 16 | Black gram | | | | |
| 17 | Cashew nuts | | | | |
| 18 | Peeper | | | | |
| 19 | Silver oak seed | | | | |
| 20 | Nepalem seed | 6.00 | 2.00 | | |
| 21 | Sunflower seed | 12489.53 | 3209.00 | 9424.00 | 4084.00 |

***Continued Table 27***

| *S. No.* | *Agricultural produce* | *1999–2000* | *2000–2001* | *2001–2002* | *2002–2003* |
|---|---|---|---|---|---|
| 1 | French beans (red) | | | | |
| 2 | French beans (white) | | | | |
| 3 | Rajama (white) | 1519.00 | 922.00 | 30.16 | 3041.12 |
| 4 | Rajama (red-big) | 2456.00 | 825.00 | 33.07 | 174.40 |
| 5 | Niger seed | 1707.00 | 278.00 | 223.45 | 18.84 |
| 6 | Redgram | 620.00 | 1206.00 | 1053.50 | 1530.67 |
| 7 | Horsegram | 5.00 | 5.00 | | |
| 8 | Coffee seed | 1205.00 | 134.00 | | |
| 9 | Annatto seed | 58.00 | 7.00 | 146.09 | 97.07 |
| 10 | White beans (rounds) | 45.00 | 154.00 | 0.72 | 576.58 |
| 11 | Cuttings | 87.00 | 16.00 | 162.03 | 136.62 |
| 12 | Turmeric | | | 151.04 | 25.37 |
| 13 | Jowar | | | | |
| 14 | Kashmir beans | 855.00 | 99.00 | | 1935.01 |
| 15 | Mustard seed | | 1.00 | | |
| 16 | Black gram | | | | |
| 17 | Cashew nuts | 93.00 | | | 102.94 |
| 18 | Peeper | | 1.00 | | |
| 19 | Silver oak seed | | | | 4.94 |
| 20 | Nepalem seed | | | | |
| 21 | Sunflower seed | | | | |

*Source*: Records of the division

**Table 28 Procurement (Rs. lakhs) of agricultural produce in Paderu division, 1992–03**

| *S. No.* | *Agricultural produce* | *1991–1992* | *1992–1993* | *1993–1994* | *1994–1995* |
|---|---|---|---|---|---|
| 1 | French beans (red) | 3.24 | 1.18 | 0.08 | 1.86 |
| 2 | French beans (white) | 1.65 | 0.64 | 0.09 | 0.51 |
| 3 | Rajama (white) | | | | |
| 4 | Rajama (red-big) | | | | |
| 5 | Niger seed | 140.40 | 100.45 | 2.62 | 28.97 |
| 6 | Redgram | 11.24 | 1.24 | 0.07 | 8.31 |
| 7 | Horsegram | 0.45 | 0.52 | 0.02 | 0.20 |
| 8 | Coffee seed | | | | |
| 9 | Annatto seed | | | | |
| 10 | White beans (rounds) | | | | |
| 11 | Cuttings | | | | |
| 12 | Turmeric | 2.82 | 0.61 | 0.50 | |
| 13 | Kashmir beans | | | | |
| 14 | Mustard seed | | | | |
| 15 | Cashew nuts | | | | |
| 16 | Peeper | | | | |
| 17 | Silver oak seed | | | | |
| 18 | Nepalem seed | 0.50 | 3.02 | 3.15 | 0.84 |
| 19 | Sunflower seed | | 0.22 | 0.09 | 0.01 |
| 20 | Total | 160.3 | 107.88 | 6.62 | 40.7 |

***Continued Table 28***

| S. No. | *Agricultural produce* | *1995–1996* | *1996–1997* | *1997–1998* | *1998–1999* |
|---|---|---|---|---|---|
| 1 | French beans (red) | | | | |
| 2 | French beans (white) | 0.30 | 0.67 | 4.19 | 9.42 |
| 3 | Rajama (white) | | | | |
| 4 | Rajama (red-big) | 1.79 | 7.58 | 4.95 | 2.98 |
| 5 | Niger seed | 146.82 | 24.17 | 101.32 | 20.76 |
| 6 | Redgram | 4.22 | 0.97 | 1.18 | 2.06 |
| 7 | Horsegram | 0.02 | | | |
| 8 | Coffee seed | 0.22 | 22.00 | 11.98 | 84.48 |
| 9 | Annatto seed | | 12.08 | 0.15 | 0.49 |
| 10 | White beans (rounds) | | | | 0.01 |
| 11 | Cuttings | | | | 0.15 |
| 12 | Turmeric | | | | 0.15 |
| 13 | Jowar | | | | 2.18 |
| 14 | Kashmir beans | | | | 0.02 |
| 15 | Mustard seed | | | | |
| 16 | Black gram | | | | |
| 17 | Cashew nuts | | | | |
| 18 | Peeper | 0.22 | 0.05 | | |
| 19 | Silver oak seed | | | | |
| 20 | Nepalem seed | | | | |
| 21 | Sunflower seed | | | | |
| 21 | Total | 153.59 | 45.52 | 123.77 | 122.70 |

***Continued Table 28***

| *S. No.* | *Agricultural produce* | *1999–2000* | *2000–2001* | *2001–2002* | *2002–2003* |
|---|---|---|---|---|---|
| 1 | French beans (red) | | | | |
| 2 | French beans (white) | | | | |
| 3 | Rajama (white) | 27.49 | 15.44 | 0.61 | 65.46 |
| 4 | Rajama (red-big) | 34.24 | 10.72 | 0.61 | 3.71 |
| 5 | Niger seed | 26.97 | 4.31 | 2.70 | 0.29 |
| 6 | Redgram | 8.26 | 14.31 | 12.59 | 19.67 |
| 7 | Horsegram | 0.04 | 0.04 | | |
| 8 | Coffee seed | 52.48 | 4.61 | | |
| 9 | Annatto seed | 0.61 | 0.07 | 4.33 | 1.81 |
| 10 | White beans (rounds) | 0.27 | 0.90 | | 6.22 |
| 11 | Cuttings | 0.67 | 0.13 | 1.33 | 1.38 |
| 12 | Turmeric | | | 4.67 | 0.92 |
| 13 | Kashmir beans | 11.10 | 1.39 | | 41.01 |
| 14 | Mustard seed | | 0.03 | | |
| 15 | Cashew nuts | 3.99 | | | 3.25 |
| 16 | Peeper | | 0.09 | | |
| 17 | Silver oak seed | | | | 2.47 |
| 18 | Nepalem seed | | | | |
| 19 | Sunflower seed | | | | |
| 20 | Total | 166.12 | 52.04 | 26.84 | 146.19 |

*Source*: Records of the division

**Table 29 (Rs. lakhs) in selected indicators in Paderu division, 1991–03**

| S. No. | Year | DRs sales | Loans issued | Total turnover |
|---|---|---|---|---|
| 1 | 1990–91 | 480.46 | 70.84 | 721.16 |
| 2 | 1991–92 | 502.17 | 31.05 | 761.26 |
| 3 | 1992–93 | 477.62 | 86.72 | 745.06 |
| 4 | 1993–94 | 603.01 | 23.01 | 746.68 |
| 5 | 1994–95 | 650.22 | 9.16 | 819.57 |
| 6 | 1995–96 | 660.89 | 18.10 | 948.70 |
| 7 | 1996–97 | 769.86 | 10.53 | 1008.26 |
| 8 | 1997–98 | 927.51 | 12.69 | 1264.25 |
| 9 | 1998–99 | 1075.75 | 13.46 | 1500.02 |
| 10 | 1999–00 | 1024.59 | 18.18 | 1448.90 |
| 11 | 2000–01 | 1946.78 | 16.12 | 2574.04 |
| 12 | 2001–02 | 1619.75 | 8.44 | 955.74 |
| 13 | 2002–03 | 1634.88 | 19.33 | 2160.90 |

*Source*: Records of the division

**Table 30 Activity-wise targets and achievements (Rs. lakhs) in Paderu division, 2002–03**

| S. No. | Activity | Target | Achievement |
|---|---|---|---|
| 1 | MFP/AP procurement | 570.00 | 360.46 |
| 2 | DRs sales | 1850.00 | 1635.05 |
| 3 | Loans disbursement | 20.00 | 19.11 |
| 4 | Loans recovery | 61.49 | 12.37 |
| 5 | R.M.D. sales | 30.00 | 32.92 |
| 6 | Total | 2531.49 | 2059.91 |

*Source*: Records of the division

**Table 31 Some basic facts about GPCMSs of Srisailam division**

| *S. No.* | *GPCMS* | *Year of establishment* | *Districts covered* | *Chenchu population* | *Membership* |
|---|---|---|---|---|---|
| 1 | Mannanur | 01.01.70 | Mahaboobnagar | 11153 | 4925 |
| | | | Nalgonda | 1110 | |
| | | | Rangareddy | 3262 | |
| 2 | Peddu Dornal | 27.10.75 | Prakasam | 12347 | 1730 |
| | | | Guntur | 5392 | |
| 3 | Nandyal | 03.03.90 | Kurnool | 6366 | 911 |
| 4 | Total | | | 39630 | 7566 |

*Source*: Records of the division

**Table 32 Procurement (quintals) of MFP in Srisailam division, 1992–03**

| *S. No.* | *MFP* | *1991–1992* | *1992–1993* | *1993–1994* | *1994–1995* | *1995–1996* | *1996–1997* |
|---|---|---|---|---|---|---|---|
| 1 | Gum karaya | 2200.13 | 1470.85 | 1418.64 | 965.18 | 854.53 | 562.63 |
| 2 | Gum kondagogu | 0.00 | 0.00 | 343.09 | 187.69 | 128.52 | 83.57 |
| 3 | Gum tiruman | 23.82 | 7.49 | 17.54 | 10.59 | 4.63 | 0.46 |
| 4 | Tamarind seeded | 142.07 | 64.68 | 3.00 | 20.00 | 8.20 | 25.09 |
| 5 | Tamarind seed | 0.00 | 0.00 | 0.00 | 7.20 | 6.10 | 5.90 |
| 6 | R.B. Honey | 198.03 | 251.82 | 126.15 | 136.47 | 320.39 | 186.03 |
| 7 | Myrobalans | 564.58 | 73.26 | 12.59 | 65.71 | 93.12 | 231.99 |
| 8 | Soapnuts | 888.58 | 2367.11 | 1185.37 | 2083.27 | 1341.92 | 1625.67 |
| 9 | Mohwa seed | 1413.26 | 1468.91 | 1271.91 | 1011.54 | 1235.11 | 1023.74 |
| 10 | Wild brooms | 168642 | 38759 | 3350 | 0 | 14193 | 1130 |
| 11 | Cleaning nuts | 49.64 | 590.26 | 977.11 | 96.03 | 63.53 | 1.73 |
| 12 | Naramamidi bark | 26.30 | 0.00 | 0.00 | 0.00 | 0.00 | 4.30 |
| 13 | Pungam seed | 433.75 | 385.31 | 284.35 | 278.77 | 233.06 | 151.53 |
| 14 | Bee wax | 12.22 | 21.21 | 16.84 | 11.60 | 20.79 | 20.71 |
| 15 | Nuxvomica | 292.76 | 662.56 | 452.25 | 498.51 | 500.53 | 147.75 |
| 16 | Tanikayalu | 0.00 | 0.00 | 0.00 | 7.00 | 55.46 | 50.02 |
| 17 | Maredugaddalu | 27.30 | 49.20 | 78.35 | 438.33 | 250.87 | 359.11 |
| 18 | Green amla | 0.00 | 0.00 | 0.00 | 0.00 | 93.22 | |
| 19 | Dry amla | | | | | | |

***Continued Table 32***

| S. No. | MFP | 1997–1998 | 1998–1999 | 1999–2000 | 2000–2001 | 2001–2002 | 2002–2003 |
|---|---|---|---|---|---|---|---|
| 1 | Gum karaya | 517.56 | 403.00 | 514.78 | 433.98 | 441.74 | 430.58 |
| 2 | Gum kondagogu | 162.27 | 141.87 | 501.78 | 615.05 | 852.60 | 901.48 |
| 3 | Gum tiruman | 1.85 | 1.19 | 0.46 | 0.00 | 2.69 | 0.16 |
| 4 | Tamarind seeded | 43.09 | 52.24 | 60.30 | 94.10 | 0.00 | 13.40 |
| 5 | Tamarind seed | 3.49 | 0.00 | 0.00 | 59.97 | 0.00 | 3.44 |
| 6 | R.B. Honey | 347.71 | 159.73 | 133.50 | 127.54 | 110.62 | 215.47 |
| 7 | Myrobalans | 253.07 | 191.43 | 89.18 | 102.92 | 18.85 | 15.19 |
| 8 | Soapnuts | 517.97 | 809.04 | 1455.79 | 1251.42 | 1697.18 | 1498.98 |
| 9 | Mohwa seed | 1140.35 | 604.88 | 1716.45 | 1743.33 | 489.59 | 1079.13 |
| 10 | Wild brooms | 10607 | 14045 | 150 | 678 | 3550 | 22576 |
| 11 | Cleaning nuts | 0.00 | 3.01 | 20.92 | 4.44 | 3.15 | 15.18 |
| 12 | Naramamidi bark | 99.96 | 68.43 | 1166.88 | 652.15 | 114.59 | 967.14 |
| 13 | Pungam seed | 211.65 | 59.47 | 237.98 | 269.34 | 171.35 | 238.12 |
| 14 | Bee wax | 18.84 | 3.79 | 3.76 | 5.436 | 3.55 | 8.64 |
| 15 | Nuxvomica | 606.12 | 126.00 | 461.22 | 110.50 | 311.45 | 817.29 |
| 16 | Tanikayalu | 338.04 | 193.72 | 46.00 | 5.98 | 0.00 | 1.33 |
| 17 | Maredugaddalu | 2396.90 | 222.25 | 213.66 | 1384.29 | 698.78 | 1804.02 |
| 18 | Green amla | | | | | 1115.00 | 664.00 |
| 19 | Dry amla | | | | | 0.85 | 26.42 |

*Source*: Records of the division

**Table 33 Growth (Rs. lakhs) in procurement of MFP in Srisailam division, 1992–03**

| S. No. | MFP | 1991–1992 | 1992–1993 | 1993–1994 | 1994–1995 | 1995–1996 | 1996–1997 |
|---|---|---|---|---|---|---|---|
| 1 | Gum karaya | 60.38 | 47.22 | 67.83 | 60.39 | 58.84 | 42.48 |
| 2 | Gum kondagogu | 0.00 | 0.00 | 13.17 | 9.48 | 7.53 | 5.16 |
| 3 | Gum tiruman | 0.50 | 0.16 | 0.39 | 0.23 | 0.10 | 0.01 |
| 4 | Tamarind seeded | 0.43 | 0.19 | 0.01 | 0.06 | 0.04 | 0.13 |
| 5 | Tamarind seed | 0.00 | 0.00 | 0.00 | 0.01 | 0.01 | 0.01 |
| 6 | R.B. Honey | 5.94 | 7.83 | 3.15 | 4.4 | 12.64 | 7.43 |
| 7 | Myrobalans | 1.36 | 0.15 | 0.02 | 0.13 | 0.24 | 0.74 |
| 8 | Soapnuts | 7.48 | 18.90 | 9.91 | 20.55 | 9.01 | 13.04 |
| 9 | Mohwa seed | 9.90 | 10.28 | 7.77 | 8.08 | 8.71 | 7.67 |
| 10 | Wild brooms | 2.53 | 0.41 | 0.03 | 0.00 | 0.24 | 0.02 |
| 11 | Cleaning nuts | 0.26 | 4.71 | 8.36 | 0.81 | 0.26 | 0.00 |
| 12 | Naramamidi bark | 0.13 | 0.00 | 0.00 | 0.00 | 0.00 | 0.05 |
| 13 | Pungam seed | 1.73 | 1.52 | 1.07 | 0.60 | 1.01 | 0.62 |
| 14 | Bee wax | 0.56 | 1.14 | 0.92 | 0.64 | 1.33 | 1.49 |
| 15 | Nuxvomica | 0.69 | 5.03 | 4.46 | 2.76 | 2.00 | 0.50 |
| 16 | Tanikayalu | 0.00 | 0.00 | 0.00 | 0.01 | 0.11 | 0.10 |
| 17 | Maredugaddalu | 0.14 | 0.35 | 0.55 | 5.18 | 2.47 | 4.10 |
| 18 | Green amla | 0.00 | 0.00 | 0.00 | 0.00 | 0.21 | |
| 19 | Dry amla | | | | | | |
| 20 | Others | 3.19 | 4.39 | 5.26 | 5.45 | 0.97 | 0.19 |
| 21 | Total | 95.22 | 102.28 | 122.90 | 118.78 | 105.72 | 83.74 |

***Continued Table 33***

| *S. No.* | *MFP* | *1997–1998* | *1998–1999* | *1999–2000* | *2000–2001* | *2001–2002* |
|---|---|---|---|---|---|---|
| 1 | Gum karaya | 37.36 | 30.83 | 47.24 | 40.08 | 41.64 |
| 2 | Gum kondagogu | 9.68 | 9.54 | 36.47 | 45.15 | 62.23 |
| 3 | Gum tiruman | 0.05 | 0.03 | 0.01 | 0.00 | 0.09 |
| 4 | Tamarind seeded | 0.24 | 0.22 | 0.34 | 0.47 | 0.00 |
| 5 | Tamarind seed | 0.01 | 0.00 | 0.00 | 0.13 | 0.00 |
| 6 | R.B. Honey | 13.56 | 4.88 | 4.18 | 5.10 | 4.42 |
| 7 | Myrobalans | 0.92 | 1.31 | 0.63 | 0.67 | 0.11 |
| 8 | Soapnuts | 3.92 | 7.71 | 15.79 | 15.37 | 19.85 |
| 9 | Mohwa seed | 1.00 | 5.86 | 16.27 | 12.20 | 2.99 |
| 10 | Wild brooms | 0.21 | 0.28 | 0.00 | 0.02 | 0.09 |
| 11 | Cleaning nuts | 0.00 | 0.01 | 0.07 | 0.01 | 0.01 |
| 12 | Naramamidi bark | 1.20 | 0.83 | 19.15 | 13.22 | 2.30 |
| 13 | Pungam seed | 0.80 | 0.22 | 1.11 | 1.21 | 0.78 |
| 14 | Bee wax | 1.30 | 0.19 | 0.19 | 0.38 | 0.24 |
| 15 | Nuxvomica | 2.23 | 0.43 | 1.56 | 0.42 | 1.67 |
| 16 | Tanikayalu | 0.68 | 0.39 | 0.06 | 0.00 | 0.00 |
| 17 | Maredugaddalu | 34.70 | 2.35 | 2.49 | 19.37 | 10.48 |
| 18 | Green amla | | | | | 2.92 |
| 19 | Dry amla | | | | | 0.03 |
| 20 | Others | 0.15 | 0.04 | 0.06 | 0.05 | 0.00 |
| 21 | Total | 108.01 | 65.12 | 145.62 | 153.85 | 149.85 |

*Source*: Records of the division

**Table 34 Growth (quintals) in procurement of agricultural produce in Srisailam division, 1992–03**

| *S. No.* | *Agricultural produce* | *1991–1992* | *1992–1993* | *1993–1994* | *1994–1995* | *1995–1996* | *1996–1997* |
|---|---|---|---|---|---|---|---|
| 1 | Jowar | 9.77 | | | | | |
| 2 | Ragi | | | | | | |
| 3 | Groundnut | 46.66 | | | | | |
| 4 | Redgram | | | | | | |
| 5 | Bengalgram | | | | | | |
| 6 | Cotton | | 902.80 | 0.95 | 505.98 | | |
| 7 | Cotton seed | | 7.80 | | | | |
| 8 | Chillies | | 92.00 | 9.70 | 7.40 | 8.81 | 28.65 |
| 9 | Paddy | 243.33 | 16.20 | | 58.31 | | |
| 10 | Bajra | | 2.25 | | | | |
| 11 | Sunflower | 30.40 | | | 11.21 | | |
| 12 | Castor | | | | 21.42 | | |

***Continued Table 34***

| *S. No.* | *Agricultural produce* | *1997–1998* | *1998–1999* | *1999–2000* | *2000–2001* | *2002–2003* |
|---|---|---|---|---|---|---|
| 1 | Jowar | | | | 29.66 | |
| 2 | Ragi | | | | | |
| 3 | Groundnut | | | | 44.00 | |
| 4 | Redgram | | | | 20.20 | |
| 5 | Bengalgram | | | | 15.00 | |
| 6 | Cotton | | | | 30.00 | |
| 7 | Cotton seed | | | | | |
| 8 | Chillies | 33.42 | 56.29 | 96.33 | 127.22 | 29.42 |
| 9 | Paddy | | | | | |
| 10 | Bajra | | | | | |
| 11 | Sunflower | | | | | |
| 12 | Castor | | | | | |

*Source*: Records of the division

**Table 35 Growth (Rs. lakhs) in procurement of agricultural produce in Srisailam division, 1992–03**

| *S. No.* | *Agriculture produce* | *1991–1992* | *1992–1993* | *1993–1994* | *1994–1995* | *1995–1996* | *1996–1997* |
|---|---|---|---|---|---|---|---|
| 1 | Jowar | 0.03 | | | | | 0.22 |
| 2 | Ragi | | | | | | 0.09 |
| 3 | Groundnut | | | | | | |
| 4 | Redgram | | | | | | |
| 5 | Bengalgram | | | | | | |
| 6 | Cotton | | 9.71 | 0.01 | 10.45 | | |
| 7 | Cotton seed | | 0.20 | | | | |
| 8 | Chillies | | 1.71 | 0.16 | 0.16 | 0.25 | 0.49 |
| 9 | Paddy | 0.69 | 0.09 | | 0.21 | | |
| 10 | Bajra | | 0.01 | | 0.00 | | |
| 11 | Sunflower | 0.27 | | | 0.12 | | |
| 12 | Castor | | | | 0.19 | | |
| 13 | Total | 1.40 | 11.72 | 0.17 | 11.49 | 0.25 | 0.80 |

***Continued Table 35***

| *S. No.* | *Agriculture produce* | *1997–1998* | *1998–1999* | *1999–2000* | *2000–2001* | *2002–2003* |
|---|---|---|---|---|---|---|
| 1 | Jowar | 0.08 | 0.01 | 0.28 | 0.39 | 0.15 |
| 2 | Ragi | | 0.01 | 0.02 | | |
| 3 | Groundnut | | | | | 0.99 |
| 4 | Redgram | | | | | 0.26 |
| 5 | Bengalgram | | | | | 0.22 |
| 6 | Cotton | | | | | 0.50 |
| 7 | Cotton seed | | | | | |
| 8 | Chillies | | 0.86 | 1.45 | | 3.58 |
| 9 | Paddy | | | | | |
| 10 | Bajra | | | | | |
| 11 | Sunflower | | | | | |
| 12 | Castor | | | | | |
| 13 | Total | 0.08 | 0.88 | 1.75 | 0.39 | 5.70 |

*Source*: Records of the division

**Table 36 GPCMSs-wise sale of essential commodities in Srisailam division, 1996–03**

| S. No. | Year | Mannanur | P. Dornal | Nandyal | Total |
|---|---|---|---|---|---|
| 1 | 1995-96 | 68.27 | 17.96 | 9.34 | 95.57 |
| 2 | 1996-97 | 89.01 | 36.02 | 11.01 | 136.04 |
| 3 | 1997-98 | 114.02 | 42.27 | 12.52 | 168.81 |
| 4 | 1998-99 | 108.35 | 43.34 | 17.43 | 169.12 |
| 5 | 1999-00 | 124.69 | 77.26 | 23.73 | 225.68 |
| 6 | 2000-01 | 217.51 | 77.04 | 36.37 | 330.92 |
| 7 | 2001-02 | 206.65 | 80.38 | 31.28 | 318.31 |
| 8 | 2002-03 | 194.37 | 83.50 | 34.48 | 312.34 |

*Source*: Records of the division

**Table 37 Growth in credit operations in Srisailam division, 1991–03**

| S. No. | Year | Villages covered | Beneficiaries | Amount disbursed (Rs. in lakhs) | Amount collected (Rs. in lakhs) | Recovery (%) |
|---|---|---|---|---|---|---|
| 1 | 1990–91 | 16 | 293 | 2.93 | 0.57 | 19.45 |
| 2 | 1991–92 | 86 | 1135 | 12.62 | 0.57 | 4.52 |
| 3 | 1992–93 | 62 | 641 | 15.67 | 2.02 | 12.89 |
| 4 | 1993–94 | 33 | 508 | 15.61 | 2.84 | 18.19 |
| 5 | 1994–95 | 13 | 99 | 3.82 | 3.10 | 81.15 |
| 6 | 1995–96 | 1 | 7 | 0.09 | 1.39 | 1544.44 |
| 7 | 1996–97 | 4 | 97 | 6.54 | 0.01 | 0.15 |
| 8 | 1997–98 | 31 | 280 | 3.83 | 1.04 | 27.15 |
| 9 | 1998–99 | 29 | 168 | 6.60 | 0.21 | 3.18 |
| 10 | 1999–00 | 13 | 219 | 8.52 | 3.02 | 35.45 |
| 11 | 2000–01 | 11 | 53 | 2.28 | 6.71 | 294.30 |
| 12 | 2001–02 | 10 | 113 | 4.61 | 1.33 | 28.85 |
| 13 | 2002–03 | 3 | 62 | 3.70 | 2.65 | 71.62 |

*Source*: Records of the division

**Table 38 Training of MFP collection in Srisailam division**

| *S. No.* | *GPCMS* | *Villages covered* | *Trainees* |
|---|---|---|---|
| 1 | Mannanur | 16 | 153 |
| 2 | P. Dornal | 13 | 94 |
| 3 | Nandyal | 12 | 82 |
| 4 | Total | 41 | 329 |

*Source*: Records of the division

**Table 39 Coverage of grain banks in Srisailam division**

| *S. No.* | *Year* | *District* | *Mandals* | *Villages* | *Families* |
|---|---|---|---|---|---|
| 1 | 1996–97 | Mahaboobnagar | 2 | 13 | 388 |
| | | Prakasam | 3 | 23 | 983 |
| | | Kurnool | 1 | 4 | 208 |
| 2 | 1997–98 | Mahaboobnagar | 4 | 26 | 511 |
| | | Prakasam | 5 | 15 | 444 |
| | | Guntur | 2 | 8 | 143 |
| | | Kurnool | 4 | 4 | 394 |
| 3 | 2000–01 | Prakasam | 4 | 12 | 462 |
| | | Kurnool | 4 | 6 | 194 |
| 4 | | Total | | 111 | 3727 |

*Source*: Records of the division

**Table 40 Productivity of GPCMSs in selected divisions, 2002–03**

| S. No. | Particulars | Divisions | | | |
|---|---|---|---|---|---|
| | | *Bhadra-chalam* | *Chinta-palli* | *Paderu* | *Srisailam* |
| 1 | GPCMSs | 8 | 3 | 6 | 3 |
| 2 | DR depots | 18 | 26 | 20 | 13 |
| 3 | Ration cards | 8279 | 12660 | 12245 | NA |
| 4 | Employees | 33 | 30 | 30 | 17 |
| 5 | MFP value (Rs. lakhs) | 33.20 | 14.30 | 60.08 | 49.95 |
| 6 | Agriculture produce (Rs. lakhs) | 5.40 | 16.13 | 24.37 | 1.9 |
| 7 | Essential commodities (Rs. lakhs) | 171.34 | 179.95 | 272.48 | 104.11 |
| 8 | Amount disbursed (Rs. lakhs) | 11.84 | 1.47 | 3.19 | 1.23 |
| 9 | Recovery (Rs. lakhs) | 9.05 | 1.08 | 2.06 | 0.88 |
| 10 | Recovery (%) | 9.55 | 24.3 | 64.73 | 23.87 |
| 11 | Turnover (Rs. lakhs) | 221.77 | 211.85 | 360.17 | 157.19 |
| 12 | Turnover/employee (Rs. lakhs) | 6.72 | 7.06 | 12.01 | 9.25 |

Figures from Sr. No. 2–12 are average for a GPCMS
*Source*: Records of the division

**Table 41 Division-wise viability of GPCMSs**

| S. No. | Grants required (as % of salaries) | Divisions | | | |
|---|---|---|---|---|---|
| | | *Bhadra-chalam* | *Chinta-palli* | *Paderu* | *Srisailam* |
| 1 | 1–25 | 2 (25.0) | 0 (0.0) | 1 (16.7) | 1 (33.3) |
| 2 | 26–50 | 3 (37.5) | 1 (25.0) | 1 (16.7) | 0 (0.0) |
| 3 | 51–75 | 2 (25.0) | 2 (50.0) | 3 (50.0) | 2 (66.7) |
| 4 | 76–100 | 1 (12.5) | 1 (25.0) | 1 (16.7) | 0 (0.0) |
| 5 | Total | 8 (100.0) | 4* (100.0) | 6 (100.0) | 3 (100.0) |

* Of the total, one belongs to Rampachodavaram division
*Source*: Records of the division

*Notes:*

1. For close supervision and monitoring of GPCMSs, divisions were created and headed by divisional managers. Divisional manager is supported by one or two CCPAs and other administrative staff. Apart from supervision of the societies, DR depots, and purchase points, divisional managers undertake centralised procurement of essential commodities, transportation of MFPs and agricultural produce procured by various GPCMSs to central godowns of traders authorised by GCC. Divisional managers are also responsible for allocation of funds for credit operatons. On the whole, he/she is the local supervisor and a nominee of the GCC.
2. Bhadrachalam is situated on the banks of river Godavari, and located 201 kms from Vijayawada. It is considered to be one of the greatest holy shrines in southern India as Lord Rama lived here for some time. Puranic and historic facts relate that Lord Rama, long after he had shed his mortal coils, manifested himself to save his devotee Bhadra Maharshi, son of Meru. Thus, the name of Bhadrachalam or Bhadradri is derived from Bhadra. It is also said that Shri Rama appeared in a dream to a woman called Pokala Dammakka and informed her about the existence of idols on Bhadragiri hills. To her surprise, she found the idols and put up a modest structure. Later, Gopanna commonly known as Ramdas renovated the temple in 17th century.
3. Division-wise data on other functions of GCC are not readily available. Within the available time, efforts were made to concentrate on credit operations.
4. Matsyagundam is known for its centuries old Sri Matsyalingeswara Swamy temple. The mythological story is that a fight between snakes (Singarajulu) and fishes (Matsyarajule) took place. The mother fish brought all the fishes here from a place called Gemmeli for safety from the snakes and eversince then the fishes lived here giving it the name Matsyagundam. It is believed that these fishes continue to be protected by Lord Matsyalingeswara Swamy. A fair is held on every Sivarathri where huge congregation of tribals over all mandals of Visakha agency and nearby Orissa takes place. It is about 11 kms from Paderu on its way towards Jolaput (3 kms off the main road).

5. Sri Mallikarjunaswamy temple at Srisailam, one of the 12 Jyothirlinga Sthalas, is dedicated to Sri Mallkarjunaswamy and his consort Bhramarambika. The sanctum enshrining Lord Mallikarjuna is a shell-like structure. The Devi is revered as Brahmani Shakti. The devout believe that one can attain mukti by taking birth at Srisailam. Sri Adi Sankara had visited the shrine and sung in praise of Lord Mallikarjuna and his consort in Sivananda Lahari. A special feature in the Srisailam temple is that anybody can go inside the sanctum and perform abhisheka and pujas. A Veerashaiva priest performs the daily pooja to the Lord, whereas the Devi's pooja is done by a Brahmin. The temple, which shines like a jewel on the Neelamalai range, is known by different names like Srigiri, Srimala and Srinagara. The famous Skanda Purana has a chapter dedicated to it. Tamil Saint poets of the past millennium have sung in praise of this temple. Early inscriptions speak of how rulers of different dynasties (Satavahanas, Vakatakas, Kakatiyas, and Vijayanagar) were ardent devotees of Lord Mallikarjuna and enriched the shrine in terms of constructions and other gifts. In later years, Maratha ruler Chatrapati Shivaji is known to have constructed a gopuram of shrine. Krishna flows four kms away from the shrine and known as Paathaala Ganga.

# 5

# Progress of Selected GPCMSs

Having analysed relative performance of selected divisions in the previous chapter, some light is thrown on working of four GPCMSs from the study area. One GPCMS each from the four selected divisions are identified. Selection of GPCMSs is based on extent of self sufficiency, and purely non-random.

## Chintapalli GPCMS

It belongs to Chintapalli division, and started in 1956 as a branch of the GCC with a view to procure MFPs and agriculture produce, to supply essential commodities through DR depots, and to provide credit. It covers Chintapalli, Ravikamatam, and Rolugunta revenue mandals from the forest ranges of Lotugedda, Chintapalli, and Narsipatnam. There are about 14,000 tribal households in the jurisdiction. Tamarind, addaleaf, sheekakai, rock bee honey, hill brooms, narmamidi bark, myrobalans, etc. are the MFPs available. Procurement season for these MFPs is provided in Table 1. Redgram, maize, beans, ginger, and turmeric are agricultural produce of the area. It has shandies at Annavaram, Lotugedda junction, Chintapalli, Lambasingi, dounuru, and Kalyanamalona.

GPCMS has three godwons, and 23 DR depots of which 16 are rented (Table 2). Daily requirements like rice, sugar, kerosene, dals, groundnut oil, chillies, soaps, onions, potatoes, etc. are sold through these DR depots. The society has 10,941 white cards, and 429 pink cards. It also took up distributing gas cylinders to women SHGs, and in all 818 were issued. In all 31 employees are working of which 24 are tribals. Total wage bill/month for the society is Rs. 2.40 lakhs. Growth in membership, share capital, turnover are provided in Appendix 27. The society has 12,013 members with a share capital of Rs. 2.61 lakhs. Turnover for 2002–03 stood at Rs. 2.55 crores.

## Procurement of MFPs and agricultural produce

Table 3 provides data on growth in procurement of MFP for 1991–03, and no discernable trend can be observed. Maximum value (Rs. 36 lakhs) was noticed during 2000–01. For an area of the size, value of MFPs procured is low on any standard. Across various MFPs, gum karaya accounted for over 40–45% of the total value. Value of agriculture produce procured too exhibited similar trend (Table 4), and french beans has been the major item in this category.

## Supply of DRs and credit operations

As mentioned above, society has over 11,000 ration cards, and the eligibility of rice/card is given in Appendix 28. Accordingly, society distributes over 176 tonnes of rice/month, 10.43 tonnes of sugar/month, and 32 kilo litres of kerosene/month. Salt, edible oil, and other domestic requirements are being distributed to the tribals (Table 5). Total value of supplies increased from Rs. 78.65 lakhs in 1990–91 to Rs. 2.15 crores in 2002–03. The growth has been steady except in 1991–92, and 2001–02.

Particulars on short-term credit operations are provided in Table 6. During 1991–03, society provided an amount of Rs. 36.21 lakhs to 3583 members giving, on an average, Rs. 1010/ member. Recovery has been over 60%, and on few occasions it was as high as 96–97%. In additition to short-term loans, society also provided consumption, and medium term loans in 1991–92, 1995–96, and 2002–03, and loans to SHGs in 1994–95. In all,

574 members were benefited out of this, and an amount of Rs. 4.7 lakhs was distributed for this, purpose of which Rs. 12.56 lakhs is overdue.

## Source of income for GPCMS

Society earns income from various sources (Appendix 29). It is to be mentioned here that PDS operations are entirely with the civil supplies department, and depends upon ration cards distributed. In other words, society has no control on this. Other sources of income are commissions on procurement of MFPs, agriculture produce, sale of essential commodities, and credit operations. As discussed in the earlier paragraphs, here again, there is constraint in increasing volumes due to topography, clientele, season, availability of MFPs, and agricultural produce. Income and expenditure incurred for month of April 2003 is provided in Table 7. Of the total expenditure, about 68% is incurred towards salaries while income is distributed across various sources. Society incurred a loss of Rs. 67,000 for this month. However, GCC has been reimbursing 60% of the total establishment charges, and thus, societies are surviving. In the absence of grants from GCC, society would incur a net loss of Rs. 8 lakhs/year. Thus, there is a need for reducing cost as also exploring the possibility of increasing income through efficiency and diversification.

## Difficulties faced by management

Discussions with officials of the GPCMS revealed following difficulties in day to day management. Non-availability and untimely release of insufficient funds, adversely affecting business operations. Concept of self sufficiency is yet to percolate down to the floor level employees. Neglect of preservation and conservation of MFP species resulted in reduced productivity. These problems are aggravated by non-availability of sincere and committed employees at vital places (in-charge of mandal level stockiest point, CCPAs , and accountants).

# Pedabayalu GPCMS

The society was started in July 1992, and covers Pedabayalu

mandal. Shandies are orgainsed at four places (Pedabayalu, Rudakota, Bondapalli, and Pedkodapalli), and tamarind is the major MFP available in this region. GPCMS has 15 DR depots with 12,562 ration cards of which 11,526 are white cards. It has 21 employees of which 16 are tribals. Average monthly salary bill is Rs. 1.50 lakhs. It has MLS godown, DRs godown, and godown for gas cylinders. Growth in membership, share capital, and turnover for the period 1992–02 is provided in Table 8. Turnover was as low as Rs. 62 lakhs in 1999–00, and reached a maximum of Rs. 200.13 lakhs in 2000–01, however there is no trend. Society has shown net profits which are based on grants received towards salaries from GCC.

## Procurement of MFPs and agricultural produce

As mentioned earlier, tamarind is the major MFP which constituted 80–90% of the total MFP procured during 1992–03 (Table 9). Addaleaf, myrobalans, and other MFPs are also procured by the GPCMS. Progress in procurement of agricultural produce is provided in Table 10. Total value of agricultural produce never increased Rs. 27 lakhs (1995–96). It was as low as Rs. 0.39 lakhs in 1993–94. On the basis of MFPs and agricultural produce procured, it can be inferred that the area has less potential.

## Supply of DRs and credit operations

Supply of domestic requirements increased from Rs. 55 lakhs in 1992–93 to 123 lakhs in 2000–03 (Table 11). Baring 1996–97, and 1999–00 growth has been steady. The share of 'other items' to total domestic requirements has also been increasing over time. Sale of other items constituted 46%, while rice accounted for 31% followed by kerosene (12%) in 2002–03.

Particulars on short-term credit operations are provided in Table 12. GPCMS provided loans to 3527 members, and an amount of Rs. 37.4 lakhs was disbursed during 1993–03. Thus, GPCMS provided, on an average, Rs. 1060/member during the study period. Percentage of recovery appears to be reasonable in this remote area.

### Viability of depots and GPCMS

Depot-wise expenditure and income for December 2003 is provided in Table 13. Barring no exception, in all depots incurred huge losses. Table 14 provides income and expenditure for the GPCMS for the month of April 2003. The GPCMS posted Rs. 5735 as profit. GPCMS posted profits only when received 75% of salaries as subsidy (Table 15).

### Problems perceived

Apart from difficulties faced in the Chintapalli GPCMS, officials of the Pedabayalu, GPCMS corroborated views expressed by Ramanan (2003) (Appendix 30).

## Peda Dornal GPCMS

GPCMS Peda Dornal was started as a branch office of GCC in October 1975. The area of operation was extended to Prakasam, Guntur, Anantapur, and Kurnool districts. As the area was too big, Nandyala GPCMS was created in 1990 covering Kurnool district. Peda Dornal was registered as GPCMS in 1994 with Prakasam, Guntur, and partially Kurnool districts as its jurisdiction. It has 9 forest ranges, and 10 DR depots. GPCMS has been supplying essential commodities and domestic requirements to tribals and government ST Ashram Schools. GPCMS covers over 18,000 chenchus who are classified as primitive tribal groups. The society is having its own office building, two MFP godowns, a DR godown. At present 11 members are working in this society, of which 7 are SCs, and 3 are STs. Monthly wage bill is Rs. 68,000.

### Procurement of MFPs and agriculture produce, and supply of DRs

Duration of various MFPs available in Peda Dornal GPCMS is provided in Table 16. Value of procurement of these MFPs for the period 1996–03 is provided in Table 17. Gum karaya, and gum kondagogu, maredugeddalu, narmamidi bark, and nuxvomica are the major MFPs. Value of procurement of MFPs was over Rs. 75 lakhs in 2002–03, while it was as low as Rs. 13 lakhs in 1998–99.

Chilies and cotton are the two principal agriculture products procured, and their share in the total turnover of the GPCMS was negligible (Table 18). DRs constituted over 50% of the total turnover. However, bifurcation of various DRs is not available. DRs increased from Rs. 30 lakhs in 1991–92 to about Rs.86 lakhs in 2002–03, and that of turnover from Rs. 67 lakhs to about Rs. 161 lakhs. Thus, there is gradual increase in procurement of MFPs, supply of DRs, and turnover during 1991–03.

## Credit operations

In tune with the objective of GPCMSs, Peda Dornal GPCM has been involved in providing both short-term, and consumption loans. Short-term loans provided for the period 1991–98 are furnished in Table 19. During the last 7 years, GPCMS covered 72 villages with 762 beneficiaries. It distributed an amount of Rs. 25.52 lakhs with a recovery of 18.8%. Recovery never increased 37%, while maximum number of loans were provided in 1992–93, 1996–97, and 1993–94 in that order. As of consumption loans, GPCMS disbursed Rs. 1.59 lakhs with a recovery of over 14% (Table 20). Off late, neither short-term loans nor cosumption loans are entertained due to lack of funds as also huge overdues.

With a view to bring self sufficiency, a tribal is posted as manager who is very active and dedicated. Through his leadership qualities as also continuous monitoring of DR depots, manager has instilled a sense of responsibility among the lower level employees. As a result, performance has improved substantially, and GPCMS is almost close to self sufficiency during 2002–03. According to him, 'a tribal officer can easily interact with tribals as also understands the problems and perceptions of the target group'. Manager also indicated that 'dedication is important while working with such clientele'. In this dedication, number of training programmes were organised for the employees as also ordinary members (Table 21). It trained 82 members in scientific collection, processing, and marketing of various MFPs. Income and expenditure for the month of January 2004 is provided in Table 22. GPCMS posted a net profit of Rs. 0.23 lakh for this period.

### Problems perceived

Apart from difficulties mentioned by the officials of earlier societies, manager Peda Dornal also mentioned about difficulties in getting beneficiaries with patta lands, and combing in forest areas by police due to insurgency of naxals.

## Yellandu GPCMS

Yellandu GPCMS falls in the Bhadrachalam division, situated on Khammam-Bhadrachalam road, and 45 kms from Khammam. The GPCMS covers 7 revenue mandals (Yellandu, Tekulapalli, Kamepalli, Singareni, Gundala, Bayyaram, and Garla). There are 32,000 tribal households dominated by Koya, Konda Reddi, Lambada, and Yerukula tribes. GPCMS has two lorries, a truck, 17 DR depots, office building, a jeep, MLS godowns, DRs godown, and two MFP godowns with 33 DR depots, and 16,773 ration cards. It distributes 373 tonnes of rice, 22.5 tonnes of sugar, 54 kilo litres of kerosene/month. Wage bill of the society is Rs. 3.41 lakhs/month. Of the total employees of 46, 50% are tribals.

### Procurement of MFPs and agriculture produce

Through narmamidi bark, hill brooms, cleaning nuts, and amla, are available in the area (Table 23), not much has been done in terms of procurement (Table 24). Gum karaya dominated MFPs procured followed by nuxvomica. Neither individual MFPs procured have shown any trend. Baring 2002–03, and 1991–92 their contribution to total turnover was negligible. Value of total MFPs procured contributed 5% to the turnover of GPCMS in 2002–03. Similar inferences can be made from Table 25. Though paddy and cotton are cultivated in the area, GPCMS failed to procure these crops during 1991–03. Chilies is the major item in the agricultural produce followed by redgram and maize.

### Supply of DRs and credit

Supply of DRs has been a major activity of the GPCMS. There has been steady improvement in these supplies (Table 26). Supply of DRs contributed about 85% of the total turnover during the last 13 years. Of the total DRs, rice contributed as much as 40%

followed by 'others', and kerosene. As mentioned earlier, rice, sugar, salt, edible oil and kerosene are controlled items and is a captive business. Any change in the sympathetic attitude of government would collapse the viability of GPCMS. Thus, there is need to concentrate on 'other DR items'.

As of short-term loans, GPCMS did considerable business during 1991–03, and the recovery has been more than satisfactory, except in 1992–93 (Table 27). Loan disbursed/member also shown positive trend during the study period. GPCMS also provided medium term loans in 1994–95, and 2002–03, and the recovery has been satisfactory.

Particulars on income and expenditure for the month of December 2003 (Table 28) have shown that income is marginally higher than expenditure probably due to recovery of transport hire charges. Profit margin due to sale of DRs is the major component of income. About 60% of the total expenditure is towards establishment charges.

### Problems perceived

Soon after appointment of a new manager, efforts were initiated to explore new areas, and also items in sales counters were increased. Regular monthly meetings of salesman and CCPAs were organised. Targets were given to each CCPA, and salesmen which are reviewed in the monthly meetings. Similarly, CCPAs were not allowed any deficits on MFPs, and agricultural produce procured. Number of meetings were organised to educate tribals about advantage of transacting with GPCMS. Prices of MFPs, and agricultural produce were published in the local newspaper for wider publicity. Manager also has been visiting DR depots regularly and motivating employees. There has been a positive change in all the employees including CCPAs. All these efforts culminated in improved turnover and margins. Management is now confident that even without controlled items, society would be self sufficient.

## Comparison of selected GPCMSs

As indicated earlier, selection of GPCMSs is non-random. Of the four, Peda Dornal attained self sufficiency while Yellandu is close to it (Table 29). On the other hand, Pedabayalu and Chintapalli are incurring heavy losses. Of the four GPCMSs, Chintapalli is oldest while Pedabayalu is of recent origin. Yellandu has maximum number of DR depots, employees, and ration cards, and outperformed other GPCMSs in terms of supply of DRs. Turnover is the highest in Yellandu and the lowest in Pedabayalu. However, turnover/employee is the highest in Peda Dornal because of its smaller number of employees.

## Summary

Working of four GPCMSs from the study area are analysed in this chapter. Chintapalli GPCMS was started in 1956 as a branch of the GCC with a view to procure MFPs and agriculture produce, to supply essential commodities through DR depots, and to provide credit. Tamarind, addaleaf, sheekakai, rock bee honey, hill brooms, narmamidi bark, myrobalans, etc. are the MFPs available. GPCMS has three godwons, and 23 DR depots of which 16 are rented. In all 31 employees are working of which 24 are tribals. Total wage bill/month for the society is Rs. 2.40 lakhs. Maximum procurement of MFP (Rs. 36 lakhs) was noticed during 2000–01. Across various MFPs, gum karaya accounted for over 40–50% of the total value. French beans has been the major item in agriculture produce. Total value of supplies increased from Rs. 78.65 lakhs in 1990–91 to Rs. 2.15 crores in 2002–03. During 1991–03, society provided an amount of Rs. 36.21 lakhs to 3583 members giving, on an average, Rs. 1010/member. Recovery has been over 60%, and on few occasions it was as high as 96–97%. Of the total expenditure, about 68% is incurred towards salaries while income is distributed across various sources. Society incurred a loss of Rs. 67,000 for April 2003. Non-availability and untimely release of insufficient funds, adversely affecting business operations. Neglect of preservation and conservation of MFP species resulted in reduced productivity.

Pedabayalu GPCMS was started in July 1992, and located in Paderu division. GPCMS has 15 DR depots with 12,526 ration cards of which 11,526 are white cards. It has 21 employees of which 16 are tribals. Average monthly salary bill is Rs. 1.50 lakhs. Total value of agriculture produce never increased Rs. 27 lakhs

(1995–96). Supply of domestic requirement increased from Rs. 55 lakhs in 1992–93 to 123 lakhs in 2002–03. GPCMS provided loans to 3527 members, and an amount of Rs. 37.4 lakhs was disbursed during 1993–03. Percentage of recovery appears to be reasonable in this remote area. Barring no exception, all depots incurred huge losses.

GPCMS Peda Dornal was started as a branch office of GCC in October 1975. It has 9 forest ranges, and 10 DR depots. At present 11 members are working in this society, of which 7 are SCs, and 3 are STs. Monthly wage bill is Rs. 68,000. Value of procurement of MFPs over Rs. 75 lakhs in 2002–03, while it was as low as Rs. 13 lakhs in 1998–99. Chilies and cotton are the two principal agriculture products procured, and their share in the total turnover of GPCMS was negligible. DRs constituted over 50% of the total turnover. GPCMS covered 72 villages with 762 beneficiaries. It distributed an amount of Rs. 25.52 lakhs with a recovery of 18.8%. Off late, neither short-term nor consumption loans are entertained due to lack of funds as also huge overdues. With a view to bring self sufficiency, a tribal is posted as manager who is very active and dedicated. Getting beneficiaries with patta lands, and combing in forest areas by police due to insurgency of naxals are problems in increasing turnover.

Yellandu GPCMS was started in 1992 and covers 7 revenue mandals. Wage bill of the society is Rs. 3.41 lakhs/month. Of the total employees of 46, 50% are tribals. Gum karaya dominated MFPs procured followed by nuxvomica. Value of total MFPs procured contributed 5% to the turnover of GPCMS in 2002–03. Supply of DRs constituted about 85% of total turnover during the last 13 years. Of the total DRs, rice contributed as much as 40% followed by 'others', and kerosene. GPCMS did considerable business during 1991–03, and the recovery has been more than satisfactory, except in 1992–93.

A comparison of performance across selected GPCMSs indicated that Peda Dornal attained self sufficiency while Yellandu is close to it. On the other hand, Pedabayalu is incurring heavy losses. Same is the case with Chintapalli. Yellandu has maximum number of DR depots, employees, and ration cards, and outperformed other GPCMSs in terms of supply of

DRs. Turnover is the highest in Yellandu and the lowest in Pedabayalu. However, turnover/employee is the highest in Peda Dornal because of its smaller number of employees.

**Table 1 Infrastructure available with Chintapalli GPCMS**

| *Sr. No.* | *Particulars* | *Place* | *Sr. No.* | *Particulars* | *Place* |
|---|---|---|---|---|---|
| 1 | Main godown | Chintapalli | 6 | DR depot | Tajangi |
| 2 | DR depot | Rajupakalu | 7 | DR depot | Chintapalli |
| 3 | Main godown | Lambasingi | 8 | DR depot | Lothugedda |
| 4 | DR depot | Lambasingi | 9 | DR depot | Lothugedda |
| 5 | Main godown | Downuru | 10 | DR depot | Downuru |

*Source:* Records of the GPCMS

**Table 2 Procurement season for various MFPs in Chintapalli GPCMS**

| *Sr. No.* | *MFP* | *Season* |
|---|---|---|
| 1 | Sheekakai | January–April |
| 2 | Seeded tamarind | February–May |
| 3 | Honey | April–June, November–December |
| 4 | Naramamidi bark | March–June |
| 5 | Marking nuts | February–March |
| 6 | Myrabalans | February–March |
| 7 | Gum | April–June, November–January |
| 8 | Pungam seed | April–May |
| 9 | Hill brooms | February–April |
| 10 | Cleaning nuts | November–January |
| 11 | Amla | November–January |

*Source :* Records of the GPCMS

**Table 3 Growth (Rs. lakhs) in purchase of MFPs in Chintapalli GPCMS, 1991–03**

| *Sr. No.* | *Year* | *Gum karaya* | *Seeded tamarind* | *Deseeded tamarind* | *Myrobalans* | *Mohwa seed* |
|---|---|---|---|---|---|---|
| 1 | 1990–91 | 20.20 | 0.20 | – | 2.93 | – |
| 2 | 1991–92 | 7.91 | 1.61 | – | 0.31 | – |
| 3 | 1992–93 | 2.77 | 1.57 | – | 0.04 | – |
| 4 | 1993–94 | 6.81 | 3.67 | – | 0.86 | 0.01 |
| 5 | 1994–95 | 4.74 | 1.84 | – | 0.38 | – |
| 6 | 1995–96 | 4.95 | 0.75 | 0.01 | 2.78 | – |
| 7 | 1996–97 | 5.13 | 2.06 | – | 0.48 | – |
| 8 | 1997–98 | 6.42 | 3.22 | – | 0.46 | – |
| 9 | 1998–99 | 4.59 | 3.77 | – | 0.86 | – |
| 10 | 1999–00 | 6.82 | 9.53 | – | 4.33 | – |
| 11 | 2000–01 | 6.05 | 25.70 | – | 3.48 | – |
| 12 | 2001–02 | 4.17 | 12.61 | – | 0.68 | – |
| 13 | 2002–03 | 4.35 | 5.67 | – | 0.29 | – |

***Continued Table 3***

| *Sr. No.* | *Year* | *Addaleaf* | *Mohwa flower* | *Nuxvomica* | *Total MFP* |
|---|---|---|---|---|---|
| 1 | 1990–91 | 4.22 | – | – | 27.55 |
| 2 | 1991–92 | 0.34 | – | – | 10.17 |
| 3 | 1992–93 | – | – | – | 4.38 |
| 4 | 1993–94 | 1.03 | – | 0.28 | 12.66 |
| 5 | 1994–95 | 0.52 | – | – | 7.48 |
| 6 | 1995–96 | 1.84 | – | – | 10.33 |
| 7 | 1996–97 | 1.10 | – | – | 8.77 |
| 8 | 1997–98 | 0.86 | – | – | 10.96 |
| 9 | 1998–99 | 0.06 | – | – | 9.38 |
| 10 | 1999–00 | 0.70 | – | – | 21.38 |
| 11 | 2000–01 | 0.56 | – | – | 35.79 |
| 12 | 2001–02 | – | – | – | 17.46 |
| 13 | 2002–03 | – | – | 0.05 | 10.36 |

*Source:* Records of the GPCMS

**Table 4 Growth (Rs. lakhs) in procurement of agricultural produce in Chintapalli GPCMS, 1991–03**

| *Sr. No.* | *Year* | *Niger seed* | *Annato seed* | *French beans* | *Redgram* | *Maize* | *Total* |
|---|---|---|---|---|---|---|---|
| 1 | 1990–91 | 3.19 | 0.03 | 32.41 | 0.23 | 0.19 | 36.05 |
| 2 | 1991–92 | 32.15 | – | 4.63 | 0.23 | 1.47 | 38.48 |
| 3 | 1992–93 | 21.72 | – | 2.89 | 0.64 | – | 25.25 |
| 4 | 1993–94 | 1. 51 | – | 0.61 | 0.39 | 0.24 | 2.75 |
| 5 | 1994–95 | 0.22 | – | 0.95 | 0.11 | – | 1.28 |
| 6 | 1995–96 | 2.82 | – | 0.59 | 0.02 | – | 3.43 |
| 7 | 1996–97 | 0.90 | 0.73 | 1.72 | – | – | 3.35 |
| 8 | 1997–98 | 3.52 | 0.12 | 3.63 | 0.15 | – | 7.42 |
| 9 | 1998–99 | 1.45 | 0.09 | 6.30 | 0.32 | – | 8.16 |
| 10 | 1999–00 | 0.39 | 0.08 | 13.81 | 0.20 | – | 14.48 |
| 11 | 2000–01 | – | 0.20 | 11.81 | – | – | 12.01 |
| 12 | 2001–02 | 0.01 | 2.52 | 0.28 | 1.16 | – | 3.97 |
| 13 | 2002–03 | – | 0.91 | 26.07 | 0.53 | – | 27.51 |

*Source* Records of the GPCMS

**Table 5 Growth (Rs. lakhs) in supply of domestic requirements Chintapalli GPCMS, 1991–03**

| *Sr. No.* | *Year* | *Rice* | *Sugar* | *Salt* | *Edible oil* | *Kerosene oil* | *Others* | *Total* |
|---|---|---|---|---|---|---|---|---|
| 1 | 1990–91 | 52.00 | 0.18 | 0.13 | 0.23 | 0.22 | 25.89 | 78.65 |
| 2 | 1991–92 | 80.15 | 0.24 | 0.12 | 0.36 | 0.36 | 28.00 | 109.23 |
| 3 | 1992–93 | 48.00 | 0.16 | 0.06 | 0.42 | 0.56 | 24.00 | 73.20 |
| 4 | 1993–94 | 82.20 | 0.28 | 0.15 | 0.55 | 0.60 | 25.53 | 109.31 |
| 5 | 1994–95 | 90.14 | 0.35 | 0.14 | 0.60 | 0.72 | 21.54 | 113.49 |
| 6 | 1995–96 | 86.65 | 0.42 | 0.12 | 0.73 | 0.83 | 17.29 | 106.04 |
| 7 | 1996–97 | 114.66 | 0.51 | 0.16 | 1.00 | 0.93 | 22.18 | 139.44 |
| 8 | 1997–98 | 113.78 | 0.34 | 0.18 | 1.00 | 0.36 | 39.34 | 154.90 |
| 9 | 1998–99 | 120.30 | 0.28 | 0.20 | 0.36 | 0.44 | 35.38 | 156.96 |
| 10 | 1999–00 | 129.77 | 0.26 | 0.10 | 0.48 | 0.30 | 33.79 | 165.30 |
| 11 | 2000–01 | 126.83 | 0.28 | 0.19 | 0.72 | 0.30 | 56.60 | 224.52 |
| 12 | 2001–02 | 115.61 | 0.16 | 0.25 | 0.80 | 0.22 | 71.21 | 188.25 |
| 13 | 2002–03 | 126.48 | 0.15 | 0.22 | 0.75 | 0.24 | 88.00 | 215.25 |

*Source:* Records of the GPCMS

**Table 6 Short term loans Chintapalli GPCMS, 1991–03**

| *Sr. No.* | *Year* | *No. of loanees* | *Amount disbursed (Rs. lakhs)* | *Recovery (Rs. lakhs)* | *Recovery (%)* |
|---|---|---|---|---|---|
| 1 | 1990–91 | 149 | 2.31 | 1.56 | 67.0 |
| 2 | 1991–92 | 350 | 2.29 | 1.53 | 66.0 |
| 3 | 1992–93 | 929 | 8.56 | 6.00 | 70.0 |
| 4 | 1993–94 | 959 | 7.19 | 4.65 | 64.0 |
| 5 | 1994–95 | 386 | 3.95 | 3.34 | 84.0 |
| 6 | 1995–96 | 346 | 3.84 | 2.97 | 77.0 |
| 7 | 1996–97 | 120 | 1.64 | 1.59 | 96.0 |
| 8 | 1997–98 | 124 | 2.36 | 1.51 | 63.0 |
| 9 | 1998–99 | 42 | 0.92 | 0.67 | 72.0 |
| 10 | 1999–00 | – | – | – | – |
| 11 | 2000–01 | 26 | 0.42 | 0.27 | 64.0 |
| 12 | 2001–02 | 45 | 0.92 | 0.90 | 97.0 |
| 13 | 2002–03 | 107 | 1.81 | 1.26 | 69.0 |

*Source:* Records of the GPCMS

**Table 7 Income and expenditure (Rs. lakhs) in Chintapalli GPCMS, April 2003**

| *Sr. No.* | *Expenditure* | *Amount* | *Sr. No.* | *Income* | *Amount* |
|---|---|---|---|---|---|
| *1* | *2* | *3* | *4* | *5* | *6* |
| 1 | Pay of establishment | 2.60 | 1 | MFP/AP commission earned as agent of GCC | 0.26 |
| 2 | MLS trade charges | 0.16 | 2 | MLS commission | 0.42 |
| 3 | DRs trade charges | 0.12 | 3 | MLS transport charges | 0.16 |
| 4 | DRs transport charges | 0.16 | 4 | Margin on ECs (difference on SP-PP of ECs | 0.34 |
| 5 | LPG trade/ transport charges | 0.03 | 5 | FFW rice transport charges | 0.14 |
| 6 | FFW rice trade/ transport | 0.18 | 6 | Margin on other DR sales | 0.05 |
| 7 | Lorry/truck maintenance | | 7 | Margins on other DRs to hotels | 0.05 |
| | a. Hiring | | | | |
| | b. Fuel | | 8 | Sale of empties | 1.12 |
| | c. Repairs and renewals | | 9 | Margins on AP trade by the society | |
| | d. Rates and taxes | 0.08 | | | |
| 8 | Jeep maintenance | | 10 | Interest on loans recovered | 0.01 |
| | a. Hiring | | | | |
| | b. Fuel | | 11 | Penalties from employees | |
| | c. Repairs and renewals | 0.03 | 12 | Deficits recovery | 0.06 |
| | d. Rates and taxes | 0.02 | 13 | Miscellaneous income (retailers margin on FFW rice) | 0.12 |
| 9 | Administrative costs | 0.02 | | | |
| | a. Electricity | | | | |
| | b. Telephone | | 14 | Margin on gas sales | 0.09 |
| | c. Licenses | | 15 | DR trade charges (hostel gas incidentals) | 0.03 |
| | | | 16 | Gas trade charges (hostel gas incidentals) | 0.03 |

*Continued*

| 1 | 2 | 3 | 4 | 5 | 6 |
|---|---|---|---|---|---|
| | d. Books and forms | | 17 | Gas transport charges (Rs. 20 on sales) | 0.03 |
| | e. Postage and telegram | 0.15 | | | |
| | | 0.00 | 18 | Miscellaneous income (check gate) | 0.01 |
| 10 | TA/DA to staff | | | | |
| 11 | Depot rents | 0.01 | | | |
| 12 | Incentives to staff (rebate) | 0.25 | | | |
| 13 | LPG. godown rent | 0.03 | | | |
| 14 | Bank commission | | | | |
| 15 | Miscellaneous expenditure | | | | |
| 16 | Typing charges | | | | |
| | Total | 3.85 | | Total | 3.18 |

*Source*: Records of the GPCMS

**Table 8 Growth (Rs. lakhs) in membership, share capital, and turnover of Pedabayalu GPCMS, 1993–02**

| *Sr. No.* | *Year* | *Membership* | *Share capital* | *Turnover* | *Net profit/ loss* |
|---|---|---|---|---|---|
| 1 | 1992–93 | 82 | 0.04 | 96.47 | 0.0 |
| 2 | 1993–94 | – | 0.04 | 82.27 | 0.0 |
| 3 | 1994–95 | 289 | 0.08 | 78.34 | 1.02 |
| 4 | 1995–96 | 1272 | 0.16 | 127.15 | –1.42 |
| 5 | 1996–97 | 114 | 0.17 | 108.57 | –4.67 |
| 6 | 1997–98 | 900 | 0.23 | 129.8 | 0.0 |
| 7 | 1998–99 | 443 | 0.25 | 160.82 | –1.62 |
| 8 | 1999–00 | 420 | 0.27 | 62.04 | 0.0 |
| 9 | 2000–01 | 270 | 0.33 | 200.13 | 3.78 |
| 10 | 2001–02 | 4 | 0.33 | 137.16 | 5.87 |

*Source:* Records of the GPCMS

**Table 9 Growth (Rs. lakhs) in purchase of MFP in Pedabayalu GPCMS, 1993–03**

| *Sr. No.* | *Year* | *Seeded tamarind* | *Deseeded tamarind* | *Myrobalans* | *Adda-leaf* | *Other MFP* | *Total MFP* |
|---|---|---|---|---|---|---|---|
| 1 | 1992–93 | 3.90 | | | | | 3.90 |
| 2 | 1993–94 | 14.01 | 1.50 | 0.02 | 0.09 | – | 15.62 |
| 3 | 1994–95 | 3.10 | 0.25 | 0.03 | 1.42 | 1.35 | 6.15 |
| 4 | 1995–96 | 5.90 | 0.51 | 0.05 | 2.18 | 1.51 | 10.15 |
| 5 | 1996–97 | 12.56 | 0.48 | 0.08 | 2.43 | 5.79 | 21.34 |
| 6 | 1997–98 | 15.91 | – | – | 1.20 | 0.02 | 17.13 |
| 7 | 1998–99 | 38.09 | 0.05 | – | 2.40 | 0.45 | 40.99 |
| 8 | 1999–00 | 9.15 | 0.19 | 0.09 | 0.56 | 1.45 | 11.44 |
| 9 | 2000–01 | 48.11 | 6.38 | 0.01 | 3.28 | 0.51 | 58.29 |
| 10 | 2001–02 | 12.69 | – | 0.02 | 0.47 | – | 13.18 |
| 11 | 2002–03 | 23.83 | – | – | 2.57 | 1.80 | 28.20 |

*Source:* Records of the GPCMS

**Table 10 Growth (Rs. lakhs) in procurement of agricultural produce in Pedabayalu GPCMS, 1993–03**

| *Sr. No.* | *Year* | *Niger seed* | *Annato seed* | *French beans* | *Redgram* | *Other AP* | *Total* |
|---|---|---|---|---|---|---|---|
| 1 | 1992–93 | 15.56 | | 0.46 | 0.11 | – | 16.13 |
| 2 | 1993–94 | 0.26 | | 0.03 | 0.10 | – | 0.39 |
| 3 | 1994–95 | 3.41 | | 1.60 | 0.27 | 0.30 | 5.58 |
| 4 | 1995–96 | 18.31 | | 6.08 | 0.56 | 2.10 | 27.05 |
| 5 | 1996–97 | 4.12 | | 2.75 | 0.31 | 1.05 | 8.23 |
| 6 | 1997–98 | 10.22 | | 0.62 | 0.01 | 2.21 | 13.06 |
| 7 | 1998–99 | 2.35 | 0.05 | 1.28 | 0.46 | 4.35 | 8.49 |
| 8 | 1999–00 | – | | – | – | – | – |
| 9 | 2000–01 | 0.17 | | 1.75 | 0.71 | – | 2.63 |
| 10 | 2001–02 | 0.01 | | – | 0.01 | – | 0.02 |
| 11 | 2002–03 | – | | 13.16 | 1.80 | 0.94 | 15.90 |

*Source:* Records of the GPCMS

**Table 11 Growth (Rs. lakhs) in supply of domestic requirements in Padabayalu GPCMS, 1993–03**

| *Sr. No.* | *Year* | *Rice* | *Sugar* | *Salt* | *Edible oils* | *Kerosene oil* | *Others* | *Total* |
|---|---|---|---|---|---|---|---|---|
| 1 | 1992–93 | 22.91 | 1.36 | 0.18 | 0.45 | 3.13 | 26.83 | 54.86 |
| 2 | 1993–94 | 29.36 | 3.16 | 0.33 | 1.42 | 4.39 | 25.15 | 63.81 |
| 3 | 1994–95 | 34.01 | 1.19 | 0.12 | 1.50 | 2.90 | 25.83 | 65.72 |
| 4 | 1995–96 | 42.36 | 3.10 | 0.38 | 1.86 | 3.92 | 36.41 | 88.03 |
| 5 | 1996–97 | 39.94 | 2.96 | 0.33 | 1.59 | 3.80 | 29.24 | 77.86 |
| 6 | 1997–98 | 52.10 | 3.95 | 0.40 | 1.98 | 4.10 | 35.50 | 98.03 |
| 7 | 1998–99 | 65.35 | 7.74 | 0.57 | 2.13 | 7.19 | 26.87 | 109.85 |
| 8 | 1999–00 | 25.10 | 2.26 | 0.26 | 1.61 | 4.09 | 15.13 | 48.45 |
| 9 | 2000–01 | 63.16 | 9.12 | 0.39 | 3.18 | 5.53 | 55.50 | 136.88 |
| 10 | 2001–02 | 63.85 | 7.74 | 0.37 | 6.36 | 16.81 | 28.14 | 123.27 |
| 11 | 2002–03 | 37.54 | 6.62 | 0.41 | 7.18 | 14.82 | 56.41 | 122.98 |

*Source:* Records of the GPCMS

**Table 12 Short-term loans (Rs. lakhs) distributed by Pedabayalu GPCMS, 1993–03**

| *Sr. No.* | *Year* | *No. of loanees* | *Amount disbursed* | *Recovery* | *Percentage* |
|---|---|---|---|---|---|
| 1 | 1992–93 | 2309 | 21.58 | 9.56 | 44 |
| 2 | 1993–94 | 290 | 2.45 | 1.77 | 72 |
| 3 | 1994–95 | 64 | 0.89 | 0.72 | 81 |
| 4 | 1995–96 | 192 | 1.92 | 1.65 | 86 |
| 5 | 1996–97 | 95 | 1.14 | 0.97 | 85 |
| 6 | 1997–98 | 122 | 1.58 | 1.38 | 87 |
| 7 | 1998–99 | 108 | 1.49 | 1.31 | 88 |
| 8 | 1999–00 | 144 | 2.15 | 1.61 | 75 |
| 9 | 2000–01 | 108 | 2.33 | 1.45 | 62 |
| 10 | 2001–02 | 41 | 0.69 | 0.58 | 84 |
| 11 | 2002–03 | 54 | 1.18 | 0.79 | 67 |

*Source:* Records of the GPCMS

**Table 13 DR depot-wise income and expenditure in Pedabayalu GPCMS, December 2003**

| *Sr. No.* | *DR depot* | *Income (Rs.)* | *Expenditure (Rs.)* | *Gap (Rs.)* |
|---|---|---|---|---|
| 1 | Pedabayalu | 3905 | 5454 | 1549 |
| 2 | Lakshipeta | 1891 | 5351 | 3460 |
| 3 | Adugulaput | 1237 | 5065 | 3828 |
| 4 | Gomangi | 3446 | 4822 | 1376 |
| 5 | Koravangi | 3309 | 8194 | 4885 |
| 6 | Rudakota | 783 | 3000 | 2217 |
| 7 | Seekari | 1457 | 3000 | 1543 |
| 8 | Peddaput | 2231 | 8110 | 5880 |
| 9 | Pedakodapalli | 2159 | 7649 | 5490 |
| 10 | Gamparai | 2443 | 6877 | 4434 |
| 11 | Bondapalli | 1912 | 8675 | 6763 |
| 12 | Kimudupalli | 3417 | 8601 | 5184 |
| 13 | Bongram | 2598 | 10935 | 8337 |
| 14 | Vanabhangi | 1821 | 6933 | 5112 |
| 15 | Aradakota | 2107 | 7029 | 4922 |
| | Total | 34716 | 99696 | 64980 |

*Source:* Records of the GPCMS

**Table 14 : Income and expenditure in pedayabalu GPCMS, april 2003**

| *Sr. No.* | *Expenditure* | *Amount* | *Sr. No.* | *Income* | *Amount* |
|---|---|---|---|---|---|
| 1 | Pay of establishment | 174983 | 1 | MFP procurement margin | 18580 |
| 2 | MLS trader charges | 13054 | 2 | Depots sales @ 2.4% | |
| 3 | DR trader charges | 1925 | | a. Rice 635 × Rs. 12.92. | 8204 |
| 4 | Trade charged (Gas FWW) | 2837 | | b. Sugar 38 × Rs. 14.52 | 551 |
| | | | | c. Kerosene 9248 × 0.18 | 1665 |
| 5 | Transport hire charges | 15981 | | d. DRs 254481 × 5% | 12724 |
| 6 | Van fuel | 17919 | 3 | Hostels supplies | |
| 7 | Van maintenace | 9235 | | a. Transport charges | 6639 |
| 8 | Insurance and taxes | 5435 | | b. Incidental charges | |
| 9 | Postage and telegram | 174 | | c. Other DRs 788 × 5% | 3944 |
| 10 | Depot rents | 2100 | 4 | Gas sales 405 cylinders × Rs. 16.55 | 6702 |
| 11 | Miscellaneous Expenditure | 555 | 5 | F.F.W. rice 1116 × Rs. 7.00 | 7816 |
| 12 | Bank commission | 1337 | 6 | Empties rice 2670 × Rs. 4.00 | 10680 |
| 13 | Rebate on sales (DRs) | 3018 | | | |
| 14 | Typing charges | 1825 | 7 | Sugar 38 × Rs. 22.00 | 836 |
| 15 | Printing and stationary | 401 | 8 | Loan interest recovery margin | 220 |
| | | | 9 | MLS commission | 19233 |
| | | | 10 | Stage-II transport | 29063 |
| | | | 11 | Gas service charges+misc. | 1400 |
| | | | 12 | Deficits recovered | — |
| | | | 13 | Grant-in-aid | 128257 |
| | Total | 250779 | | Total | 256514 |

*Source*: Records of the GPCMS

**Table 15 Viability Pedabayalu GPCMS, December 2003**

| *Sr. No.* | *% of subsidy* | *Income (Rs. lakhs)* | *Expenditure (Rs. lakhs)* | *Gap (Rs. lakhs)* |
|---|---|---|---|---|
| 1 | Without subsidy | 1.10 | 2.31 | 1.21 |
| 2 | With 25% subsidy | 1.57 | 2.31 | 0.74 |
| 3 | With 50% subsidy | 2.03 | 2.31 | 0.28 |
| 4 | With 60% subsidy | 2.22 | 2.31 | 0.09 |
| 5 | With 75% subsidy | 2.50 | 2.31 | 0.19 |

*Source:* Records of the GPCMS

**Table 16 Duration and availability of MFP in Peda Dornal GPCMS**

| *Sr. No.* | *MFP* | *Season* |
|---|---|---|
| 1 | Gum karaya | September–March |
| 2 | Maredugeddalu | Throughout year |
| 3 | Nuxvomica | November–March |
| 4 | Soapnuts | February–April |
| 5 | Amla fruits | November–February |
| 6 | Honey | April–July |

*Source:* Records of the GPCMS

**Table 17 Growth (Rs. lakhs ) in procurement of MFPs in Peda Dornal GPCMS, 1996–03**

| *Sr. No.* | *MFP* | *1995–96* | *1996–97* | *1997–98* | *1998–99* |
|---|---|---|---|---|---|
| 1 | Gum karaya | 14.11 | 8.72 | 8.69 | 7.62 |
| 2 | Gum kondagogu | 0.76 | 0.51 | 1.14 | 1.01 |
| 3 | Gum tiruman | 0.03 | 0.01 | 0.01 | 0.01 |
| 4 | Seeded tamarind | 0.03 | 0.13 | | 0.02 |
| 5 | Tamarind seed | | 0.01 | | |
| 6 | R.B. honey | 6.99 | 2.78 | 5.46 | 1.61 |
| 7 | Myrobalans | 0.08 | 0.44 | 0.45 | 0.72 |
| 8 | Soapnuts | 6.01 | 6.38 | 0.21 | 1.13 |
| 9 | Mohwa seed | 0.35 | 0.10 | 0.16 | 0.17 |
| 10 | Cleaning nuts | 0.06 | | | |
| 11 | Naramamidi bark | | 0.05 | 1.20 | 0.14 |
| 12 | Pungam seed | 0.04 | 0.01 | 0.02 | 0.01 |
| 13 | Bee wax | 0.31 | 0.25 | 0.34 | 0.01 |
| 14 | Nuxvomica | 0.61 | 0.13 | 0.25 | 0.10 |
| 15 | Tanikayalu | 0.05 | 0.07 | 0.06 | 0.04 |
| 16 | Maredugeddalu | 1.14 | 2.11 | 5.45 | 0.52 |
| 17 | Green amla | 0.21 | | | |
| 18 | Dry amla | | | | |
| 19 | Others | | | | |
| 20 | Total | 30.78 | 2.17 | 23.44 | 13.11 |

**Continued Table 17**

| Sr. No. | MFP | 1999–00 | 2000–01 | 2001–02 | 2002–03 |
|---|---|---|---|---|---|
| 1 | Gum karaya | 9.45 | 7.19 | 6.35 | 9.92 |
| 2 | Gum kondagogu | 6.83 | 11.05 | 20.26 | 26.81 |
| 3 | Gum tiruman | | | | |
| 4 | Seeded tamarind | | 0.16 | | |
| 5 | Tamarind seed | | 0.07 | | |
| 6 | R.B. honey | 1.32 | 0.85 | 2.04 | 1.85 |
| 7 | Myrobalans | 0.07 | 0.12 | 0.07 | |
| 8 | Soapnuts | 3.55 | 3.59 | 0.54 | 1.07 |
| 9 | Mohwa seed | 0.32 | 0.01 | 0.23 | 0.07 |
| 10 | Cleaning nuts | | | | 0.01 |
| 11 | Naramamidi bark | 7.55 | 9.31 | 0.30 | 6.46 |
| 12 | Pungam seed | 0.11 | 0.05 | 0.11 | 0.04 |
| 13 | Bee wax | 0.02 | 0.04 | 0.02 | 0.04 |
| 14 | Nuxvomica | 0.07 | 0.10 | 0.17 | 4.49 |
| 15 | Tanikayalu | | | 5.09 | |
| 16 | Maredugeddalu | 0.33 | 10.34 | 2.79 | 20.66 |
| 17 | Green amla | | | | 3.32 |
| 18 | Dry amla | | | | 0.51 |
| 19 | Others | | | | |
| 20 | Total | 29.62 | 42.88 | 37.97 | 75.25 |

*Source* : Records of the GPCMS

**Table 18 Growth (Rs. lakhs) in procurement of MFP, agriculture produce, and DRs in Peda Dornal GPCMS, 1991–03**

| *Sr. No.* | *Year* | *MFP* | *Agricultural produce* | *DRs* | *Turnover* |
|---|---|---|---|---|---|
| 1 | 1990–91 | 34.99 | 0.67 | 30.14 | 67.11 |
| 2 | 1991–92 | 21.92 | 0.95 | 38.93 | 62.55 |
| 3 | 1992–93 | 20.71 | 11.72 | 49.39 | 89.07 |
| 4 | 1993–94 | 25.39 | 0.14 | 36.46 | 67.35 |
| 5 | 1994–95 | 34.68 | 0.04 | 53.16 | 90.33 |
| 6 | 1995–96 | 30.78 | | 24.05 | 61.37 |
| 7 | 1996–97 | 21.7 | | 37.30 | 60.86 |
| 8 | 1997–98 | 23.44 | | 42.57 | 66.01 |
| 9 | 1998–99 | 13.11 | | 44.05 | 57.16 |
| 10 | 1999–00 | 29.62 | | 78.58 | 108.02 |
| 11 | 2000–01 | 42.88 | | 87.11 | 129.99 |
| 12 | 2001–02 | 37.97 | | 85.67 | 123.64 |
| 13 | 2002–03 | 75.25 | | 85.72 | 160.97 |

*Source:* Records of the GPCMS

**Table 19 Short-term loan operations in Peda Dornal GPCMS, 1991–99**

| *Sr. No.* | *Year* | *Villages covered* | *Beneficiaries* | *Amount disbursed (Rs. lakhs)* | *Amount collected (Rs. lakhs)* | *Recovery (%)* |
|---|---|---|---|---|---|---|
| 1 | 1990–91 | 3 | 79 | 1.31 | 0.10 | 7.63 |
| 2 | 1991–92 | 8 | 58 | 0.75 | 0.14 | 18.67 |
| 3 | 1992–93 | 20 | 189 | 7.25 | 1.13 | 15.59 |
| 4 | 1993–94 | 13 | 119 | 5.36 | 1.43 | 26.68 |
| 5 | 1994–95 | 6 | 58 | 2.45 | 0.89 | 36.33 |
| 6 | 1996–97 | 4 | 97 | 6.54 | 1.04 | 15.90 |
| 7 | 1997–98 | 18 | 162 | 1.86 | 0.04 | 3.76 |
| 8 | Total | 72 | 762 | 25.52 | 4.80 | 18.81 |

*Source:* Records of the GPCMS

**Table 20 Consumption loans disbursed in Peda Dornal GPCMS**

| *Sr. No.* | *Year* | *Villages covered* | *Beneficiaries* | *Amount disbursed (Rs. lakhs)* | *Amount collected (Rs. lakhs)* | *Recovery (%)* |
|---|---|---|---|---|---|---|
| 1 | 1991–92 | 13 | 136 | 0.62 | 0.06 | 9.68 |
| 2 | 1994–95 | 13 | 131 | 0.97 | 0.17 | 17.53 |
| 3 | Total | 26 | 267 | 1.59 | 0.23 | 14.47 |

*Source:* Records of the GPCMS

**Table 21 Training provided in Peda Dornal GPCMS**

| *Sr. No.* | *Date* | *Place* | *Village attached* | *Trainees* | *Total* |
|---|---|---|---|---|---|
| 1 | 12.07.03 | Nallaguntla | Nallaguntla gudem | 15 | |
| | | | Peda penta | 4 | |
| | | | Iannakunta | 11 | |
| | | | Peddapaka | 2 | |
| | | | Cheruvugudem | 1 | 35 |
| 2 | 14.07.03 | Diguvametta | Pillipalli | 5 | |
| | | | Konapalli | 5 | |
| | | | Diguvametta | 7 | 17 |
| 3 | 15.07.03 | Gannepalli | Gannepalli | 10 | |
| | | | Papinenipalli | 5 | |
| | | | Bommilingam | 2 | |
| | | | Damchenchugudem | 13 | 30 |

*Source:* Records of the GPCMS

**Table 22 Income and expenditure in Peda Dornal GPCMS, January 2004**

| *Sr. No.* | *Expenditure* | *Amount (Rs.)* | *Sr. No.* | *Income* | *Amount (Rs.)* |
|---|---|---|---|---|---|
| 1 | DRs trade charges | 2602 | 1 | Rice | 12462 |
| 2 | Lorry hire charges (DRs) | 7525 | 2 | Sugar | |
| 3 | Rebate on sales | 3854 | 3 | Kerosene oil (litres) | 667 |
| 4 | Pay of establishment | 69.647 | 4 | ECS credit sales (hostel rice) | 4646 |
| 5 | Postage and telegram | 194 | 5 | Others DRs cash sales | 20778 |
| 6 | Miscellaneous expenditure | 866 | 6 | Others DRs credit sales | 25734 |
| 7 | Typing charges | 2450 | 7 | Sale of empties | 6209 |
| 8 | Depot commission (honorarium) | 4000 | 8 | DRs transport hire charges | 12631 |
| 9 | Depot rents | 1650 | 9 | MFP transport claims | 6097 |
| 10 | Truck fuel | 9046 | 10 | Miscellaneous income | – |
| 11 | Truck maintenance | 2065 | 11 | Depot commission (honorarium) | 4000 |
| 12 | Electricity charges | 2173 | 12 | 3% commission on MFP | 26317 |
| 13 | Bank commission | 30 | 13 | Gunnies | 10075 |
| 14 | Hospitality charges | 491 | | | |
| 15 | Printing and stationary | 162 | | | |
| 16 | Total | 106845 | 14 | Total | 129632 |

*Source:* Records of the GPCMS

**Table 23 Duration and availability of MFPs in Yellandu GPCMS**

| *Sr. No.* | *MFP* | *Season* |
|---|---|---|
| 1 | Gum karaya | Entire year |
| 2 | Nuxvomica | December–March |
| 3 | Mohwa seed | June–August |
| 4 | Mohwa flower | March–June |
| 5 | Amla pulp | November–January |
| 6 | Naramamidi bark | December–March |
| 7 | Brooms | November–February |
| 8 | Cleaning nuts | December–March |

*Source:* Records of the GPCMS

**Table 24 Growth (Rs. lakhs) in procurement of MFPs in Yellandu GPCMS, 1991–03**

| *Sr. No.* | *Year* | *Gum karaya* | *Seeded tamarind* | *Deseeded tamarind* | *Myrob-alans* | *Mohwa seed* | *Mohwa flower* | *Nux-vomica* | *Total MFP* |
|---|---|---|---|---|---|---|---|---|---|
| 1 | 1990–91 | 1.15 | 0.048 | – | 0.59 | 0.17 | 0.01 | 0.73 | 2.70 |
| 2 | 1991–92 | 13.52 | 0.191 | – | 0.29 | 0.27 | 1.25 | 1.18 | 16.69 |
| 3 | 1992–93 | 1.44 | – | – | 0.06 | 0.03 | – | 0.24 | 1.73 |
| 4 | 1993–94 | 0.70 | – | – | 0.00 | – | – | 0.01 | 0.70 |
| 5 | 1994-95 | 0.65 | 0.06 | 0.07 | 0.00 | 0.09 | – | 0.10 | 0.96 |
| 6 | 1995–96 | 1.23 | – | – | 0.00 | 0.10 | – | 1.48 | 2.81 |
| 7 | 1996–97 | 1.47 | – | – | 0.03 | 0.04 | – | 0.71 | 2.25 |
| 8 | 1997–98 | 0.87 | – | – | 0.01 | 0.09 | – | 2.71 | 3.67 |
| 9 | 1998–99 | 0.70 | – | – | 0.00 | 0.59 | – | 0.06 | 1.35 |
| 10 | 1999–00 | 0.59 | – | – | 0.04 | 0.06 | – | 0.82 | 1.51 |
| 11 | 2000–01 | 0.77 | – | – | 0.00 | 0.11 | – | 0.92 | 1.80 |
| 12 | 2001–02 | 2.75 | – | – | 0.07 | 0.07 | 1.73 | 2.18 | 6.81 |
| 13 | 2002–03 | 9.81 | 0.14 | – | 0.01 | 0.40 | 4.28 | 8.68 | 23.32 |

*Source:* Records of the GPCMS

**Table 25 Growth (Rs. lakhs) in procurement of agricultural produce in Yellandu GPCMS, 1991–03**

| Sr. | Year | Redgram | Chilies | Maize | Total |
|---|---|---|---|---|---|
| 1 | 1990–91 | 1.84 | – | – | 1.84 |
| 2 | 1991–92 | – | 2.32 | 0.82 | 3.14 |
| 3 | 1992–93 | – | – | – | – |
| 4 | 1993–94 | – | 0.05 | 2.34 | 2.39 |
| 5 | 1994–95 | – | – | – | – |
| 6 | 1995–96 | – | – | 0.40 | 0.40 |
| 7 | 1996–97 | – | – | 0.51 | 0.51 |
| 8 | 1997–98 | – | 0.89 | – | 0.89 |
| 9 | 1998–99 | – | 0.74 | – | 0.74 |
| 10 | 1999–00 | – | 7.93 | – | 7.93 |
| 11 | 2000–01 | – | 15.54 | – | 15.54 |
| 12 | 2001–02 | – | 2.77 | – | 2.77 |
| 13 | 2002–03 | 2.18 | 12.26 | 0.50 | 14.94 |

*Source:* Records of the GPCMS

**Table 26 Growth (Rs. lakhs) in supply of domestic requirements in Yellandu GPCMS, 1991–03**

| Sr. No. | Year | Rice | Sugar | Salt | Edible oils | Kerosene oil | Others | Total |
|---|---|---|---|---|---|---|---|---|
| 1 | 1990–91 | 99.09 | 15.91 | 0.87 | 6.76 | 8.65 | 74.66 | 205.94 |
| 2 | 1991–92 | 169.39 | 22.52 | 0.01 | 8.04 | 7.32 | 41.97 | 249.25 |
| 3 | 1992–93 | 63.90 | 24.03 | 0.08 | 34.32 | 16.12 | 108.04 | 246.49 |
| 4 | 1993–94 | 104.12 | 24.55 | 0.08 | 3.72 | 7.29 | 30.08 | 169.84 |
| 5 | 1994–95 | 83.33 | 24.78 | 0.02 | 6.25 | 8.14 | 66.42 | 188.94 |
| 6 | 1995–96 | 80.01 | 24.81 | 2.08 | 5.90 | 8.61 | 34.58 | 155.99 |
| 7 | 1996–97 | 140.35 | 36.37 | 1.42 | 7.79 | 10.18 | 23.38 | 219.49 |
| 8 | 1997–98 | 134.30 | 35.84 | 1.11 | 10.20 | 11.50 | 26.24 | 229.19 |
| 9 | 1998–99 | 142.50 | 27.43 | 0.97 | 15.90 | 12.88 | 76.90 | 276.58 |
| 10 | 1999–00 | 150.85 | 20.97 | 0.83 | 6.15 | 14.92 | 103.76 | 297.48 |
| 11 | 2000–01 | 177.29 | 38.65 | 0.45 | 1.56 | 31.00 | 87.35 | 336.30 |
| 12 | 2001–02 | 175.24 | 27.22 | 2.87 | 14.63 | 34.93 | 108.56 | 363.45 |
| 13 | 2002–03 | 165.85 | 18.45 | 2.35 | 24.18 | 38.55 | 162.85 | 412.23 |

*Source:* Records of the GPCMS

**Table 27**
**Short-term loan operations (Rs. lakhs) in Yellandu GPCMS, 1991–03**

| Sr. No. | Year | No. of loanees | Amount disbursed | Recovery | Percentage |
|---|---|---|---|---|---|
| 1 | 1990–91 | 312 | 6.33 | 6.06 | 96 |
| 2 | 1991–92 | 448 | 7.69 | 4.48 | 58 |
| 3 | 1992–93 | 984 | 24.88 | 9.38 | 37 |
| 4 | 1993–94 | 872 | 21.70 | 20.93 | 96 |
| 5 | 1994–95 | 602 | 12.56 | 17.39 | 100 |
| 6 | 1995–96 | 705 | 17.10 | 20.47 | 100 |
| 7 | 1996–97 | 1036 | 20.05 | 21.52 | 100 |
| 8 | 1997–98 | 768 | 20.85 | 16.87 | 81 |
| 9 | 1998–99 | 608 | 22.27 | 22.42 | 100 |
| 10 | 1999–00 | 1023 | 39.93 | 32.39 | 81 |
| 11 | 2000–01 | 1047 | 51.92 | 39.95 | 77 |
| 12 | 2001–02 | 919 | 35.37 | 29.55 | 83 |
| 13 | 2002–03 | 468 | 24.38 | 17.98 | 74 |

*Source:* Records of the GPCMS

## Table 28 Income and expenditure in Yellandu GPCMS, December 2003

| *Sr. No.* | *Expenditure* | *Amount (Rs.)* | *Sr. No.* | *Income* | *Amount (Rs.)* |
|---|---|---|---|---|---|
| 1 | MLS trade charges | 0.37 | 1 | Profit margin on ECs | 0.50 |
| 2 | DRs trade charges | 0.26 | 2 | Profit on credit sales. | 0.35 |
| 3 | DR depot rent | 0.06 | 3 | Profit margin on other DRs | 1.29 |
| 4 | Transport hire charges | 0.83 | 4 | RMD sales | 0.44 |
| 5 | Conveyance vehicle expenditure (fuel/repair) | 0.07 | 5 | Rice | 0.32 |
| 6 | Transport vehicle expenditure | 0.43 | 6 | Sugar | 0.04 |
| 7 | Establishment charges | 3.09 | 7 | MLS trade charges | 0.60 |
| 8 | Other miscellaneous expenditure | 0.02 | 8 | Commission on MFP | 0.37 |
| 9 | Bank commission | 0.04 | 9 | HRA | 0.07 |
| 10 | Printing and stationary | 0.07 | 10 | Transport hire charges recovered | 1.24 |
| 11 | Postage and telegram | 0.01 | 11 | Retailer dealer margin on FFW | 0.21 |
| 12 | Typing charges | 0.02 | | | |
| 13 | Electricity charges | 0.03 | | | |
| 14 | License and renewals | 0.02 | | | |
| 15 | Rebate on sales | 0.07 | | | |
| 16 | Total | 5.32 | | Total | 5.43 |

*Source* Records of the GPCMS

**Table 29 A comparison of selected GPCMSs**

| Sr. No. | Indicator | Chintapalli | Pedabayalu | Peda Dornal | Yellandu |
|---|---|---|---|---|---|
| 1 | Year of starting | 1956 | 1992 | 1975 | 1972 |
| 2 | DR depots | 23 | 15 | 10 | 33 |
| 3 | Employees | 31 | 21 | 11 | 46 |
| 4 | Ration cards | 11000 | 12562 | – | 16773 |
| 5 | Monthly salaries (Rs. lakhs) | 2.40 | 1.50 | 0.68 | 3.41 |
| 6 | Share capital (Rs. lakhs) | 2.61 | 0.33 | – | 0.32 |
| 7 | Procurement of MFP (Rs. lakhs) | 10.36 | 28.20 | 75.25 | 23.32 |
| 8 | Procurement of AP (Rs. lakhs) | 27.51 | 15.90 | 3.40 | 14.94 |
| 9 | DR sales (Rs. lakhs) | 215.25 | 122.98 | 85.72 | 412.23 |
| 10 | Credit (Rs. lakhs) | 1.81 | 1.18 | 25.52 | 24.38 |
| 11 | Turnover (Rs. lakhs) | 2.55 | 1.37 | 1.61 | 4.75 |
| 12 | Turnover/employee (Rs. lakhs) | 8.23 | 6.52 | 14.64 | 10.33 |
| 13 | Estimated income (Rs. lakhs) | 15.33 | 36.75* | 13.13 | 60.33 |
| 14 | Estimated expenditure (Rs. lakhs) | 19.88 | 30.79 | 12.82 | 62.89 |
| 15 | Estimated net profit/loss (Rs. lakhs) | -4.55 | 5.96 | 0.31 | -2.56 |
| 16 | % of loss/profit | 29.68 | 16.22 | 2.36 | 4.0 |

*Includes 60% of salaries received from GCC

*Source*: Records of the selected GPCMSs

# 6

# Profile and Participation in SHGs

This chapter is aimed at providing socio-economic profiles of sample respondents, and their involvement in SHGs. As indicated in Chapter 1, results are based on 105 women drawn from 21 GPCMSs situated in four divisions of GCC. Ample care is taken to cover major tribes as also different regions of the state.

## Socio-economic profiles

These include age, size of family, land holding, and working persons. Results on these indicators for selected divisions are contained in Table 1 Average age of the respondents is 30 years with a range of 25.6 in Paderu to 37.6 in Srisailam. Average size of family is around 5. It is slightly higher in Srisailam, and on lower side in Paderu. Proximity to plains and interactions with non-tribals could be the reasons for the variation. Tribals own both irrigated lands as also podu lands. Podu lands have no pattas, and thus hereditary. Ownership of irrigated land is low compared to podu lands. Due to increase in population, podu land is declining, and yields are also minimal. Further, it is subjected to vagaries of monsoon as also wild animals. Crops are grown with no inorganic fertilisers on these podu lands. Respondents, on an average, had 2.15 areas of land with two working persons/ family.

Educational status of respondents is provided in Table 2. As expected, majority (62%) of them are illiterates, and 28% are literate. Those who reported as literates studied to a maximum of 5th standard. Adult education classes organised by various developmental agencies as also SHGs contributed significantly to literacy. As much as 10% of total sample indicated ability to sign. Across divisions, Paderu reported higher levels of literacy followed by Bhadrachalam and Srisailam.

Tribal marriage has been a topic of interest to both sociologists and anthropologists. As the economy is primitive so is the case with daily life. Profiles of respondents marriages revealed four types (love and arrange, love and elopement, arranged, and captured) (Table 3). Love and arranged marriages are most frequent followed by arranged, love and elopement, and captured in that order. The latter one is almost non-existent in the younger generations. Attempts are made to provide minute details on tribe-wise marriage (Chapter 8). Trends in nature of marriages across divisions are uniform. Dances are part and parcel of festive occasions, and each tribe has its own dance.

## Rules of succession and inheritance

Acceptance of the principle of male hegemony from primordial band life to present day family life resulted in patrilineal descent, patriarchal authority, and patrilocal residence among these tribes. As a corollary of patriarchal authority, partilineal descent might be imitation of the heterotypic provided by the immigrant and neighbouring plain population. Hereditary succession to property in the male line is adopted. The property is usually divided among male siblings with the son who looks after the aged parents getting higher share than the others. Primogeniture was also followed in modified form by some tribal groups. Concept of property also varies from tribe to tribe. MFP yielding trees in the forest are property of the community living in the vicinity. The village headman assisted by traditional council allot these trees according to family capacity for exploitation and their needs. Honey combs in Nallamalai hills are traditional clan property.

Each tribe has a traditional council to enforce customary law of its tribes. Jurisdiction of the traditional council is religiously obeyed by members concerned. It is self contained in their system of self management, and is based on beliefs, values, traditions and world view of each tribe and their social heritage. In view of their varied cultural values and physical environment, there is diversity in the customary laws of various tribes of the state.

## Pattern of workload

Work of a tribal woman is distributed on household chores, agriculture, and collection of fire wood, animal husbandry, wage employment, and off-farm activities. In all, workload is divided into 12 activities (Table 4). Total workload ranged between 10 hours and 50 minutes/day in Paderu division to 13 hours and 58 minutes in Bhadrachalam. Across divisions, women worked, on an average, 12 and 10 minutes/day. MFP and agricultural labour are the two major components accounting for 44% of the total workload. It is customary for these women to complete household responsibilities in the early hours and proceed to forest for collection of MFP and/or attending wage employment.

Cooking consumed as much as 11% of the total workload/ day. As source of water is located far away from household, they need to spend long hours in fetching water. Tribal women used to carry drinking water from a local stream. Not many differences in workload are observed across divisions. A mention about shandy and pounding cereals are in order here. All women, invariably, attended shandies once a week. They attend shandies for selling MFP and agriculture produce, and also to purchase domestic requirements. More importantly, it is considered as a social activity and recreation. Even if there is no sale/purchase, women attend these shandies. As mentioned elsewhere, tribal life is dry without shandies. Similarly, pounding cereals is a routine activity. In the absence of hullers and floor mills, it is the reasonability of the women to pound grains which consumed about 3% of the total workload. Majority of the women opined that their counterparts (men) work for lesser hours. Similar opinions too were expressed by male members as also accompanying employees.

Occupation-wise distribution of income (Table 5) has revealed interesting results. Annual income is the highest in Paderu ad the lowest in Chintapalli. At the aggregate level, annual income/ household is lower by Rs. 1140 to cross poverty line. Thus, invariably majority of them are poor. Primary occupation contributed around 61% of the total annual income and balance by secondary occupation. Primary occupations mentioned are MFP, agriculture, agriculture labour, wage employment, and on rare occasions, petty trade and contracts.

## Benefits availed from government schemes

A number of welfare schemes were introduced by Government of Andhra Pradesh for the socio-economic upliftment of these marginalised people. They include improving standards of tribals with emphasis on rehabilitation, settled cultivation, distribution of mulch animals, improving education standards, providing better health, and drinking water facilities. Craftsman training centres were introduced in the tribal areas to provide vocational guidance. Efforts were also made to build appropriate administrative infrastructure. Emphasis was laid on enactment and enforcement of laws relating to transfer of lands, money lending, bonded labour, and laying appropriate policy in respect of liquor vending. Text books are being provided free of cost to tribal children unto 10th standard. In addition, scholarships are arranged to graduate students in engineering and medical colleges. IRDP, DWACRA, TRYSEM, SGSY, etc. programmes are also being implemented in these areas. Respondents were asked to indicate facilities received under various government programmes (Table 6). Interestingly, all respondents received one or other facility. Houses and house sites were received by majority of respondents. Other benefits received are gas stoves, investment for petty trade, mulch animals, sheep and goats, etc. Relatively higher percentage of respondents from Bhadrachalam and Chintapalli received house sites and houses.

## Supply of daily requirements through DR depots

Ownership of ration cards and facilities available on these cards is provided in Table 7 About 82% of the respondents have cards and they have been receiving rice, kerosene, and sugar uniformly across divisions. Tribals receive these ration items from the nearby DR depots owned by the local GPCMS. Respondents are asked to express their views on the services provided at DR depot. Opinion is obtained on quality, quantity, and price of goods supplied. Baring price, majority of the respondents are not happy with the services, and it is more so in Bhadrachalam and Paderu (Table 8). Respondents are also provided suggestions for improving the viability of DR depots (Table 9). They included supply of proper quantity, supply at less than market prices, regularity in opening depots, convenient timings, small quantity packs, variety of items, good display, cleanliness, good behaviour, and awareness generation programs. Of all the suggestions mentioned, proper quantity, variety of items, supply at less than market price, and supply in small quantity packs were mentioned by majority of the respondents.

Basic facilities available in the study area are provided in Table 10. Many villages are deprived of play ground, bus stand, regular water supply, and health care centre. Other facilities mentioned are primary schools, anganwadi centre, approach road, and electricity. An attempt is made in the following sections to describe involvement of women in SHGs.

## Self help groups[1]

Self help groups (SHGs) comprise of people with poor financial background, and size ranging between 10 to 20 who come together for addressing common problems. These like-minded individuals representing a homogenous class volunteer to save small amounts of money in common pool. Need-based loans are provided to members from the pool for meeting emergent credit requirements based on priorities decided by the group. The process helps imbibe essentials of financial intermediation including prioritisation of needs, setting terms and conditions, and accounts keeping. Thus, SHGs can be referred to as a group of persons who own, manage, and control a micro bank of their own. As a result, members learn to handle resources of a size that is much beyond their individual capacities. Banks are encouraged to provide loans in certain multiples of accumulated savings of SHGs without any collateral at market interest rates. Groups decide terms of loans to their members. Since group's own accumulated savings are part and parcel of aggregate loans made by groups to their members, peer pressure ensures timely repayments.

Essential features of SHG are aptly provided in DWCD, 1999. They include (a) group members come together voluntarily. (b) basis of coming together is mutual help, (c) homogenous group, (d) regular interaction among group members, (e) group independently takes decisions and manages its activities, (f) basis of people's coming together is affinity, (g) all group members participate in the process, (h) cooperation (not competition), and discussion (dialogue) are cornerstone of its functioning, and (i) group maintains its own accounts. SHGs have both qualitative and quantitative benefits (Table 11). A succinct review of characteristics of various micro-finance delivery models are provided by Sinha (2003) (Table 12), and a growth of these operations during 1993–02 is brought out in Table 13. Cumulatively 4.61 lakh SHGs were organised, and a bank loan of Rs. 545.46 cores were provided to these groups.

## Women and SHGs

Concept of SHG is not new in Andhra Pradesh. Awareness of women has considerably increased during Telugu Desam Party period, and its efforts in sensitising women needs appreciation. Party has been able to bring a revolution in awareness through janmabhumi program. Further, infrastructure facilities in the form of approach roads, protected drinking water, anganwadi centres, health care centres, free housing loans, ashram schools, food for work program, etc. too helped in improving socio-economic status of these tribals. Number of state departments, non-governmental organisations, and social workers have been promoting self help groups in these areas for the last over 10 years. Around

61% of the respondents are involved in groups (Table 14). Involvement of respondents in groups is relatively more (73%) in Paderu and low (47%) in Srisailam.

Among various reasons identified for joining SHGs, vast majority (41%) of them indicated savings as the main purpose followed by self help, opportunity for availing loans, inculcation of discipline, and force by others. Across divisions, 46% from Bhadrachalam indicated savings as main reason while reasons are not uniform in other divisions (Table 15).

Salient features of selected SHGs are provided in Table 16. Average membership in these groups is 17 with a savings of Rs. 34/month. In terms of age of the group, it varied between 28 to 36 months. Thus, 31 months is the average age. Installments are to be paid on second day of every month in Bhadrachalam while it is 7th day in Paderu, and no definite time periods are agreed upon both Chintapalli and Srisailam.

Forty-four out of 64 (69%) respondents participating SHGs availed loans ranging between Rs. 1535/member in Srisailam to Rs. 2435/member in Bhadrachalam. Members agreed upon a minimum interest rate of 24%/annum to a maximum of 36%/annum. Repayment periods varied between 6–9 months in Bhadrachalam, 4–9 months in Chintapalli, and 6 months each in Paderu and Srisailam. Thus, average repayment period is worked out as 6½ months. All the groups have been maintaining individual accounts, register for meetings, resolutions, and have opened accounts either in nationalised banks or regional rural banks. Majority of respondents are happy with functioning of SHGs, which is evident from the opinions provided in Table 16.

## Purpose-wise utilisation of loans

Loans availed from groups are further analysed by purpose (Table 17). These purposes are divided into production, and consumption. Loans for production purpose include cultivation of food crops, vegetable crops, and commercial crops, purchase of sheep and goats, petty shop, business, and others. These categories consumed as much as 65% of the total loans availed/member. Proportion of loan used for production purpose is relatively more in Paderu while it is less in Chintapalli. Across various production purposes, food crops consumed over a quarter of the total loan availed. Petty trade is next important purpose for which loans are used.

On the other hand, consumption purpose constituted 35% of the total loan availed. This category includes purchase of household provisions, social function, and arrack. Diversion of loan amounts for such non-productive purposes results in overdues and chokes the credit channel.

## Rating of SHGs

Following a modified version of NISIT (2003), an attempt is made to rank sample SHGs, and following criterias like group size, composition, age of the group, monthly meeting, attendance in meetings, participation in discussions, regularity of savings, recovery, documentation, knowledge about group rules and functions, educational status, and maintenance of records are used The score ranged between 5 to 120 (Table 18). An observation of the Table reveals that SHGs from Paderu performed better than their counterparts in other three divisions. Rating of SHGs from Srisailam is far from satisfactory.

## Income-generating activities by SHGs

Sample respondents represent 12 SHGs of which four are maintaining daily requirement depots of GPCMSs. These group members deposited amount of Rs. 25,000 with project officer (ITDA), and got permission to run DR depot for which a monthly honorarium of Rs. 2,000 is paid. As the women members are mostly illiterate, accounts and records keeping are looked after by a male person who is paid monthly salary, and balance is distributed among 2–3 active members who are running the depots. In another case, group got permission for running depot while deposit was paid by a third party who is paying Rs. 500/ month to secretary and leader of the group. 'Before involvement in SHG things get grimmer with every passing day, with rising mercury, water getting scarcer, and meager savings vanishing. However, things changed favourably after joining SHG. There is no more wife beating in the area, and women became pressure groups', beamed Kanthamma from Bhadrachalam division.

Kucha Ramulamma hails from Chintapalli division and belongs to Nuka Dora tribe. The family has only an acre of podu land, and thus depended mainly on income from agriculture sector. She joined SHG with meager savings and availed loan to purchase a sewing machine. Ramulamma attends 6–7 shandies a month and earns Rs. 800 towards tailoring charges. Ramulamma repaid loan, and now planning to send her daughter to Waltair for further studies. So is the case with Kasulamma of Paderu division who belongs to Konda Reddy tribe. Having educated upto 5th standard, Kasulamma organised SHG in the village, took loan and working as commission agent in minor forest produce. She purchases MFP by visiting door to door in the interior villages, sells the same at GPCMS. Thus, she has been earning Rs. 1100–1200/month, and happy with the functioning of SHG. However, such successful cases are not many. In the absence of income-generating activities, illiteracy, and locational disadvantageous, most of these women are finding it difficult to find out productive avenues.

## Summary

Socio-economic profiles of sample respondents, and their involvement in SHGs are provided in this chapter. Average age of respondents is 30 years while average size of family is around 5. Respondents, on an average, had 2.15 acres of land with two working persons/family. Majority (62%) of them are illiterates, and 28% are literates. Love and arranged marriages are most frequent followed by arranged, love and elopement, and captured in that order. Patrilineal descent, patriarchal authority, and patrilocal residence is observed. Each tribe has a traditional council to enforce customary law of its tribes. Across divisions, women worked, on an average, 12 hours and 10 minutes/day. MFP, and agricultural labour are the two major components accounting for 44% of the total workload. Annual income is the highest in Paderu and the lowest in Chintapalli, and primary occupation contributed around 61% of the total income. Interestingly, all respondents received one or other facility from the government. About 82% of the respondents have ration cards, and have been receiving rice, kerosene, and sugar uniformly across divisions. Baring price, majority of the respondents are not happy with the services of GPCMSs. Respondents requested supply of proper quantity, supply at less than market prices, regularity in opening depots, convenient timings, small quantity packs, variety of items, good display, etc.

Study revealed that about 2/3rd of respondents are participating in the groups, and savings is the main reason for joining such groups. On an average, this group have a membership of 17 with a savings of Rs. 34/month. Forty four out of 64 respondents participating in SHGs availed loans to the tune of Rs. 1961/ member. In most of the cases date of deposit, interest rates, and availed from SHGs. Starting with small thrift and credit activities, these groups have become platforms for empowering the rural poor. Membership in SHGs offered opportunities for leadership

**Table 1 Socio-economic status of respondents**

| *Sr. No.* | *Indicator* | *Division* Bhadra-chalam (n=40) | Chinta-palli (n=20) | Paderu (n=30) | Srisailam (n=15) | *Overall* (n=105) |
|---|---|---|---|---|---|---|
| 1 | Age | 35.8 | 29.3 | 25.6 | 37.6 | 30.1 |
| 2 | Size of family | 2.4 | 2.2 | 2.3 | 2.8 | 2.4 |
| | Adults | | | | | |
| | Sons | 1.4 | 1.5 | 1.2 | 2.3 | 1.6 |
| | Daughters | 1.3 | 1.7 | 0.9 | 1.1 | 1.3 |
| | Total | 5.1 | 5.4 | 4.4 | 6.2 | 5.3 |
| 3 | Land holding | | | | | |
| | Irrigated | 0.3 | 0.4 | 0.5 | 0.2 | 0.35 |
| | Podu* | 2.2 | 1.6 | 2.2 | 1.2 | 1.80 |
| | Total | 2.5 | 2.0 | 2.7 | 1.4 | 2.15 |
| 4 | Working Persons | 2.0 | 2.0 | 1.7 | 1.9 | 1.9 |

*Hill slopes and terraces with no official titles

*Source*: Field visits

development and managerial skills at village level. Creditworthiness of rural poor has been enhanced and banks and other financial institutions are now forthcoming to extend repayment schedules are clearly spelt out and have accounts in the nearby banks. About 65% of the loans so availed were used for productions purpose of which food crops accounted for as much as 27%. These groups are involved in managing daily requirement depots, and some of them benefited from loans capital to the poor. Sustainability of these groups is an area of concern as their contribution to the development process at large.

**Table 2 Educational status of respondents**

| *Sr. No.* | *Status* | *Division* | | | | *Overall* |
|---|---|---|---|---|---|---|
| | | *Bhadra-chalam* | *Chinta-palli* | *Paderu* | *Srisailam* | |
| 1 | Illiterate | 20<br>(50.0) | 11<br>(55.0) | 27<br>(90.0) | 7<br>(46.7) | 65<br>(61.9) |
| 2 | Can sign | 3<br>(7.5) | 4<br>(20.0) | 1<br>(33.3) | 2<br>(13.3) | 10<br>(9.5) |
| 3 | Literate* | 17<br>(42.5) | 5<br>(25.0) | 2<br>(66.7) | 6<br>(40.0) | 30<br>(28.6) |
| 4 | Total | 40<br>(100.0) | 20<br>(100.0) | 30<br>(100.0) | 15<br>(100.0) | 105<br>(100.0) |

*Most of them studied upto 5th standard
*Source:* Field visits

**Table 3 Nature of marriage**

| *Sr. No.* | *Status* | *Division* | | | | *Overall* |
|---|---|---|---|---|---|---|
| | | *Bhadra-chalam* | *Chinta-palli* | *Paderu* | *Srisailam* | |
| 1 | Love and arranged | 18<br>(45.0) | 9<br>(45.0) | 16<br>(53.3) | 8<br>(53.4) | 51<br>(48.5) |
| 2 | Arranged | 11<br>(27.5) | 6<br>(30.0) | 7<br>(23.3) | 2<br>(13.3) | 26<br>(24.8) |
| 3 | Love & elopement | 7<br>(17.5) | 2<br>(10.0) | 5<br>(16.7) | 3<br>(20.0) | 17<br>(16.2) |
| 4 | Captured | 4<br>(10.0) | 3<br>(15.0) | 2<br>(6.7) | 2<br>(13.3) | 11<br>(10.5) |
| 5 | Total | 40<br>(100.0) | 20<br>(100.0) | 30<br>(100.0) | 15<br>(100.0) | 105<br>(100.0) |

*Source:* Field visits

**Table 4 Division-wise changes in pattern of workload (minutes/day)**

| Sr. No. | Activity | Division | | | | Overall |
|---|---|---|---|---|---|---|
| | | *Bhadra-chalam* | *Chinta-palli* | *Paderu* | *Srisailam* | |
| 1 | Cooking | 103 (12.3) | 84 (11.1) | 70 (10.8) | 74 (11.0) | 82 (11.2) |
| 2 | Cleaning | 65 (7.7) | 52 (6.8) | 49 (7.5) | 56 (8.3) | 56 (7.7) |
| 3 | Fetching water | 49 (5.8) | 43 (5.7) | 37 (5.7) | 56 (8.3) | 46 (6.3) |
| 4 | Child care | 12 (1.4) | 40 (5.3) | 16 (2.5) | 36 (5.3) | 26 (3.6) |
| 5 | Washing cloths | 55 (6.5) | 32 (4.2) | 19 (2.9) | 24 (3.6) | 33 (4.5) |
| 6 | Collecting firewood | 34 (4.1) | 39 (5.1) | 45 (6.9) | 27 (4.0) | 36 (4.9) |
| 7 | MFP | 196 (23.4) | 174 (23.0) | 129 (19.8) | 162 (24.0) | 165 (22.6) |
| 8 | Agricultural labour | 205 (24.5) | 157 (20.7) | 135 (20.8) | 124 (18.4) | 155 (21.2) |
| 9 | Feeding animals | 25 (3.0) | 28 (3.7) | 34 (5.2) | 30 (4.5) | 29 (4.0) |
| 10 | Shandy | 65 (7.8) | 51 (6.7) | 40 (6.2) | 42 (6.2) | 50 (6.8) |
| 11 | Pounding cereals | 15 (1.8) | 22 (2.9) | 31 (4.8) | 14 (2.1) | 21 (3.0) |
| 12 | Others* | 14 (1.7) | 36 (4.7) | 45 (6.9) | 29 (4.3) | 31 (4.2) |
| 13 | Total | 838 (100.0) | 758 (100.0) | 650 (100.0) | 674 (100.0) | 730 (100.0) |

*Include petty trade, contracts, commission agent, business, tailoring, maid servant, etc.

*Source:* Field visits

**Table 5 Occupation-wise distribution of income (rupees/annum)**

| Sr. No. | Activity | Division: Bhadra-chalam | Chinta-palli | Paderu | Srisailam | Overall |
|---|---|---|---|---|---|---|
| 1 | Primary | 6540 (68.0) | 6054 (63.4) | 7698 (66.1) | 6060 (57.0) | 6588 (60.6) |
| 2 | Secondary | 5079 (32.0) | 3501 (31.4) | 3940 (33.9) | 4567 (43.0) | 4272 (39.4) |
| 3 | Total | 11619 (100.0) | 9555 (100.0) | 11638 (100.0) | 10627 (100.0) | 10860 (100.0) |
| 4 | Share of MFP (%) | 35.5 | 18.0 | 20.0 | 26.0 | 25.2 |

*Source*: Field visits

**Table 6 Benefits received from government***

| Sr. No. | Benefit | Division: Bhadra-chalam | Chinta-palli | Paderu | Srisailam | Overall |
|---|---|---|---|---|---|---|
| 1 | House site | 18 (45.0) | 8 (40.0) | 9 (30.0) | 2 (13.3) | 37 (35.2) |
| 2 | House | 14 (35.0) | 5 (25.0) | 10 (33.3) | 9 (60.0) | 38 (36.2) |
| 3 | Milch animals | 4 (10.0) | 1 (5.0) | 0 (0.0) | 0 (0.0) | 5 (4.8) |
| 4 | Gas stove | 2 (5.0) | 2 (10.0) | 4 (13.3) | 0 (0.0) | 8 (7.6) |
| 5 | Sheep and goats | 1 (2.5) | 2 (10.0) | 2 (6.7) | 0 (0.0) | 5 (4.8) |
| 6 | Petty trade | 1 (2.5) | 1 (5.0) | 3 (10.0) | 2 (13.3) | 7 (6.6) |
| 7 | Any other | 0 (0.0) | 1 (5.0) | 2 (6.7) | 2 (13.3) | 5 (4.8) |
| 8 | Total | 40 (100.0) | 20 (100.0) | 30 (100.0) | 15 (100.0) | 105 (100.0) |

*Other than wage employment

*Source*: Field visits

### Table 7 Quantities received on ration card

| *Sr. No.* | *Item* | *Division* | | | | *Overall* |
|---|---|---|---|---|---|---|
| | | *Bhadra-chalam* | *Chinta-palli* | *Paderu* | *Srisailam* | |
| 1 | Percentage of respondents having ration cards | 82.5 | 85.0 | 80.0 | 80.0 | 81.9 |
| 2 | Rice (kgs) | 14.2 | 14.6 | 20.0 | 18.5 | 16.8 |
| 3 | Kerosene (litres) | 3.0 | 3.0 | 3.0 | 3.0 | 3.0 |
| 4 | Sugar (kgs) | 1.0 | 1.0 | 1.0 | 1.0 | 1.0 |

*Source*: Field visits

### Table 8 Opinion on services provided on ration card

| *Sr. No.* | *Benefit* | *Division* | | | | *Overall* |
|---|---|---|---|---|---|---|
| | | *Bhadra-chalam* | *Chinta-palli* | *Paderu* | *Srisailam* | |
| 1 | Quality | | | | | |
| | a. Yes | 13<br>(39.4) | 10<br>(58.8) | 10<br>(41.7) | 8<br>(66.7) | 41<br>(47.7) |
| | b. No | 20<br>(60.6) | 7<br>(41.2) | 14<br>(58.3) | 4<br>(33.3) | 45<br>(52.3) |
| 2 | Quantity | | | | | |
| | a. Yes | 7<br>(21.2) | 7<br>(41.2) | 4<br>(16.7) | 2<br>(16.7) | 20<br>(23.3) |
| | b. No | 26<br>(78.8) | 10<br>(58.8) | 20<br>(83.3) | 10<br>(83.3) | 66<br>(76.7) |
| 3 | Price | | | | | |
| | a. Yes | 17<br>(51.5) | 11<br>(64.7) | 13<br>(54.2) | 7<br>(58.3) | 48<br>(55.8) |
| | b. No | 16<br>(48.5) | 6<br>(35.3) | 11<br>(45.8) | 5<br>(41.7) | 38<br>(44.2) |

*Source*: Field visits

**Table 9 Suggestions (%) for improving viability of daily requirement depots***

| *Sr. No.* | *Suggestion* | *Division* | | | | *Overall* |
|---|---|---|---|---|---|---|
| | | *Bhadra-chalam* | *Chinta-palli* | *Paderu* | *Srisailam* | |
| 1 | Proper quantity | 75.8 | 70.6 | 75.0 | 66.7 | 73.2 |
| 2 | Less than market price | 57.6 | 64.7 | 66.7 | 41.7 | 59.3 |
| 3 | Regularity in opening depot | 21.2 | 47.0 | 45.8 | 41.7 | 36.0 |
| 4 | Convenient timings | 15.1 | 35.3 | 25.0 | 33.3 | 24.4 |
| 5 | Small quantity packs | 39.4 | 58.8 | 62.5 | 66.7 | 53.5 |
| 6 | Variety of items | 57.6 | 70.6 | 62.5 | 83.3 | 65.1 |
| 7 | Good display | 33.3 | 35.3 | 16.7 | 25.0 | 27.9 |
| 8 | Cleanliness | 18.2 | 23.5 | 25.0 | 25.0 | 22.1 |
| 9 | Good behaviour | 21.2 | 23.5 | 12.5 | 25.0 | 19.8 |
| 10 | Awareness generation | 15.1 | 17.6 | 12.5 | 16.7 | 15.1 |

*Based on the views of respondents having ration cards, and multiple anwers are provided

*Source*: Field visits

**Table 10 Proportion of respondents acknowledging access to basic facilities**

| *Sr. No.* | *Facility* | *Division* | | | | *Overall* |
|---|---|---|---|---|---|---|
| | | *Bhadra-chalam* | *Chinta-palli* | *Paderu* | *Srisailam* | |
| 1 | Primary school | 63.6 | 70.0 | 62.5 | 71.4 | 65.9 |
| 2 | Health care centre | 27.2 | 40.0 | 43.8 | 42.9 | 38.6 |
| 3 | Anganwadi centre | 63.6 | 70.0 | 62.5 | 71.4 | 65.9 |
| 4 | Regular water supply | 54.5 | 60.0 | 50.0 | 57.1 | 54.5 |
| 5 | Approach road | 72.7 | 70.0 | 81.3 | 85.7 | 77.3 |
| 6 | Bus stand | 36.4 | 40.0 | 68.8 | 57.1 | 52.3 |
| 7 | Electricity | 81.8 | 70.0 | 56.3 | 71.4 | 68.2 |
| 8 | Play groud | 50.0 | 50.0 | 75.0 | 33.3 | 47.6 |

*Source*: Field visits

**Table 11 Overall benefits due to SHGs**

| *Sr. No.* | *Project component* | *Output and benefits* |
|---|---|---|
| *1* | *2* | *3* |
| 1 | Capacity building of self-reliant women's groups | 1. Mutual support enabling women to manage their own affairs.<br>2. Increased self-reliance and self confidence to address constraints faced by women.<br>3. Framework for cost effective delivery of financial and technical services.<br>4. Increased ability of women to mobiles public and private sector services for their benefit and Improvement in social status of women in family.<br>5. Community. |
| 2 | Strengthen participating agencies to support women's development | 1. Improved orientation and attitude of support agencies, enabling them to be aware of women's priorities, and more proactive and effective in addressing women's specific needs, and<br>2 Improvement in levels of services received by women from banks and line departments |
| 3 | Mobilisation of investment funds | 1 Inculcation of savings habit and development of credit management skills. |

| *1* | *2* | *3* |
|---|---|---|
| | | 2 Building a pool of creditworthy clients.<br>3 Increased long term access of women to credit through integration into mainstream delivery mechanisms for credit, and<br>Reduction in risks and transaction costs of banks as<br>4 a result of high repayment rates of women's groups leading to greater willingness on the part of banks to lend to poor women. |
| 4 | Provision of business management and technical support services to SHG members | 1 Increased income in the hands of women used for welfare of family, resulting in improved child health and nutrition and reduced poverty<br>Improved management and technical skills, and<br>2 Establishment of linkages of SHG members with service providers required to sustain and expand<br>3 economic activities undertaken by women. |

*Source:* Field visits

**Table 12 Characteristics of micro-finance delivery models**

| *Sr. No.* | *Financial service* | *Characteristic* | *Description* |
|---|---|---|---|
| *1* | *2* | *3* | *4* |
| 1 | Credit | Loan amount | Determined by the longevity of the client's association with the MFI. Not often directly related to the credit needs of the borrower. |
| | | Loan term | Usually 12 months, occasionally less, sometimes greater. |
| | | Repayment installments | Monthly or weekly–usually fixed, equal amounts. |
| | | Interest charge | Range of 24–36% usually levied as a flat charge, partly to simplify calculations for both the MFI and the client. Some MFIs charge lower rates but suffer from poory sustainability as a result. |
| | | Collateral | No physical collateral but often linked to some compulsory savings component which acts as financial collateral. Reinforced by joint liability with other clients or peer pressure arising from membership of a community group revolving its own as well as borrowed funds. Some MFIs also create reserve funds to cover the risk of default. |
| 2 | Savings | Amount deposited | *Grameen*: compulsory–usually a fixed proportion of the repayment installment. *SHG*: Compulsory–fixed amounts (weekly or monthly) permiting to be deposited as part of the group fund; occasionally also voluntary. Some MFIs now offer long terms fixed deposits. |
| | | Withdrawals | Compulsory savings cannot be withdrawn except when the client leaves the group. |

*Continued*

| *1* | *2* | *3* | *4* |
|---|---|---|---|
| | | | Voluntary savings often require some notice of withdrawal. |
| | | Interest paid | Most programmes pay 4–6% interest (not consistent). |
| 3 | Insurance | Life | Some MFIs are starting to offer life insurance covering client loan repayments plus a small payment to the family in case of the death of the client. |
| | | Annual premium | Usually linked with a formal insurance company which obtains bulk business from the MFI while the latter provides the service of premium collection; assists in the verification of claims. |

*Source*: Sinha (2003)

**Table 13 Growth in micro-finance (Rs. crores)**

| *Sr. No.* | *Year* | *No. of SHGs* | *Bank loan* | *NABARD refinance* |
|---|---|---|---|---|
| 1 | 1992–93 | 255 | 0.29 | 0.27 |
| 2 | 1993–94 | 620 | 0.65 | 0.46 |
| 3 | 1994–95 | 2112 | 2.44 | 2.30 |
| 4 | 1995–96 | 4757 | 6.06 | 5.66 |
| 5 | 1996–97 | 8598 | 11.84 | 10.65 |
| 6 | 1997–98 | 14317 | 23.76 | 21.38 |
| 7 | 1998–99 | 32995 | 57.07 | 52.06 |
| 8 | 1999–00 | 114775 | 192.87 | 150.13 |
| 9 | 2000–01 | 262825 | 480.87 | 250.62 |
| 10 | 2001–02 | 461478 | 545.46 | 395.73 |

*Source*: NABARD (various years)

**Table 14 Involvement of respondents in SHGs**

| *S.No.* | *Division* | *Yes* | *No* | *Total* |
|---|---|---|---|---|
| 1 | Bhadrachalam | 22<br>(55.0) | 18<br>(45.0) | 40<br>(100.0) |
| 2 | Chintapalli | 13<br>(65.0) | 7<br>(35.0) | 20<br>(100.0) |
| 3 | Paderu | 22<br>(73.3) | 8<br>(26.7) | 30<br>(100.0) |
| 4 | Srisailam | 7<br>(46.7) | 8<br>(53.3) | 15<br>(100.0) |
| 5 | Overall | 64<br>(61.0) | 41<br>(39.0) | 105<br>(100.0) |

*Source*: Field visits

**Table 15 Reasons to join SHG**

| *Sr. No.* | *Benefit* | *Division* | | | | *Overall* |
|---|---|---|---|---|---|---|
| | | *Bhadra-chalam* | *Chinta-palli* | *Paderu* | *Srisailam* | |
| 1 | Savings | 5<br>(45.5) | 4<br>(40.0) | 7<br>(43.8) | 2<br>(28.6) | 18<br>(40.9) |
| 2 | Self help | 3<br>(27.3) | 2<br>(20.0) | 3-<br>(18.8) | 1<br>(14.3) | 9<br>(20.4) |
| 3 | Loans | 2<br>(18.2) | 3<br>(30.0) | 2<br>(12.5) | 2<br>(28.6) | 9<br>(20.4) |
| 4 | Discipline | 0<br>(0.0) | 1<br>(10.0) | 1<br>(6.2) | 1<br>(14.3) | 3<br>(6.8) |
| 5 | Force | 1<br>(9.0) | 0<br>(0.0) | 2<br>(12.5) | 1<br>(14.3) | 4<br>(9.1) |
| 6 | Others | 0<br>(0.0) | 0<br>(0.0) | 1<br>(6.2) | 0<br>(0.0) | 1<br>(2.3) |
| 7 | Total | 11<br>(100.0) | 10<br>(100.0) | 16<br>(100.0) | 7<br>(100.0) | 44<br>(100.0) |

*Source*: Filed visits

**Table 16 Salient features of selected SHGs**

| Sr. No. | Content | Division | | | | Overall (n=64) |
|---|---|---|---|---|---|---|
| | | Bhadra-chalam (n=22) | Chinta-palli (n=13) | Paderu (n=22) | Srisailam (n=7) | |
| 1 | Average members | 18 | 18 | 16 | 17 | 17.2 |
| 2 | Average savings/month (rupees) | 35 | 33 | 33 | 35 | 34 |
| 3 | Age of SHGs (months) | 36 | 32 | 30 | 28 | 31.5 |
| 4 | Total savings/member | 1020 | 1056 | 990 | 980 | 1072 |
| 5 | Respondents availing loan | 11 | 10 | 16 | 7 | 11 |
| 6 | Average amount of loan (rupees) | 2435 | 2130 | 1745 | 1534 | 1961 |
| 7 | Rate of interest (%) | 24 | 30 | 30 | 36 | 30.0 |
| 8 | Repayment period (month) | 6–9 | 4–9 | 6 | 6 | 6.5 |
| 9 | Repayment (%) | 92 | 87 | 90 | 82 | 88 |
| 10 | Opinion about functioning of SHGs | | | | | |
| | a. Not satisfactory | 11 | 6 | 9 | 5 | 31 |
| | b. Satisfactory | 7 | 3 | 6 | 0 | 16 |
| | c. Good | 4 | 4 | 7 | 2 | 17 |

*Source*: Field visits

## Table 17 Purpose-wise loans availed by respondents

| *Sr. No.* | *Particulars* | *Division* | | | | *Overall (n=44)* |
|---|---|---|---|---|---|---|
| | | *Bhadra-chalam (n=11)* | *Chinta-palli (n=10)* | *Paderu (n=16)* | *Srisailam (n=7)* | |
| 1 | Production purpose | | | | | |
| | a. Food crops | 715 | 474 | 407 | 484 | 520 |
| | | (29.4) | (22.2) | (23.3) | (31.5) | (26.5) |
| | b. Vegetable culti- | 333 | 122 | 259 | 0 | 179 |
| | vation | (13.7) | (5.7) | (14.8) | (0.0) | (9.1) |
| | c. Commercial crops | 0 | 208 | 0 | 0 | 52 |
| | | (0.0) | (9.8) | (0.0) | (0.0) | (2.7) |
| | d. Purchase of sheep | 74 | 120 | 145 | 246 | 146 |
| | and goat | (3.0) | (5.6) | (8.3) | (16.0) | (7.4) |
| | e. Petty shop | 212 | 125 | 275 | 305 | 229 |
| | | (8.7) | (5.9) | (15.8) | (19.9) | (11.7) |
| | f. Business | 134 | 195 | 0 | 0 | 82 |
| | | (5.5) | (9.2) | (0.0) | (0.0) | (4.2) |
| | g. Others | 120 | 0 | 143 | 0 | 66 |
| | | (4.9) | (0.0) | (8.3) | (0.0) | (3.4) |
| | h. Sub-total | 1588 | 1244 | 1229 | 1035 | 1274 |
| | | (65.2) | (58.4) | (70.4) | (67.6) | (65.0) |
| 2 | Consumption purpose | 356 | 506 | 302 | 276 | 360 |
| | a. Provisions* | (14.6) | (23.7) | (17.3) | (18.0) | (18.4) |
| | b. Social functions | 372 | 225 | 186 | 185 | 242 |
| | | (15.3) | (10.6) | (10.6) | (12.2) | (12.3) |
| | c. Arrack | 119 | 155 | 28 | 38 | 85 |
| | | (4.9) | (7.3) | (1.6) | (2.5) | (4.3) |
| | d. Sub-total | 847 | 886 | 516 | 499 | 687 |
| | | (34.8) | (41.6) | (29.6) | (32.5) | (35.0) |
| | Grand total | 2435 | 2130 | 1745 | 1534 | 1961 |
| | | (100.0) | (100.0) | (100.0) | (100.0) | (100.0) |

*Includes expenditure on medicines

*Source*: Field visits

**Table 18 Rating of sample SHGs**

| *Sr. No.* | *Criteria for rating* | *Division* | | | | *Overall* |
|---|---|---|---|---|---|---|
| | | *Bhadra-chalam* | *Chinta-palli* | *Paderu* | *Srisailam* | |
| 1 | Group size | 6.4 | 7.5 | 8.7 | 5.0 | 6.9 |
| 2 | Composition | 6.5 | 7.0 | 8.0 | 5.0 | 6.6 |
| 3 | Age of the group | 7.2 | 8.0 | 10.0 | 6.0 | 7.8 |
| 4 | Monthly meeting | 4.5 | 5.4 | 6.5 | 4.0 | 5.1 |
| 5 | Attendance in meetings | 5.8 | 6.5 | 7.5 | 5.0 | 6.2 |
| 6 | Participation in discussions | 6.0 | 7.0 | 8.0 | 5.0 | 6.5 |
| 7 | Regularity of savings | 3.0 | 3.8 | 4.4 | 3.0 | 3.6 |
| 8 | Recovery (%) | 7.0 | 8.0 | 10.0 | 6.0 | 7.8 |
| 9 | Documenation | 4.0 | 4.5 | 5.4 | 4.0 | 4.5 |
| 10 | Knowledge about group rules and functions | 4.0 | 4.0 | 5.0 | 3.0 | 4.0 |
| 11 | Educational status | 2.0 | 3.0 | 3.0 | 2.0 | 2.5 |
| 12 | Maintenance of records | 4.0 | 5.0 | 6.0 | 4.0 | 4.8 |
| 13 | Total | 60.4 | 69.7 | 82.5 | 52 | 66.3 |

*Source* : Field visits

*Note* :

1. This section of the report is presented at a national seminar on revitalisation of SHGs held at NISIET, Hyderabad during March 4–5, 2004 (Rao, 2004).

# 7

# Procurement and Marketing of MFP by Women

Participation of women in procurement, processing, preservation, and marketing of MFPs, income from sale of MFP, and difficulties faced in procurement and marketing of MFP and agricultural produce are discussed in this chapter.

## Contribution of various activities to total time required for MFP

Distribution of workload/day respondents across various activities were discussed in the previous chapter (Table 4). A quick look at distribution of workload indicated that MFP activities consumed as much as 165 minutes/day, and constituted 23% of the daily workload. Various stages in MFP included procurement, processing, preservation, and marketing. Relative shares of various stages to total time involved in MFP are provided in Table 1. As expected, procurement came out to be the major activity followed by processing, and marketing. At the aggregate level, procurement accounted for 55% of the total time spent. It's share is slightly higher (62%) in Srisailam and low (49%) in Chintapalli. Distance from the village, productivity, and thickness of forest covered could be reasons for the above variations. Preservation consumed about 9% of the total time spent on MFP.

Depending upon various stages involved in procurement, processing, and preservation, time required varies across various MFPs. For example, preparation of addaleaf for market involves leaf cutting, gathering leaves from ground, bundling leaves, drying, storing, cutting of stem, storing, bundling, and marketing [Ramanujam, *et.al.* (1998)]. Stages involved for various MFPs are provided in Appendix 31.

Relative shares of various persons to procurement are provided in Table 2. Women contributed about 16% of the total time required in procurement while 'both' (men and women) accounted for 47%, followed by 1/3rd from husbands. Though their contribution varied, women, husband, 'both', and others (children, in-laws, etc.) are involved in these operations

Surprisingly, women are the major agents in processing contributing over 61% of total time associated (Table 3). As expected, husband's role is just 13% in processing, and so is the case with preservation (Table 4) where women's involvement is as high as 73%. Contribution of women in marketing is 24% (Table 5), and respondents who mentioned 'both' contributed 38%. Thus, women accounted for 43% (24% plus half of time devoted by both) of the total time required for marketing. The above analysis indicates that women are the major contributors in processing, preservation, and marketing while their role is on par with male counterparts in procurement. Thus, it can concluded that 65–70% of the work involved in MFPs is contributed by women.

## Involvement in GPCMSs activities

These societies distributed giri cards to MFP pickers. The card provides information on head of the household, wife/husband, children, land holding, type of house, number of trees owned, annual income, etc. along with space for recording volumes of MFPs sold, and prices received. Ownership of this card entails compensation at the time of accidents, death, etc. The cards also help in procurement of MFP from forest areas by avoiding harassment by police and forest officials. Unfortunately, only

1/3rd of members interviewed were issued such important cards (Table 6). Relatively higher percentage of respondents from Bhadrachalam and Srisailam indicated possession of cards.

Depending upon the volume of MFP procured, perishability, urgency of money, space for storage, and availability of sale point/depot, tribals dispose-off MFP. Frequency of visits to GPCMSs are provided in Table 7, and about 40% of them visited once a week while 36% reported twice a week. Across divisions, there are wide variations in frequency of visits.

## Income from MFP and utilisation

As can be expected, there are wide variations in availability of MFPs across divisions (Table 8). Gum karaya, and narmamidi bark are the two common items avaibable in all divisions. Similary, there are wide fluctuations in income earned from MFPs across divisions. Respondents of Chintapalli received the lowest income (Rs. 1720) while in Bhadrachalam it is the highest (Rs. 4125). At the aggregate level, income from MFP stood at over Rs. 2700, constituting about a quarter to the total income. It's contribution is high as 35% in Bhadrachalam, and as low as 18% in Chintapalli.

Income earned from sale of MFP is utilised for purchasing household provisions, social functions, dresses, gifts to children, utensils, arrack, savings, electronic goods, chilren's education, gambling, agricultural inputs, and medical expenses (Table 9). Purchase of household provisions is the single major item reported by as many as 85% of sample respondents. Social functions are second order of priority for which money was spent followed by dresses ad gifts to children. Not many variations are observed in the spending pattern across divisions.

Though women contributed substantially, men have major say in utilisation of income earned from sale of MFPs (Table 10). At the aggregate level, 22% of the respondents mentioned themselves as decision makers while in 29% of the cases it is husbands. On the whole, men dominated in utilisation of income. Traditional social systems could be responsible for such decision making pattern.

## Difficulties in procurement and marketing

Difficulties faced in procurement of MFPs are brought out in Table 11. They included decline in MFP, productivity, longer distances, wild animals, harassment by forest officials, lack of knowledge, training, tools and equipments, and harassment by police and naxalites. Across divisions, decline in MFP followed by longer distances are the two major problems noticed by respondents. Difficulties mentioned are, nevertheless, uniform in the sample.

As of marketing, malpractices in irregular weighment, working days at purchase points, misbehaviour, not entering in giri cards, malpractices in payment, purchase of limited items, inconvenient timings at purchase points, and longer distances are the difficulties encountered (Table 12). Weighment, and irregular working days at purchase points are ranked one and two. Across divisions, variations in ranking of difficulties in marketing are not many.

## Sale of agricultural produce

A close observation at Chapters 3, 4, and 5 revealed that tribals not only sell MFPs but also agricultural produce at GPCMSs. However, they have no monopoly rights in procurement of these commodities. Further, tribals have age-old contacts with traders who are mostly non-tribals. Due to various advantages mentioned elsewhere in the report, tribals trade with these non-tribals. Only 30% of the respondents interviewed mentioned selling agricultural produce to GPCMSs (Table 13). It could be paddy, cotton, rajama, niger seed, redgram, horsegram, annatto seed, turmeric, jowar, mustard, black gram, cashew nuts, pepper, white beans, sunflower, etc. Average amount received from the sale of agricultural produce is Rs. 721 with marginal differences across divisions. Being irrigated zone, respondents from Paderu division earned as much as Rs. 833. However, this amount is very low on any standard. The value of sale of agricultural produce/ household may not be less than Rs. 4000 to 5000/annum. Thus, not even 25% of the agricultural produce is sold to GPCMSs, and this is an area of concern for the officials. While majority of them mentioned prompt payment (immediate), 68% opined

GPCMSs price as reasonable. Similarly, 23% of the respondents mentioned not receiving correct payment.

As majority of the agricultural produce is sold to private traders, women were asked to indicate reasons for the same (Table 14). Loans in advance, age-old relations with the trader, intimacy with trader, trader as extension worker, and malpractices in weighment and payment at GPCMSs are some of the factors mentioned.

Based on the above discussions, one can infer that substantial portion of MFPs and agricultural produce are sold to private, traders, and tribals are not happy with officials of GPCMSs. Women were asked to express their opinion about these officials. As expected, 13% of them mentioned either very good or good, and 36% are not satisfied with their services. Responses are uniform across divisions.

As of assistance expected from GPCMSs (Table 16), reasonable price received first rank followed by timely finance, and convenient timings. Close supervisions of DR depots and purchase points, and training received sixth and seventh ranks respectively. Other assistances expected included convenient timings at DR depots and purchase points, tools and equipments, DR depots in village, compulsory giri cards with insurance facility, and identity cards.

## Summary

This chapter looked at participation of women in procurement, processing preservation, and marketing of MFPs, income from sale of MFPs, etc. Various stages in MFP included procurement, processing, preservation, and marketing. At the aggregate level, procurement accounted for 55% of the total time spent. It's share is slightly higher (62%) in Srisailam, and low (49%) in Chintapalli. Depending upon different stages involved in procurement, processing, and preservation, time required varied across various MFPs. Women contributed 16%, 61%, 73%, and 24% on procurement, processing, preservation, and marketing of MFPs respectively. Thus, 60–65% of the work involved in MFPs is contributed by women.

As of giri cards, only 1/3rd of members interviewed were issued, and 40% of women visited GPCMSs once a week. At the aggregate level, income from MFP is worked out as Rs. 2700 constituting about a quarter of the total income. It's contribution is as high as 35% in Bhadrachalam, and as low as 18% in Chintapalli. Income earned from sale of MFP was utilised for a variety of purposes. Though women contributed substantially, men have major say in utilisation of income earned from sale of MFPs. Difficulties faced in procurement of MFPs included decline in MFP, low productivity. Longer distances, wild animals, harassment by forest officials, lack of knowledge, lack of training, tools and equipments, and harassment by police and naxalites. As of marketing, weighment, and irregular working days at purchase points are ranked as most important difficulties.

Only 30% of the respondents interviewed mentioned selling agricultural produce to GPCMSs. Thus, not even 25% of the agricultural produce is procured by GPCMSs. Loans in advance, age-old relations with the trader, intimacy with trader, trader as extension worker, and malpractices in weighment and payment at GPCMSs are some of the factors mentioned in favour of traders. About 36% of respondents are not satisfied with the services of employees. As of assistance expected from GPCMSs, reasonable price received first rank followed by timely finance, and convenient timings.

**Table 1 Components of work involved in MFP (minutes/day)**

| *Sr. No.* | *Component* | *Division* | | | | *Overall* |
|---|---|---|---|---|---|---|
| | | *Bhadra-chalam* | *Chinta-palli* | *Paderu* | *Srisailam* | |
| 1 | Procurement | 105<br>(53.6) | 85<br>(48.9) | 71<br>(55.1) | 100<br>(61.7) | 90<br>(54.5) |
| 2 | Processing | 35<br>(17.9) | 36<br>(20.7) | 24<br>(18.6) | 28<br>(17.3) | 31<br>(18.8) |
| 3 | Preservation | 15<br>(7.6) | 19<br>(10.9) | 11<br>(8.5) | 15<br>(9.3) | 15<br>(9.1) |
| 4 | Marketing | 41<br>(20.9) | 34<br>(19.5) | 23<br>(17.8) | 19<br>(11.7) | 29<br>(17.6) |
| 5 | Total | 196<br>(100.0) | 174<br>(100.0) | 129<br>(100.0) | 162<br>(100.0) | 165<br>(100.0) |

*Source:* Field visits

**Table 2 Relative shares (%) of time involved in procurement**

| Sr. No. | Person | Division | | | | Overall |
|---|---|---|---|---|---|---|
| | | Bhadra-chalam | Chinta-palli | Paderu | Srisailam | |
| 1 | Self | 13.3 | 9.4 | 18.3 | 21.0 | 15.5 |
| 2 | Husband | 34.3 | 41.2 | 19.7 | 23.0 | 30.0 |
| 3 | Both | 43.8 | 44.7 | 52.1 | 49.0 | 46.7 |
| 4 | Others | 8.6 | 4.7 | 9.9 | 7.0 | 7.8 |
| 5 | Total | 100.0 | 100.0 | 100.0 | 100.0 | 100.0 |

*Source:* Field visits

**Table 3 Relative shares (%) of time involved in processing**

| Sr. No. | Person | Division | | | | Overall |
|---|---|---|---|---|---|---|
| | | Bhadra-chalam | Chinta-palli | Paderu | Srisailam | |
| 1 | Self | 62.9 | 58.4 | 62.5 | 64.4 | 61.3 |
| 2 | Husband | 11.7 | 8.3 | 16.7 | 17.8 | 12.9 |
| 3 | Both | 17.1 | 25.0 | 20.8 | 17.8 | 19.4 |
| 4 | Others | 8.6 | 8.3 | 0.0 | 0.0 | 6.4 |
| 5 | Total | 100.0 | 100.0 | 100.0 | 100.0 | 100.0 |

*Source:* Field visits

**Table 4 Relative shares (%) of time involved in preservation**

| Sr. No. | Person | Division | | | | Overall |
|---|---|---|---|---|---|---|
| | | Bhadra-chalam | Chinta-palli | Paderu | Srisailam | |
| 1 | Self | 66.7 | 68.4 | 63.6 | 80.0 | 73.3 |
| 2 | Husband | 0.0 | 10.5 | 9.1 | 0.0 | 6.7 |
| 3 | Both | 20.0 | 21.1 | 27.3 | 20.0 | 20.0 |
| 4 | Others | 13.3 | 0.0 | 0.0 | 0.0 | 0.0 |
| 5 | Total | 100.0 | 100.0 | 100.0 | 100.0 | 100.0 |

*Source:* Field visits

**Table 5 Relative shares (%) of time involved in marketing**

| Sr. No. | Person | Division | | | | Overall |
|---|---|---|---|---|---|---|
| | | *Bhadra-chalam* | *Chinta-palli* | *Paderu* | *Srisailam* | |
| 1 | Self | 22.5 | 20.0 | 30.0 | 33.3 | 23.8 |
| 2 | Husband | 25.0 | 25.0 | 16.7 | 20.0 | 21.9 |
| 3 | Both | 37.5 | 40.0 | 33.3 | 46.7 | 38.1 |
| 4 | Others | 15.0 | 15.0 | 20.0 | 0.0 | 14.2 |
| 5 | Total | 100.0 | 100.0 | 100.0 | 100.0 | 100.0 |

*Source:* Field visits

**Table 6 Ownership of giri cards**

| *S.No.* | *Division* | *Yes* | *No* | *Total* |
|---|---|---|---|---|
| 1 | Bhadrachalam | 17<br>(42.5) | 23<br>(57.5) | 40<br>(100.0) |
| 2 | Chintapalli | 4<br>(20.0) | 16<br>(80.0) | 20<br>(100.0) |
| 3 | Paderu | 9<br>(30.0) | 21<br>(70.0) | 30<br>(100.0) |
| 4 | Srisailam | 6<br>(40.0) | 9<br>(60.0) | 15<br>(100.0) |
| 5 | Overall | 36<br>(34.3) | 69<br>(65.7) | 105<br>(100.0) |

*Source:* Field visits

**Table 7 Frequency of visits to GPCMSs**

| Sr. No. | Visit | Division | | | | Overall |
|---|---|---|---|---|---|---|
| | | *Bhadra-chalam* | *Chinta-palli* | *Paderu* | *Srisailam* | |
| 1 | Twice a week | 22<br>(55.0) | 3<br>(15.0) | 8<br>(26.7) | 5<br>(33.3) | 38<br>(36.2) |
| 2 | Once a week | 10<br>(25.0) | 10<br>(50.0) | 13<br>(43.3) | 9<br>(60.0) | 42<br>(40.0) |
| 3 | Fortnightly | 4<br>(10.0) | 4<br>(20.0) | 3<br>(10.0) | 0<br>(0.0) | 11<br>(10.5) |
| 4 | As and when required | 4<br>(10.0) | 3<br>(15.0) | 6<br>(20.0) | 1<br>(6.7) | 14<br>(13.3) |
| 5 | Total | 40<br>(100.0) | 20<br>(100.0) | 30<br>(100.0) | 15<br>(100.0) | 105<br>(100.0) |

*Source:* Field visits

**Table 8 Item-wise income from sale of MFP across divisions**

| *Sr. No.* | *Item* | *Division* | | | | *Overall* |
|---|---|---|---|---|---|---|
| | | *Bhadra-chalam* | *Chinta-palli* | *Paderu* | *Srisailam* | |
| 1 | Gum | 2871 | 202 | 349 | 848 | 1069 |
| 2 | Maredugeddalu | | | | 673 | 168 |
| 3 | Gum kondagogu | | | | 533 | 133 |
| 4 | Soapnuts | | | | 384 | 96 |
| 5 | Narmamidi bark | 377 | 373 | 344 | 178 | 319 |
| 6 | Mohwa seed | 195 | | | 147 | 86 |
| 7 | Seeded tamarind | | 280 | 1131 | | 353 |
| 8 | Addaleaf | | | 304 | | 76 |
| 9 | Rock bee honey | 93 | 231 | 101 | | 106 |
| 10 | Amla pulp | | 344 | 99 | | 111 |
| 11 | Nuxvomica | 307 | | | | 77 |
| 12 | Mohwa flower | 110 | | | | 28 |
| 13 | Wild/hill brooms | 172 | | | | 43 |
| 14 | Sheekakai | | 265 | | | 66 |
| 15 | Pungam seed | | 25 | | | 6 |
| 16 | Total | 4125 | 1720 | 2328 | 2763 | 2737 |

*Source:* Field visits

**Table 9 Purpose-wise utilisation (%) of income from MFP**

| Sr. No. | Item | Division | | | | Overall |
|---|---|---|---|---|---|---|
| | | *Bhadra-chalam* | *Chinta-palli* | *Paderu* | *Srisailam* | |
| 1 | Household provisions | 80.0 | 85.0 | 90.0 | 86.7 | 84.8 |
| 2 | Social functions | 62.5 | 60.0 | 60.0 | 40.0 | 58.1 |
| 3 | Dresses | 57.5 | 50.0 | 40.0 | 40.0 | 48.6 |
| 4 | Gifts to children | 55.0 | 50.0 | 33.3 | 46.7 | 46.7 |
| 5 | Utensils | 47.5 | 45.0 | 43.3 | 33.3 | 43.8 |
| 6 | Arrack | 42.5 | 35.0 | 36.7 | 33.3 | 38.1 |
| 7 | Savings | 37.5 | 40.0 | 33.3 | 13.3 | 33.3 |
| 8 | Electronic goods | 25.0 | 30.0 | 50.0 | 20.0 | 32.4 |
| 9 | Children's education | 17.5 | 20.0 | 26.7 | 26.7 | 21.9 |
| 10 | Gambling | 12.5 | 15.0 | 23.3 | 33.3 | 19.0 |
| 11 | Agricultural inputs | 10.0 | 20.0 | 16.7 | 26.7 | 16.2 |
| 12 | Medical expenses | 12.5 | 10.0 | 23.3 | 20.0 | 16.2 |

Multiple answers are provided

*Source:* Field visits

**Table 10 Decision-maker in utilisation of income earned from sale of MFP**

| Sr. No. | Item | Division | | | | Overall |
|---|---|---|---|---|---|---|
| | | *Bhadra-chalam* | *Chinta-palli* | *Paderu* | *Srisailam* | |
| 1 | Self | 7 (17.5) | 4 (20.0) | 4 (13.3) | 7 (46.7) | 22 (21.0) |
| 2 | Husband | 14 (35.0) | 9 (45.0) | 4 (13.3) | 3 (20.0) | 30 (28.6) |
| 3 | Both | 13 (32.5) | 5 (25.0) | 15 (50.0) | 4 (26.7) | 37 (35.2) |
| 4 | Others | 6 (15.0) | 2 (10.0) | 7 (23.4) | 1 (6.7) | 16 (15.2) |
| 5 | Total | 40 (100.0) | 20 (100.0) | 30 (100.0) | 15 (100.0) | 105 (100.0) |

*Source:* Field visits

**Table 11 Ranking of difficulties faced in procurement of MFP**

| *Sr. No.* | *Difficulty* | *Division* | | | | *Overall* |
|---|---|---|---|---|---|---|
| | | *Bhadra-chalam* | *Chinta-palli* | *Paderu* | *Srisailam* | |
| 1 | Decline in MFP | I | I | I | I | I |
| 2 | Longer distance | II | II | III | II | II |
| 3 | Wild animals | III | III | II | IV | III |
| 4 | Harassment by forest officials | IV | IV | IV | III | IV |
| 5 | Lack of knowledge | VI | V | VI | IV | V |
| 6 | Lack of training | V | VI | VII | VI | VI |
| 7 | Lack of tools and equipments | VII | VII | V | V | VII |
| 8 | Harassment by police | VIII | VIII | VIII | VII | VIII |
| 9 | Harassment by naxalites | IX | IX | IX | VIII | IX |

*Source:* Field visits

**Table 12 Ranking of difficulties faced in marketing of MFP**

| *Sr. No.* | *Difficulty* | *Division* | | | | *Overall* |
|---|---|---|---|---|---|---|
| | | *Bhadra-chalam* | *Chinta-palli* | *Paderu* | *Srisailam* | |
| 1 | Malpractices in weighment | I | I | I | I | I |
| 2 | Irregular working days at purchase point | II | II | II | III | II |
| 3 | Misbehaviour | III | IV | V | IV | III |
| 4 | Not entering in giri cards | V | VII | III | II | IV |
| 5 | Malpractices in payment | IV | VI | IV | VI | V |
| 6 | Purchase of limited items | VI | V | VI | V | VI |
| 7 | In-convenient timings at purchase points | VII | V | VII | IV | VII |
| 8 | Longer distances | VIII | III | VIII | VII | VIII |

*Source:* Field visits

**Table 13 Particulars of sale of agricultural produce to GPCMSs**

| *Sr. No.* | *Purpose* | *Division* | | | | *Overall* |
|---|---|---|---|---|---|---|
| | | *Bhadra-chalam* | *Chinta-palli* | *Paderu* | *Srisailam* | |
| 1 | Respondents selling agricultural produce to GPCMSs (%) | 35.0 | 30.0 | 23.3 | 26.7 | 29.5 |
| 2 | Average amount received (rupees) | 525 | 714 | 833 | 811 | 721 |
| 3 | Reasonable price (%) | 64.3 | 66.7 | 71.4 | 75.0 | 67.7 |
| 4 | Prompt payment (%) | 85.7 | 83.3 | 85.7 | 100.0 | 87.1 |
| 5 | Correct payment (%) | 78.6 | 66.7 | 71.4 | 100.0 | 77.4 |

*Source:* Field visits

**Table 14 Factors responsible (%) for selling agricultural produce to private traders**

| *Sr. No.* | *Factor* | *Division* | | | | *Overall* |
|---|---|---|---|---|---|---|
| | | *Bhadra-chalam* | *Chinta-palli* | *Paderu* | *Srisailam* | |
| 1 | Loans in advance | 57.9 | 85.7 | 87.0 | 81.8 | 75.7 |
| 2 | Age old relations with trader | 69.2 | 78.6 | 73.9 | 81.8 | 74.3 |
| 3 | Intimacy with trader | 28.4 | 71.4 | 78.3 | 63.6 | 75.7 |
| 4 | Trader as extension worker | 10.8 | 42.8 | 43.5 | 27.3 | 36.5 |
| 5 | Malpractices in weighment at GPCMS | 57.7 | 57.1 | 65.2 | 36.4 | 56.7 |
| 6 | Malpractices in payment at GPCMS | 16.2 | 50.0 | 52.2 | 45.5 | 48.6 |

*Source:* Field visits

**Table 15 Respondents opinion about GPCMSs officials**

| *Sr. No.* | *Opinion* | *Division* | | | | *Overall* |
|---|---|---|---|---|---|---|
| | | *Bhadra-chalam* | *Chinta-palli* | *Paderu* | *Srisailam* | |
| 1 | Very good | 6<br>(15.0) | 2<br>(10.0) | 5<br>(16.7) | 2<br>(13.3) | 15<br>(14.3) |
| 2 | Good | 6<br>(15.0) | 4<br>(20.0) | 5<br>(16.7) | 3<br>(20.0) | 18<br>(17.1) |
| 3 | Satisfactory | 15<br>(37.5) | 6<br>(30.0) | 9<br>(30.0) | 4<br>(26.7) | 34<br>(32.4) |
| 4 | Not satisfactory | 13<br>(32.5) | 8<br>(40.0) | 11<br>(36.6) | 6<br>(40.0) | 38<br>(36.2) |
| 5 | Total | 40<br>(100.0) | 20<br>(100.0) | 30<br>(100.0) | 15<br>(100.0) | 105<br>(100.0) |

*Source:* Field visits

**Table 16 Ranking of assistance expected from GPCMSs**

| *Sr. No.* | *Assistance* | *Division* | | | | *Overall* |
|---|---|---|---|---|---|---|
| | | *Bhadra-chalam* | *Chinta-palli* | *Paderu* | *Srisailam* | |
| 1 | Reasonable price | II | I | I | I | I |
| 2 | Finance | I | II | II | III | II |
| 3 | Convenient timings | IV | III | III | II | III |
| 4 | Tools and equipments | V | IV | IV | V | IV |
| 5 | DR depot in village | III | V | | IV | V |
| 6 | Close supervision | VI | VI | V | VII | VI |
| 7 | Training | VII | V | VI | VI | VII |
| 8 | Compulsory giri cards with insurance facility | VII | VII | VII | VIII | VIII |
| 9 | Identity cards | VIII | VIII | VIII | IX | IX |

*Source:* Field visits

# 8

# Selected Case Histories

Discussions were centred around averages in all the previous chapters. Efforts are made in this chapter to look at micro level case studies so as to have finer details of selected women. In all, details on four women are provided representing four divisions.

## Mrs. Ragala Bayamma

Bayamma is an illiterate, belongs to Chenchu[1] tribe, and 30 years old. Chenchus live in conical huts, and are endogamous (requires an individual to marry within a specified or defined group of which he/she is member) tribe. They are dark black or brown people of slender build. They claim their origin from Lord Mallikarjuna and his wife Chenchita (Goddess Bhramarambika). Bayamma got married at the age of 13 to Nagulu who owns 1.5 acres of podu land, and yields are uncertain. They both hails from the same village. There are two types of marriages prevalent in this community [marriage by negotiations (*pelli*), and marriage by elopement (*raji*)]. However, 'we fall in love at a very young age and later informed parents who arranged the marriage as per our custom. Husband paid an amount of Rs. 750 as bride price. He also brought a saree and some ornaments for my mother. Of course, a big feast is compulsory'.

She has three sons, and all of them are studying in ashram school. Though she is illiterate, she is determined to educate children. Nagulu is, more or less, an ideal husband who obeys Bayamma's orders. Both work together for about 12–13 hours/day in field as also forest. She is proud of her husband who is cooperative and understanding. Major source of income for the family comes from MFP which is substituted by income from wage labour and agriculture. Motivated by a health worker, she underwent tubectomy soon after third delivery. Thus, she has set an example in the village in favour of family planning operations.

Family's annual income is around Rs. 15,500 of which approximately Rs. 2000 are spent on children's educational expenses. Looking into the difficulties, she also joined the podupu sangham (SHG), and has been having Rs. 75/month for the last 35 months. Couple has a radio, bicycle, and a saving of Rs. 5000. She owns a ration card as also giri card, and happy with behaviour of the salesman. Her only complaint is about under weighment of MFP and un-remunerative prices. 'Today, I sold nuxvomica at the sale point. Salesman has deducted money towards weight loss (produce is wet, and I mixed them with immature seeds!).' Honey is another important MFP available in the area. Honey collectors go in group during nights for collection. They see to it that there is no blood relation between group members (consanguinal), and prefer brother-in-laws (affinal).

'We both go to forest for putting knots to trees as also collecting gum on fourth day. Trees in the forest are demarcated among various tribals, and generally there is no encroachment. However, gum is spoiled and by the monkeys, and wild bears. Collecting gum has become a difficult task these days because of wild animals as also naxals. Once my husband was bitten by snake, luckily he was cured by a local quack.

Bayamma would like to maintain a DR depot, and is aware of Rs. 2000 honorarium for the service. Husband is active in local politics, and also close to officials of the GPCMS who assured giving such license. However, we have to deposit Rs. 25,000, quips the enthusiastic lady.

Electricity and water are the two major problems in our village. I spend 35–45 minutes/day in fetching water. 'Men have bicycles but rarely do they offer to carry water on them. Being the responsibility of women, it is this fraternity of all ages that religiously and dedicatedly ensures there is water for home. Young girls of ten years onwards helping their mothers fetch water.'

Chunce couples are made for each other. Except for collection of rock bee honey, they go together. Bayamma was reluctant to show her house in the absence of husband as it might invite wrath of Nagulu. Accompanying manager informed such incidents might lead to divorce.

## Mrs. Vetti Dulamma

Dulamma is native of Kaliganda from Chintur GPCMS (Bhadrachalam division). She married to Gangayya at the age of 14, and both are illiterate. It was a marriage by capture. Initially, her in-laws brought proposal. As bride price was not agreed upon, Dulamma's fathter rejected the offer. While she was in forest for collecting firewood, her husband (would be) with the help of four neighbours took her away. She was kept at her sister-in-law's (would be) for a week. Though I was new, I was treated and looked after well during those seven days. Her parents came to know about this, and marriage was solemnised as per the caste rirual. 'Fortunately, I have a son and daughter, I will neither be taking bride price for my daughter nor pay for my son, and both are attending school. Koya[2] woman has lot of freedom before marriage. Marriage keeps us in bondage and our contribution never recognised. I have sacrificed my entire life for the welfare of this house but my husband has no time to listen to me. I feel deceived, and exploited. Had I concentrated on God, it would have been more satisfied, and contended soul. I am not consulted in any decision making process. I believe that this is true with all other okay women.'

Ugadi, kothal, dacha pandaga, konda velpulu, etc. are celebrated along with other Hindu festivals. Bhadrachalam is the nearest shopping centre, which she visited once along with her husband. During the trip, the also visited Sri Rama temple. According to her, koya people helped Sri Rama during his stay in forest.

They have less than as acre of podu land where paddy is cultivated, and no surplus produce to sell. She got ration card with the help of local MLA. 'We need to bribe people at every stage to get small favours', grumbles Dulamma. Home produced grains, and ration obtained from DR depot keeps family going. My husband has all bad habits with limited sources of income. She was given plastic sheets, forceps, and scissors for collecting and drying gum. 'I go to forest regularly and gum, nuxvomica, cleaning nuts, and tamarind are the MFP available.' She works for about 13 hours/day whereas husband works 4–5 hours/day only, anyway he is my husband! Major source of income comes from MFP, and agricultural labour. 'Total annual income is around Rs. 10,000 of which my contribution may be more than 70%', groans this hard working lady. She is a regular visitor to shandy. This is a day for them to deck up in colourful sarees, and get together to make merry.

When enquired about DR depot, she complained that it is not kept open regularly and salesman attends at his convenience. 'As per ration card, we should get 20 kgs of rice while we receive only 15–16 kgs. There is cheating in both supplying essential commodities as also purchasing MFPs. We have no one to approach.' She is not happy with the officials of GPCMSs, and she suggested keep all consumable items in DR depots at less than market prices. 'If the prices are same, we prefer to go to private shop.' Dulamma has five hundred rupees with her without husband's knowledge. Recently, she was informed about SHG, and would like to be a member.

## Mrs. Korra Sundaramma

Sheer beauty and tranquility of Paderu is something that cannot be described, it has to be experienced. Silence of the early morning was so profound that suddenly out of no wave came fading memories of long forgotten lines from Waltar de la Mare's hauntingly beautiful poen 'someone':s

*'Someone came knocking my small door*
*someone came knocking, I am sure, sure, sure,*
*I listened, I opened, I looked to left and right,*
*but naught there was a string in the still dark night'*

Substitute 'early morning light' for still dark night, and there, you have it. Here time does not stands still, and the following story is drawn from this beautiful place.

Sundaramma belongs to Konda Reddi[3], a primitive tribal group. Balarama Murty is her husband who owns two acres of podu land, and an acre of coffee plantation. It was a love marriage. 'My husband gave two goats, 150 kgs of rice, Rs. 500, and dresses to myself and my parents at the time of marriage.' They have two sons, and all of them are illiterate. Average family income is Rs. 17,000 of which Rs. 9000 is contributed by coffee plantation. She also earns around Rs. 2500 from wage labour, and saved an amount of Rs. 4000 in SHG. Though, they both work, she feels that her day is long (17 hours). My husband underwent major operation and is bed-ridden for the last three years. He is a chronic alcoholic. They have no assets worth mentioning except land without patta. She also availed a loan of Rs. 3000 in 2002, which is yet to be repaid.

As of marketing of MFP and agricultural produce, also opined that 'we are cheated in selling and purchasing by traders in shandy. Traders give us token advances and take our commitment. We go to any extent to honour our word. Thus, they curtail our freedom to dispose off the produce at higher price. Misappropriation in weighment and payment is common. GPCMS is not coming to our rescue.' Sundaramma has been visiting DR depot since childhood. They have ration card and they receive 20 kgs of rice, 3 litres of kerosene oil, and a kg of sugar. She makes it a point to bring these items every months. Though she is not happy with the DR depot, she felt that it should be continued.

MFP collection is declining gradually, while the MFP collectors are increasing gradually. As a result, we are forced to go deep into reserved forest. Forest officials are harassing, and expect favours from us. These thick forests are also homes for naxals. We are sandwiched between naxals and police. Both believe that we are informers. Combing of forests is eating into our earnings. One day I was in the forest and was attacked by a tiger. Fortunately, I climbed nearby tree and was there for one and half day till tiger left the place. On the other day, a women was killed by tiger from our village.

Income from MFP is provided in Table 1. In addition, some portion of MFP as also all agricultural produce is sold to private traders. According to them, services offered by GPCMS, and prices are not reasonable. Korinte bark is available in Paderu region and private traders are purchasing at Rs. 150 kg. It is used in the preparation of varnishes and certain medicines. Corinte is a creeper tribals make it as a pulp which is sold at a through away price. A tribal can earn Rs. 20/day which is not economical. There is need for GPCMS to work as an all-in-one organisation.

She expects loans, and training from GPCMS. Sundaramma is neither aware of the constitution of GPCMS nor its functions. According to her, GPCMS is a government department. She is also not happy about facilities provided by the government to their community.

## Mrs. Dipalla Seetamma

Seetamma belongs to Bagata[4] tribe who enjoys celebrating Korrakotha, Jolda, Nandi panduga, and ltukula panduga. She is 45 years old, and eldest wife of Bojjayya. Seetamma has six children of which four are sons. When asked about her husband, Seetamma got angry. It was love and arranged marriage. Her natal village is 10 kms from Bojjayya's place. She came to know about him through a relative, and eloped with him. Later, parents approved the marriage. My husband paid only Rs. 300 to in-laws, and due Rs. 1300, thus the marriage is yet to be solemnised.

The sad part of the story is that Bojjayya got fancied to another lady, and had a second marriage. Bojjayya visits Seetamma once or twice a month. Thus, she is the actual head of household. Fortunately, all children are good and obey her instructions. Of the six children, half of them are married, and leading a satisfactory life.

I work from 5 a.m. to 8 p.m. without any selfish mottos and devote half of my time for the well being of my husband. But he cannot spare 15 minutes. Neither my views are given due weightage nor work recognised and appreciated. We work like labourers and the work is taken as granted. Last year, I earned Rs. 7000 through sale of goats which was wasted by my husband on arrack and gambling. I too drink but cannot afford during day time.[5]

My parents worked hard to send my younger brother to an ashram school. He is now employed and settled in Visakhapatnam. It is a big city, but air is clean in our village. I found lot of difficulties in those busy roads. My brother has a television, motor-cycle, and number of electric appliances. Everything is available in the house itself. Supply of water and electricity is regular there, they need not have to walk for miles like me to fetch water and firewood. My sister-in-law is lucky but selfish and pround. I watched serials like eanati ramayanam, talambralu, jayam, padmaviewham, namgodu nakusontham, and priyanka. Is is a luxury to think those facilities in the village. So called approach road leading to our homes is all slush. We have no political leader to bring facilities to our door step. We have made frequent representations at the manual office but they are yet to respond to our request. There is resentment among tribals, due to shortage of drinking water and non-availability of power.

Sundaramma briefed us about Naimalapedu, a tiny village in Visakhapatnam district, experience. Tribals of Naimalapedu fought with Birlas when the latter were given a lease to mine calcite in their backyards in 1997. Samata, a tribal NGO took the case to high court and then to Supreme Court on behalf of villagers. Judgment ruled that, 'state had no right to grant lease to private companies in areas governed by 5th schedule of the constitution'. She is confident about their unity and power. 'Though we are rich in resources, we do not have education, health services, and cash for additional food.' Answer lies in converting resources into productive assets.

GCC gave plastic sheets, scissors, and training in collection, and preservation of MFPs, but she is not happy with their weighment and behaviour. Basket weaving is also a practice here. Tamarind, gum, myrobalans are three major MFPs available in area, and she earns Rs. 2500–3000/annum on sale of MFP. Her total income is Rs. 16,000/annum of which agricultural labour contributes 63%. Depending upon the work, I go to forest twice a week. Apart from this kuchha house, I have 4 sheeps, and 10 birds. She has been a member of SHG, and saving Rs. 30/month for the last 36 months. Though, I am poor I am deprived of a ration card. Gram Bora has not helped me in getting one, she complained.

## Summary

Micro level case studies of four women respondents are discussed in this chapter. Majority of them are in their middle age with no literacy, and got married at a very early age. Love and arranged marriages are common. They are imitating non-tribals, and celebrating Hindu festivals too. Women are also sending children to schools. They worked for 13–16 hours/day, and average income hovered around Rs. 15,000/annum. Within the meager incomes, they have been able to save through SHGs. Women have complaints about their husbands who are not contributing to household income. Three out of four have ration cards, and have been associated with GPCMSs of DR depots since childhood. They are not happy with the services provided at these depots. Women also complained about police, and problems due to naxals. Despite being illiterate and poor, women are hopeful of their future, abundant forest resources with medicinal herbs, and aromatic plants are available in these areas. Answer lies in converting them into productive assets.

**Table 1 Supply of forest produce by Sundaramma**

| *Sr. No.* | *Particulars* | *Quantity (kgs)* | *Amount Received* |
|---|---|---|---|
| 1 | Gum | 10 | 750 |
| 2 | Honey and wax | 50 | 3000 |
| 3 | Marking nuts | 10 | 300 |
| 4 | Cleaning nuts | 20 | 240 |
| 5 | Naxvomica | 20 | 260 |
| 6 | Wild brooms | 10 | 20 |
| | Total | | 4570 |

*Source:* Field visits

*Notes:*

1. Chenchus inhabit Nallamalai forests (Kurnool, Prakasam and Mahboobnagar), and are expert honey collectors, food gatherers, and hunters. Social system of chenchu is exogamous (prohibit marriage between members of certain groups), and institution of levirate is common. The social control sytem of chenchus is headed by 'Pedda Manishi or Chenchu Pedda' at the chenchu settlement. Resolution of disputes between members of a chenchu settlement is the sole domain of chenchu traditional council consisting of 'Pedda Manishi' and the elders of each clan of the chenchu settlement.
2. Koyas live is East and West Godavaris, Khammam, and Visakhapatnam districts. They are of medium stature with dark and coarse features. Each clan has its own deity (devara). Koya marriages are monogamous but polygamy is allowed. Marriage by capture and marriage by negotiations are common in this tribe. Marriages, within the same clan is a taboo. Cross cousins marriages are allowed. Marriage negotiations is time consuming, and proposal is always from groom's side.
3. Konda Reddi, a primitive tribe lives in hilly and forest tracts of eastern ghats in West Godavari, East Godavari, and Khammam and practicing podu cultivation. Besides being hunters and gatherers with bow and arrow and digging stick, they are experts in forest cutting operations. Further, they are very skilled craftsmen of bamboo products like winnowing, fans, baskets etc. and speak Telugu. Their social organisation is based on exogamous sects. The consumption of beef is a taboo for Konda Reddies. Majority of them are still addicted to drinking caryota sap and palmyrah sap (toddy). The widow remarriage and divorce are socially permitted levirate system of marriage by means of which it is the customary duty of the younger brother to marry the widow of the deceased elder brother is also in vogue.
4. Bagatas are mainly involved in cultivation, and strong and sturdy in comparison to other communities. They are polygamous, and tattooing is common practice in the tribe. Bagatas practice marriage by negotiation (*lagnapupendi*), bringing girl with consent of the parents (*theculakonuta*), taking other's wife without

his consent (*maganali*), marriage by elopement (*udidiya uttigola*), and marriage by service (*gorjuvai kabebaka*). Marriages other than the consanguious ones, weekly bazaars provide ample opportunities for boys and their parents. Venue for marriage is the groom's village. Marriage expenditure of Bagatas is sizeable because they invite and feed Konda Doras and Dombs who accept food from them.

5. Toddy is the choicest the tribal people and irrespective of age and sex they drink toddy from January to June. The tribals subsist on toddy alone for days together without taking food.

# 9

# Summary and Policy Prescriptions

## Background

Tribal population is highly heterogeneous, and wide variations exist across tribes and within a tribe. This is mainly due to topography, lack of script, and seclusion for 100s of years, which made them suspicious about alien objects, including non-tribal. Being a light hearted people, it is a cultural shock to them to interact with shrewd non-tribals, imbibe new qualities, and habits. Initial thinking about tribal development was based on five principles suggested by Late Prime Minister Jawaharlal Nehru. They included (a) people should develop along the lines of their own genius and we should avoid imposing anything on them, (b) tribal rights in land and forest should be respected, (c) we should try to train and build up a team of their own people to do the work of administration and development, (d) we should not over-administer these areas or overwhelm them with a multiplicity of schemes, and (e) we should judge results, not by statistics or the amount of money spent, but by the quality of human that is evolved (Verrier, 1988).

During the last 55 years a number of developmental programs were introduced which helped them bringing closer to modern world. With improved infrastructure and communication facilities, tribals are now in transition from barter to money system. Statutory provisions, education and communication helped them in getting employment, contracts, entering business, and politics. Shandies still play a major role in their lives as also economies. They are now celebrating more of Hindu festivals and slowly forgetting their traditional customs and values, started using polyester dress, radio, televisions, edible oils, soaps, spicy foods, etc. They are also sending children, including girls, to schools.

Presence of bride price, and substantial contribution to household incomes by women has not been able to increase their status in terms of decision making process. They are yet not part of any tribal panchayat. Unmarried females enjoy better freedom than married ones. Married life brings misery, and freedom is limited to toiling and sacrifices. Though, female is anchor point in the household, she is conditioned by number of restrictions. Major problems being faced are illiteracy, limited mobility, lack of access to information and health care, absence of political knowledge, and lack of experience in publicly advocating their interest.

Organisation of GCC is one of the milestones initiated by the Government of Andhra Pradesh for the overall development of tribals. GCC has a mandate to procure MFPs and agricultural produce, and supply domestic requirements and credit in the tribal areas. Government has been providing budgetary allocations to support GCC over the last 40 years. GCC through its affiliated GPCMSs have been trying to achieve above objectives.

## Objectives

The study aims at evaluating performance of GCC, and enhancing participation of women in the management of GPCMSs. Specific objectives of the study are:

a. to provide an overview of various government programs for emancipation of tribals,
b. to analyse performance of Girijan Cooperative Corporation in terms of procurement of MFP and agricultural produce, supply of essential commodities, and provision of credit,

c. to evaluate progress of selected divisions, and GPCMSs,
d. to observe socio-economic background of tribal women, and their involvement in SHGs,
e. to understand participation of women in procurement, processing, and marketing of MFPs, and
f. to suggest measures enhancing participation of women in GPCMSs which intern help increasing the business.

## Methodology

Girijan Cooperative Corporation (Andhra Pradesh) is selected for the study mainly because of its long standing, and variety of services being extended. Secondary data for the period 1992–03 were collected to evaluate performance of GCC. Based on membership, turnover, and facilities extended, a moderate sample of 21 GPCMSs (49% of total GPCMSs) from 4 divisions (Bhadrachalam, Chintapalli, Paderu, and Srisailam) (30% of total divisions) representing 3 regions of Andhra Pradesh were selected. In all, 105 women from these societies were interviewed. Data were collected during October 2003 to February 2004.

## Policy initiatives for tribal development

The special status accorded to scheduled areas under Scheduled Districts Act of 1874 was continued under the Government of India Act, 1935 under which tribal areas were called partially excluded areas. Article 46 of the constitution places special responsibility on the state. Articles 15, 16, 17, and 19 make exceptions in favour scheduled tribes to pursue noble directives. The Bawa Committee (1971) recommended large sized agricultural multipurpose cooperative societies as a part of tribal sub-plan areas. Greater attention on tribals was focused during Fifth Five Year Plan. Tribal sub-plan is being used to allot funds and planned development. State Level Cooperative Tribal Development Federations were also organised to promote marketing of minor forest produce and also supply of essential consumer goods. Further, TRIFED was constituted in 1987 with a view to provide marketing requirements of forest and agriculture produce of forest people and to ensure remunerative prices.

Government of India constituted Ministry of Tribal Affairs in October 1999 to give more focused attention to the development of STs. Further, a National Commission for Scheduled Areas and Scheduled Tribes was set up to report on administration of the scheduled areas and welfare of STs followed by a national policy on tribals which seeks to bring STs into mainstream. The draft policy focuses its attention on education, health, preservation of culture, and traditional knowledge.

## Performance of GCC

GCC was registered as a cooperative society in 1970. Management of GCC shall vest in a board of directors consisting of not more than 18 members. Over the years, GCC appointed number of employees which currently stood at over 1500, and most of them are tribals. Initially, GCC opened branches to undertake various activities (procurement MFP and agricultural produce, supply of daily requirements, and cedit). Over the period, these branches were registered as Girijan Primary Cooperative Marketing Societies (GPCMSs). GCC has monopoly rights on procurement of selected MFPs. Procurement is normally done through shandies (weekly markets) by credit-cum-procurement assistants (CCPAs) of GPCMSs. Establishment of processing units, and a separate retail marketing division were started to plough back remunerative prices to tribals and quality products to consumers. Conscious efforts for building brand image through advertisement are also being made, and products of GCC are sold under the brand name of 'Girijan'.

GCC has 33 branch offices during 1980–81 which were registered as GPCMSs during 1994–95, and currently 45 such GPCMSs are functional. Composition of share capital revealed that 96% of it comes from Government of Andhra Pradesh. The federation recorded profits in 10 out of the 22 years considered. Value of procurement was Rs. 40.58 lakes in 1972–73 which increased to Rs. 16.44 cores by 2002–03. There are substantial changes in the relative contribution of various MFPs over the study period. Trend equations estimated for 18 commodities shown significant results for 12. $R^{-2}$ ranged between as low as 0.02 to as high as 0.80 across commodities and same is true with

F-values. A comparison of trends in values of various MFPs indicated maximum increase in gum, while maximum decrease in apiary honey. Trends in prices of various MFPs noticed positive and significant results.

Total value of agriculture produce procured was Rs. 5.84 crores in 1990–91 and has an erratic trend, it was just Rs. 40 lakhs in 2001–02. Cotton, french beans, niger seed, and redgram were the major commodities contributing 78.5% to the total value in 1990–91. Cashewnuts constituted as much as 1/3rd to total procurement in 2002–03 followed by french beans (31.7%). Thus, there are wide variations in the relative contribution across years and items.

Total value of domestic requirements (rice, sugar, salt, edible oil, kerosene oil, etc.) supplied increased from Rs. 4.91 crores in 1980–81 to Rs. 80.05 crores in 2002–03. Rice constituted 42% of the total value of domestic requirements supplied in 2002–03. As of credit operations, huge amounts of loans were provided during 1992–93, 1993–94, and 1994–95. Loan amount/borrower has shown no trend which, nevertheless, increased from Rs. 2017 to Rs. 3575 during study period. Recovery was less than satisfactory during 1991–96, and 1999–00. As on today, GCC has to recover Rs. 8 crores from previous borrowers. Trend equations for borrowers, and amount disbursed were satisfactory, in that borrowers and loan amount/borrower, and recovery were significant. Loans disbursed for medium term, consumption purpose, SHGs, and 'others' are insignificant.

## Progress of selected divisions of GCC

Progress in various functions (procurement of MFPs and agriculture produce, supply of daily requirements, and credit operations) of selected divisions are studied in Chapter 4. There are 10 divisions with 45 GPCMSs, and 3.72 lakhs membership. All GPCMSs together contributed Rs. 82.44 lakhs to the share capital of GCC. Recovery is less than satisfactory across divisions. Utnoor has the highest (Rs. 2.76 crores) outstanding, and Sirpurkagaznagar has the lowest (Rs. 3.88 lakhs).

Bhadrachalam division has 8 GPCMSs with 73,000 membership, and Rs. 2.56 lakhs share capital. Gum karaya, mohwa seed, microbalans, and nuxvomica are the major MFPs in the area, and gum karaya contributed 2/3rds to the total value of MFP procured. According to local officials, as much as 20% of the produce is sold to outside agencies. Chilies are the single major item in agricultural produce. In all, division covers 30 revenue mandals, and has 66,232 ration cards. Supply or domestic requirements increased from Rs. 6.60 cores in 1990–91 to Rs. 13.71 crores in 2002–03 registering more than 100% growth during the last 13 years. 'Rest' constituted as much as 40–45% of the total domestic supplies. Though there is no trend in the amounts disbursed, recovery has been over 80% during the study period.

Chintapalli division was carved out of Paderu in November 1990, and functioned during 1990–01. The division has 683 revenue villages with a tribal population of 1.40 lakhs. In all, 16 shandies are there in the division. Gum karaya, tamarind, and microbalans are three major MFPs procured. Total value of MFPs procured declined steadily during the period under observation. Procurement in gum karaya has shown no trend, while tamarind has increased its share substantially during 1991–03. Procurement of agriculture produce never increased Rs. 50 lakhs during the 13 years for which data are available, and touched a low of Rs. 8.15 lakhs in 1997–98. Of the total procurement in 2002–03, french beans accounts for 93%. Supply of domestic requirements steadily increased from Rs. 1.67 crores in 1990–91 to Rs. 5.40 crores in 2002–03. Across various commodities, rice constituted 62.5% of the total supplies while 'others' contributed 25%. Maximum loaning operations were carried out during 1992–95, and as much as Rs. 2.62 crores were disbursed. Loan disbursed/member has shown steady increase and stood at Rs. 6067 in 2001–02 which dwindled to Rs. 1706 in 2002–03. Grain banks were established covering 746 families from 16 villages of primitive tribal groups during 2003.

Paderu division has 6 GPCMSs. The division has 119 DR depots with about 73,000 ration cards. Tamarind, addaleaf, gum, myrobalans, marking nuts, and pungam seed are major items of MFPs in the division. Value of MFPs procured increasd steadily from Rs. 66 lakhs in 1991–92 to Rs. 360.5 lakhs in 2002–03, while maximum value of procurement was noticed in 2000–01 (Rs. 5.59 crores). As of procurement of agriculture produce, french beans, niger seed, redgram, and nipalem seed were the major items during 1992–95, while rajama, redgram, white beans, and Kashmir beans during 2000–03. Value of agriculture produce too underwent wide fluctuations. DR sales increased from Rs. 4.8 cores in 1990–91 to Rs. 16.35 cores in 2002–03 constituting approximately 3/4ths of the total division's turnover. Tornover, in terms of procurement of MFP, agriculture produce, supply of essential commodities, and loans issued, is around Rs. 22 crores in 2002–03 of which 17% is contributed by MFP, and 16.75% by agricultural produce. Division fall short of 19% of the total targets fixed for 2002–03. Flower tamarind cake making units were established at eight places, and seeded tamarind is processed into consumable packs at these processing centres.

Srisailam division has three GPCMSs with 39,630 chenchus. Important MFPs available in the division are gum karaya, gum dondagogu, mohwa seed, rock bee honey, nuxvomica, soapnuts, naramamidi bark, maredugeddalu, ama, and myrobalans. Gum karaya decreased from 220 tonnes in 1991–92 to 43 tonnes in 2002–03, and that of gum kondagogu increased from 34 tonnes in 1993–94 to 90 tonnes by 2002–03. Total value of MFPs procured was the lowest (Rs. 65.12 lakhs) in 1998–99, and the highest (Rs. 202.04 lakhs) in 2002–03. Major agricultural produce available in the area are cotton, chillies, paddy, and sunflower. Sales increased from Rs. 95.57 lakhs in 1995–96 to Rs. 3.12 crores in 2002–03. Of the total sales in 2002–03, 62% was contributed by Mannanur GPCMS. As of short term credit operations, division has provided Rs. 83.12 lakhs during 1991–03 of which Rs. 24.89 lakhs was collected. Training on scientific collection of MFPs was imparted to 329 MFP collectors during 2002–03. About 111 grain banks have been established during 1996–97, 1997–98, and 2000–01.

Across divisions, essential commodities constituted major chunk of the business followed by MFP, and agriculture produce. Employees/society is the lowest in Srisailam division and the highest in Bhadrachalam, while turnover/employee is the highest in Paderu followed by Srisailam. Majority of the GPCMSs fall short of 51–75% of their salaries, which is reimbursed by the GCC.

## Progress of selected GPCMSs

Working of four GPCMSs from the study area are analysed in Chapter 5. Chintapalli GPCMS was started in 1956 as a branch of the GCC with a view to procure MFPs and agriculture produce, to supply essential commodities through DR depots, and to provide credit. Tamarind, addaleaf, sheekakai, rock bee honey, hill brooms, narmamimdi bark, myrobalans, etc. are the MFPs available. GPCMS has three godowns, and 23 DR depots of which 16 are rented. In all, 31 employees are working of which 24 are tribals. Total wage bill/month for the society is Rs. 2.40 lakhs. Maximum procurement of MFP (Rs. 36 lakhs) was noticed during 2000–01. Across various MFPs, gum karaya accounted for over 40–50% of the total value. French beans has been the major item in agriculture produce. Total value of supplies increased from Rs. 78.65 lakhs in 1990–91 to Rs. 2.15 crores in 2002–03. During 1991–03, society provided an amount of Rs. 36.21 lakhs to 3583 members giving, on an average, Rs. 1010/member. Recovery has been over 60% and on few occasions it was as high as 96–97%. Of the total expenditure, about 68% is incurred towards salaries while income is distributed across various sources. Society incurred a loss of Rs. 67,000 for April 2003. Non-availability and untimely release of insufficient funds, adversely affecting business operations. Neglect of preservation and conservation of MFP species resulted in reduced productivity.

Pedabayalu GPCMS was started in July 1992, and located in Paderu division. GPCMS has 15 DR depots with 12,562 ration cards of which 11,526 are white cards. It has 21employees of which 16 are tribals. Average monthly salary bill is Rs. 1.50 lakhs. Total value of agriculture produce never increased Rs. 27 lakhs (1995–96). Supply of domestic requirements increased from Rs. 55 lakhs in 1992–93 to 123 lakhs in 2000–03. GPCMS provided loans to 3527 members, and an amount of Rs. 37.4 lakhs was disbursed during 1993–03. Percentage of recovery appears to be reasonable in this remote area. Baring no exception, all depots incurred huge losses.

GPCMS Peda Dornal was started as a branch office of GCC in October 1975. It has 9 forest ranges, and 10 DR depots. At present 11 members are working in this society, of which 7 are

SCs, and 3 are STs. Monthly wage bill is Rs. 68,000. Value of procurement of MFPs was over Rs. 75 lakhs in 2002–03, while it was as low as Rs. 13 lakhs in 1998–99. Chilies and cotton are the two principal agriculture products procured, and their share in the total turnover of the GPCMS was negligible. DRs constituted over 50% of the total turnover. GPCMS covered 72 villages with 762 beneficiaries. It distributed an amount of Rs. 25.52 lakhs with a recovery of 18.8%. Off late, neither short-term nor consumption loans are entertained due to lack of funds as also huge overdues. With a view to bring self sufficiency, a tribal is posted as manager who is very active and dedicated. Getting beneficiaries with patta lands, and combing in forest areas by police due to insurgency of naxals are problems in increasing turnover.

Yellandu GPCMS was started in 1992 and covers 7 revenue manuals. Wage bill of the society is Rs. 3.41 lakhs/month. Of the total employees of 46, 50% are tribals. Gum karaya dominated MFPs procured followed by noxvomica. Value of total MFPs procured contributed 5% to the turnover of GPCMS in 2002–03. Supply of DRs constituted about 85% of total turnover during the last 13 years. Of the total DRs, rice contributed as much as 40% followed by 'others', and kerosene. GPCMS did considerable business during 1991–03, and the recovery has been more than satisfactory, except in 1992–93.

A comparison of performance across selected GPCMSs indicated that Peda Dornal attained self sufficiency while Yellandu is close to it. On the other hand, Pedabayalu is incurring heavy losses. Same is the case with Chintapalli. Yellandu has maximum number of DR depots, employees and ration cards, and outperformed other GPCMSs in terms of supply of DRs. Turnover is the highest in Yellandu and the lowest in Pedabayalu. However, turnover/employee is the highest in Peda Dornal because of its smaller number of employees.

## Profile and participation in SHGs

Socio-economic profiles of sample respondents, and their involvement in SHGs are provided in Chapter 6. Average age of respondents is 30 years while average size of family is around

5. Respondents, on an average, had 2.15 acres of land with two working persons/family. Majority (62%) of them are illiterates, and 28% are literates. Love and arranged marriages are most frequent followed by arranged, love and elopement, and captured in that order. Patrilineal descent, patriarchal authority, and partilocal residence is observed. Each tribe has a traditional council to enforce customary law of its tribes. Across divisions, women worked, on an average, 12 and 10 minutes/day. MFP, and agricultural labour are the two major components accounting for 44% of the total workload. Annual income is the highest in Paderu and the lowest in Chintapalli, and primary occupation contributed around 61% of the total income. Interestingly, all respondents received one or other facility from the government. About 82% of the respondents have ration cards, and have been receiving rice, kerosene, and sugar uniformly across divisions. Baring price, majority of the respondents are not happy with the services of GPCMSs. Respondents requested supply of proper quantity, supply at less than market prices, regularity in opening depots, convenient timings, small quantity packs, variety of items, good display, etc.

Study revealed that about 2/3rd of respondents are participating in the groups, and savings is the main reason for joining such groups. On an average, these groups have a membership of 17 with a savings of Rs. 34/month. Forty-four out of sixty-four respondents participating in SHGs availed loans to the tune of Rs. 1961/member. In most of the cases date of deposit, interest rates, and repayment schedules are clearly spelt out and have accounts in the nearly banks. About 65% of the loans so availed were used for production purpose of which food crops accounted for as much as 27%. These groups are involved in managing daily requirement depots, and some of them benefited from loans availed from SHGs. Starting with small thrift and credit activities, these groups have become platforms for empowering the rural poor. Membership in SHGs offered opportunities for leadership development and managerial skills at village level. Creditworthiness of rural poor has been enhanced and banks and other financial institutions are now forthcoming to extend capital to the poor. Sustainability of these groups is an area of concern as their contribution to the development process at large.

## Procurement and marketing of MFP by women

Chapter 7 looked at participation of women in procurement, processing, preservation, and marketing of MFPs, income from sale of MFPs, etc. Various stages in MFP included procurement, processing, preservation, and marketing. At the aggregate level, procurement account for 55% of the total time spent. It's share is slightly higher (62%) in Srisailam, and low (49%) in Chintapalli. Depending upon different stages involved in procurement, processing, and preservation, time required varied across various MFPs. Women contributed 16%, 61%, 73%, and 24% on procorement, processing, preservation, and marketing of MFPs respectively. Thus, 60–65% of the work involved in MFPs is contributed by women.

As of girl cards, only 1/3rd of members interviewed were issued, and 40% of women visited GPCMSs once a week. At the aggregate level, income from MFP is worked out as Rs. 2700 constituting about a quarter of the total income. It's contribution is as high as 35% in Bhardrachalam, and as low as 18% in Chintapalli. Income earned from sale of MFP was utilised for a variety of purposes Though women contributed substantially, men have major say in utilisation of income earned from sale of MFPs. Difficulties faced in procurement of MFPs included decline in MFP, low productivity, longer distances, wild animals, harassment by forest officials, lack of knowledge, lack of training, tools and equipments, and harassment by police and naxalities. As of marketing, weighment, and irregular working days at purchase points are ranked as most important difficulties.

Only 30% of the respondents interviewed mentioned selling agricultural produce to GPCMSs. Thus, not even 25% of the agricultural produce is procured by GPCMSs. Loans in advance, age-old relations with the trader, intimacy with trader, trader as extension worker, and malpractices in weighment and payment at GPCMSs are some of the factors mentioned in favour of traders. About 36% of respondents are not satisfied with the services of employees. As of assistance expected from GPCMSs, reasonable price received first rank followed by timely finance, and convenient timings.

## Selected case histories

Micro level case studies of four women respondents are discussed in Chapter 8. Majority of them are in their middle age with no literacy, and got married at a very early age. Love and arranged marriages are common. They are imitating non-tribal, and celebrating Hindu festivals too. Women are also sending children to schools. They worked for 13–16 hours/day, and average income hovered around Rs. 15,000/annum. Within the meager incomes, they have been able to save through SHGs. Women have complaints about their husbands who are not contributing to household income. Three out of four have ration cards, and have been associated with GPCMSs or DR depots since childhood. They are not happy with the service provided at these depots. Women also complained about police, and problems due to naxals. Despite being illiterate and poor, women are hopeful of their future. Abundant forest resources with medicinal herbs, and aromatic plants are available in these areas. Answer lies in converting them into productive assets.

## Policy prescriptions

A close observation of above discussions revealed that GCC was conceived as a development and welfare organisation. Accordingly, number of under-educated, un-qualified, and untrained tribal were employed alongwith non-tribals. DR depots were started in inaccessible and far-flung areas. These DR depots provided excellent services, which were till then alien to tribals. GPCMSs were organised to offer a more efficient and just alternative to private traders. They can realise these goals only if they can compete with private on a one-to-one footing. GPCMSs have higher unit costs than traders, and if necessary, traders can operate on surprisingly narrow margins. Further, traders can operate far more flexible and can evade taxes and other legal stipulation, which GPCMSs cannot. On the top of it, members goals in GPCMSs do not coincide fully with employees goals and thus, there is bureaucracy.

Lack of long term planning, sound financial management, escalation in cost of etablishment, leakages, pilferages, undue delays in decision making process, and politicisation made the organisation sick. Step-motherly treatment from government is also partly responsible for the state of affairs. Erratic supply of money from GCC, blockage of scarce capital with ITDAs, lack of trained and committed personnel, unnecessary controls by GCC, violent fluctuations in prices of MFPs, agricultural produce and daily requirements, huge overdues, lack of democratic control, etc. are responsible for failure of GPCMSs. At the moment, they are working as extension of government departments with little regard to priciples and philosophy of cooperation. In case it is difficult to adhere to principles of cooperation, let us not call them as cooperatives (corporation or a department may be appropriate word!). A separate research study on viability of GPCMSs can throw more light in this regard.

As the focus of the study is not on viability of GPCMSs, following general observations are made to strengthen them. At the outset, intention should be to make viable and vibrant organisations. GPCMSs should meet all requirements of tribals, be it procurement of MFP and agricultural produce, and supply of essential commodities and credit. Availability of adequate funds on time, and more importantly, commitment and dedication by employees are prerequisites to achieve this objective. GPCMSs should be free from unnecessary controls and regulations.

Value addition, and diversification of activities in tune with changing requirements are order of the day. Cost reduction, plugging leakages/pilferages, productivity linked incentives, finding out domestic and international markets for their products, ISO certification, application of voluntary retirement scheme, posting of non-performers in far off places, etc. would make them viable. Plantation of high value species should be taken up by tribals on commercial basis so as to have uninterrupted supply of MFPs[1]. There is a need for networking among GPCMSs. Above issues can be divided into internal and external to GPCMS, and Table 1 provides the summary. Internal factors are endogenous to society and can be controlled locally, while external factors are outside the control of the GPCMS. They need structural changes and support from government.

## Suggested structure of the management committee

Currently, there is hardly any participation by tribals in the day-to-day management of GPCMS. All tribals should be made members, and a management committee constituting of nine members be drawn (5 elected members of which 3 should be women, manager, divisional manager, project officer ITDA, and BDO). Board of directors should be held responsible for decisions taken. Similar pattern can also be thought of for GCC. Members, local leaders, and government officials should be made to understand repercussions of popular decisions, and in case of difficulty nothing to fall back. If the government is interested in a particular scheme/activity, required funding should be provided in advance for implementation. Viability should be the touch stone, and no more un-economical operations. Idea is to develop an outward looking, vibrant, dynamic, and cooperative organisation.

## Modalities for increasing women's participation

It is clear from the study that women have no say in the day-to-day management of GPCMS[2] (when vast majority of men are not members what to talk about women). Women should be made to realise that GPCMSs are member owned, controlled, and managed societies. Services provided should be of better quality or at least on par with traders. For availing benefits, membership in GPCMSs should be made compulsory, and all women should have membership along with their men. Regularisation of podu lands in the name of both wife and husband would enable them ownership, and associated benefits. This should be supported by adult education, training in income generating activities, soft loans, market support, quality consciousness, gender sensitisation, incentives to girl children, pre- and post-natal services, etc. Table 2 summarises these suggestions.

**Table 1 Suggested internal and external factors for viability of GPCMSs**

| *Sr. No.* | *Internal* | *Sr. No.* | *External* |
|---|---|---|---|
| 1 | Good intentions | 1 | Value addition through processing. |
| 2 | Coverage of remote areas | 2 | Exploring domestic and international markets. |
| 3 | Supply of all items required by tribals | 3 | Brand promotion. |
| 4 | Procurement of all MFPs available with tribals (all-in-one organisation) | 4 | Obtaining quality certification (ISO, organic, etc.). |
| 5 | Closing unavailable DR depots | 5 | Restructuring bye-laws and entrusting management to elected boards in a phased manner. |
| 6 | Fixing targets for both salesmen and CCPAs, and incentive based payment | 6 | Reconstitution of the board. |
| 7 | Freeze on DA, and pay revision | 7 | Ban on recruitment. |
| 8 | Involvement of tribals into day to day management | 8 | Redeployment of existing staff. |
| 9 | Promotion and preservation of MFP species of high value | 9 | Cleansing the balance sheet with one time grants |
| 10 | Training to tribals in MFP procurement, preservation, and processing | 10 | Introduction of voluntary retirement schemes. |
| 11 | Training to employees on procurement, sales management, financial management, ethics, governance, democratic control, leadership, qualities, etc. | 11 | Promotion of medicinal aromatic plants and their processing and marketing. |
| 12 | Liaison with local governments to increase sales of DRs and other items | 12 | Networking of GPCMSs. |
| 13 | Fee-based compulsory membership to tirbals | 13 | Good governance. |
| 14 | Diversification of activities, wherever possible | | |
| 15 | Austerity in travelling, establishment, etc. | | |
| 16 | Posting of non-performers in far off places. | | |

*Source:* Field study

Lijjat papad has been providing gainful employment to women in low-income societies. Material is supplied at the doorstep and women-folk roll papads. Product is picked up by the organisation for packaging marketing. Is it possible to introduce such experiments in these hilly and tribal areas with other altruistic non-governmental organisations? Group approach has started showing positive results. This is another area which would increase self-esteem, and awareness among women and be encouraged to continue momentum. Women dairy project being funded by the Department of Women and Child Development, Ministry of Human Resource Development (Gcvernment of India is another example in this direction). (For more details on WDP, see Rao, 2003, 2004). We need a blue print of what exactly need of these hard working but innocent women. The plan should supplement development programs of the government. It should be a joint venture between local women, NGOs, government departments, social workers, and GPCMSs.

**Table 2 Modalities for increasing women's participation**

| *Sr. No.* | *Modalities* |
|---|---|
| 1 | Compulsory membership in GPCMSs. |
| 2 | Representation on the board of directors. |
| 3 | Representation in panchayats. |
| 4 | Regularisation of podu lands in the joint names of both wife and husband. |
| 5 | Soft loans. |
| 6 | Promoting GPCMSs as all-in-one organisations. |
| 7 | Inculcating quality consciousness. |
| 8 | Promotion of SHGs. |
| 9 | Creating awareness on principles and philosophy of cooperation. |
| 10 | Adult education. |
| 11 | Training in income generating activities. |
| 12 | Gender sensitisation. |
| 13 | Pre- and post-natal services. |
| 14 | Incentives to girl children. |

*Source:* Field study

---

*Notes:*

1 For the last couple of years, GCC has been providing grants to van samrakshan samittees (forest protection committees) for promoting species having commercial value. However, these grants are inadequate to take up plantation on a large scale. GCC should involve tribals by promoting plantation on hill slopes, marginal lands, bunds, and kitchen gardens so as to have a continuous supply of MFPs.

2 As mentioned elsewhere, membership in GPCMSs has a different connotation. Membership is required only for availing loan. Ownership of land is a prerequisite for availing loan. Thus, in the given circumstances women cannot be members of GPCMSs. Not even a single lady reported having a land on her name in the sample.

# References Cited

Anonymous (2004), Reviving tribes highlighting major achievements of the Ministry of Tribal Affairs, Alliance Darpan, January–February, pp. 96–99.

Apte, U.K. (1982), Vaidic Hindu and Tribal Marriage: A Study in Culture Change, AWARE, Hyderabad.

Department of budgets (2002), Scheme of establishment of grain banks in tribal villages, Government of Andhra Pradesh, Hyderabad.

Department of Women and Child Development (1999), Savings and Credit Groups: Need for Formation and Stages in Formation, Ministry of Human Resource Development, Government of India, New Delhi.

GCC (1989), Perspective Plan of GCC for 1989 to 1991 and Action Plan for 1988, GCC, Visakhapatnam.

GCC (1993), Note on Activities of GCC, Visakhapatnam.

GCC (1999), Bye laws: Amended upto December 31st, 1998, GCC, Visakhaptnam.

NABARD (various years), Various Annual Reports of NABARD, NABARD, Mumbai.

NISIET (2003), Reading Material on Workshop on Project Approach for SHGs, micro enterprises held during December 17–19, 2003, NISIET, Hyderabad.

Ram, K.S. (2004), Tribals Lives Close to Nature and God, Times of India, January 6.

Ramanan, M.V. (2003), Report on Comprehensive Studies of Paderu, Bhadrachalam, and Chittoor GPCMS of GCC, Andhra Pradesh Productivity Council, Hyderabad.

Ramanujam, M.S.; N.K. Anand; S.B.L. Saxena.; I.C. Awasthi; S.L. Arora; and U. S. Bhandari (1998), Pricing of Minor Forest Products Procured by the Girijan Cooperative Corporation Limited, Institute of Applied Manpower Research, New Delhi.

Rao, K.M. (undated), Strategy for Operationalisation of Provisions of the Panchayats (Extension to Scheduled Areas Act, 1996) in Andhra Pradesh (mimeo), Government of Andhra Pradesh, Hyderabad.

Rao, N.G., and N. Ramgopal (1996), Prospectus of Value Addition to Tribal Produce: A Study of Selected Commodities in Tribal Areas of Andhra Pradesh, AERC, Visakhapatnam.

Rao, N.S. (1990), The Role of Cooperatives (LAMPS) in Tribal Development, Indian Cooperative Review, 28(2): 124–134.

Rao, V.M. (2003), Evaluation of Women Dairy Project in Rajasthan, Regency Publications, New Delhi.

Rao, V.M. (2004a) Self Help Groups in Agency Areas of Andhra Pradesh, paper presented at a national seminar on revitalisation of self help groups held at NISIET during March 4–5, 2004.

Rao, V.M. (2004b), Empowering Rural Women Through Dairy Cooperatives, Anmol Publications, New Delhi.

Rao, V.M. (2004c), Changing Destiny of Rural Women Through Dairy Cooperative in Bihar, Mittal Publication, New Delhi.

Ray, A.K. (1997), Credit Operation for Tribals: A Study of GCC, Andhra Pradesh, Cooperative Perspective, 32(2), 17–27.

Sinha, S. (2003), Financial Services for Low Income Families: An Appraisal, Management Review, 15(2): 54–65.

Swa-Shakti Project (undated), Swa-Shakti, Ministry of Human Resource Development, Government of India, New Delhi.

Verrier, E. (1998), A Philosophy for North East Frontier Agency, Directorate of Research, Government of Arunachal Pradesh, Itanagar.

Vidyasagar, A. (2003), Tribal Development and Marketing of NTFP Products for Poverty Alleviation, GCC, Visakhapatnam.

# Appendices

**Appendix 1 Division-wise distribution of GPCMSs**

| *Sr. No.* | *Division* | *GPCMSs* |
|---|---|---|
| *1* | *2* | *3* |
| 1 | Seethampeta | a. Pathapatnam |
| | | b. Seethampeta |
| 2 | Parvathipuram | a. G.L. Puram |
| | | b. Parvathipuram |
| | | c. Salur |
| 3 | Paderu | a. Paderu |
| | | b. Araku |
| | | c. Munchingput |
| | | d. Pedabayalu |
| | | e. Gangaraju Madadugula |
| | | f. Kasipatnam |
| | | g. Chintapalli |
| | | h. Gudem Kotha Veedhi |
| | | i. Koyurru |

| *1* | *2* | *3* |
|---|---|---|
| 4 | Rampachodavaram | a. Rampachodavaram |
| | | b. Addateegala |
| | | c. Rajavommangi |
| | | d. Maredumilli |
| | | e. Kote Ramchandrapuram |
| 5 | Trupathi | a. Nellore |
| | | b. Chittoor |
| | | c. Cuddapah |
| 6 | Srisailam | a. Nandyala |
| | | b. Peda Dornala |
| | | c. Mannanur |
| 7 | Bhardachalam | a. Bhadrachalam |
| | | b. Venkatapuram |
| | | c. Chintur |
| | | d. Palwancha |
| | | e. Dammapeta |
| | | f. Yellandu |
| | | g. Mangur |
| | | h. Kuknoor |
| 8 | Eturunagaram | a. Eturunagaram |
| | | b. Mulugu |
| | | c. Narasampeta |
| | | d. Mahadevpur |
| 9 | Utnoor | a. Utnoor |
| | | b. Itchada |
| | | c. Adilabad |
| | | d. Asifabad |
| | | e. Sirpurkagaznagar |
| | | f. Jannaram |

*Source*: Records of the GCC

# Appendix 2 Alluri Sitarama Raju's Uprising (1992–94)

Alluri Sitarama Raju was a Kshatriya young man from the West Godavari District. He was a student of Yoga and Astrology. He gave up his studies at the age of eighteen and retreated into the forest in order to undertake a life of meditation and prayer. He ended up living like a hermit in one of the tribal villages and thus came into direct contact with the tribes. The British administrators were demanding free labour from the tribals for the construction of roads in the forest areas. The tribals were not accustomed to hard labour, and the non-tribals were unwilling to work in malarial tracts. The petty officers began to insist on forced labour from the Koya and Konda Reddi, and force was also employed to make the tribals construct the roads. The exactions of unscrupulous road-builders were responsible for outbreaks in the tribal areas. It should be remembered that those were also the days of the Non-cooperation and Civil Disobedience Movements launched by Mahatma Gandhi.

Alluri Sitarama Raju is said to have been greatly influenced by Indian National Movement and Gandhi, and he asked the tribes to non-cooperate with the Britishers. While putting an end to the ruthless exploitation of outsiders in tribal areas, he resolved to revolt against the British with the help of tribals to further freedom struggle. He resorted to guerilla warfare for two years and defeated the local police in many encounters even capturing some police stations. The British government retaliated by completely cutting off the agency tracts. They encircled the area with police and troops and obstructed the flow of all supplies of goods and material into agency. The British officers intensified their raids on tribal hamlets and molested the women and destroyed the crops.

Witnessing the unpleasant consequences for the tribals of his activities Alluri Sitarama Raju himself surrendered to the police at Koyyuru. He was shot dead and his body was buried at Krishanadevipet. Before the end of September 1324 neraly all his followers had been captured or shot dead.

**Apendix 3 Scheduled MFP items covered under GCC**

| *S. No.* | *Name of the commodity* | *Rs./kg.** |
|---|---|---|
| *1* | *2* | *3* |
| 1 | Gum karaya grade 1 | 125.00 |
| 2 | Gum karaya grade 2 | 90.00 |
| 3 | Gum karaya grade 3 | 60.00 |
| 4 | Gum kondagogu 1 | 100.00 |
| 5 | Gum kondagogu 2 | 60.00 |
| 6 | Gum kondagogu 3 | 42.00 |
| 7 | Gum Tiruman 1 | 60.00 |
| 8 | Gum Tiruman 2 | 50.00 |
| 9 | Gum Tiruman 3 | 30.00 |
| 10 | R.B. Honey | 50.00 |
| 11 | Honey Wax | 70.00 |
| 12 | Naramamidi bark | 20.00 |
| 13 | Maredugadelu | 17.00 |
| 14 | Mohwa flower | 5.00 |
| 15 | Mohwa seed | 10.00 |
| 16 | Pungam seed | 5.50 |
| 17 | Dry amla | 25.00 |
| 18 | Green amla | 3.00–5.00 |
| 19 | Myrobalans | 1.50 |
| 20 | Soapnuts | 5.00–7.00 |
| 21 | Tamarind seeded | 4.00 |
| 22 | Tamarind deseeded | 5.00 |
| 23 | Tamarind green | |
| 24 | Tamarind seed | 2.50 |
| 25 | Tamarind shell | |
| 26 | Cleaning nuts | 8.00 |
| 27 | Marking nuts | |
| 28 | Nuxvomica | 13.00 |
| 29 | Wild brooms | 3.00 |
| 30 | Hill brooms | |
| 31 | Addaleaf | |

*Continued*

| 1 | 2 | 3 |
|---|---|---|
| 32 | Chiranji | |
| 33 | Apiary honey | |
| 34 | Amla fruit and seed | |
| 35 | Kusum oilseed | |
| 36 | Rauwolfia serpentina | |
| 37 | Sheekakai | |
| 38 | Teripods | |
| 39 | R.S. roots | |
| 40 | Sugandhipala | |

*Prevailing rates in 2004

*Source:* Records of GCC

**Appendix 4 Commodities procured by GCC**

| *Sr. No.* | *Local name* | *Botanical name* | *Procurement season* | *Known uses* |
|---|---|---|---|---|
| *1* | *2* | *3* | *4* | *5* |
| 1 | Gum karaya | *Sterculia urens* | Throughout the year | Pharmaceutical, food, and textile industries |
| 2 | Gum olibanum | *Boswellia serrata* | Feb.–May | Ulcers, perfumery works, calico printing |
| 3 | Gum dikamali | *Gardenia gummifera.* | Feb.–May | Ayurveda, unani medicines |
| 4 | Gum Thiruman | *Anegeissus latifolia* | Feb.–May | Cosmetic, food pharmaceutical industries |
| 5 | Cleaning nuts | *Strychnos potatorum* | Nov.–Mar. | Clarifying muddy waters, ayurveda, unani |
| 6 | Tamarind | *Tamarindus indica* | Jan.–June | Cuisine |
| 7 | Tamarind seeds | *Tamarindus indica* | Mar.–July | Starch, paper, and jute industries |

*Continued*

| 1 | 2 | 3 | 4 | 5 |
|---|---|---|---|---|
| 8 | Sheekakai | *Acacia concinna* | Jan.–Mar. | Soaps, shampoos, detergents |
| 9 | Soapnuts | *Sapindus emerginatus* | Mar.–May | Detergents, washing woolens and jewellery |
| 10 | Niger seed | *Guizotia abyssinica* | Dec.–Feb. | Edible oil, bird feed |
| 11 | Pungam seed | *Pongamia glabra* | Feb.–June | Lubricant, soap, tanning industries |
| 12 | Mohwa seed | *Madhuca longifolia* | May–Aug. | Vanaspati, wool & jute, soap industries |
| 13 | Myrabalans | *Terminalia chebula* | Oct.–Apr. | Tanning, alankari printing, ayurveda |
| 14 | Nuxvomica | *Strychnos nuxvomica* | Nov.–Mar. | Pharmaceuticals, rat-poison |
| 15 | Honey | — | Mar.–July & Oct.–Jan. | Calorie rich food, food industry, curative agents, ayurveda |
| 16 | Bees wax | — | Mar.–July & Oct.–Jan. | Paints, varnishes, binder |
| 17 | Sarpagandha | *Rauwolfia serpentina* | Dec.–Jan. | Epilepsy, snake bite, stomach disorders, anti-hypertensive |
| 18 | Marking nuts | *Semecarpus anacardium* | Jan.–May | Chemicals, paint industries, ayurveda, ink |
| 19 | Mohwa flower | *Madhuca longifolia* | Mar.–June | Pharmaceutical, food and beverages |
| 20 | Naramamidi bark and other items | *Terminalia arjuna* | Jan.–June | Agarbathi industry |

*Source:* Records of the GCC

## Appendix 5 List of medicinal herbs available in forest areas of Andhra Pradesh

| *Sr. No.* | *Botanical* | *Telugu* | *Hindi* | *Useful Part* | *Availability* |
|---|---|---|---|---|---|
| *1* | *2* | *3* | *4* | *5* | *6* |
| 1 | *Abrus precatorius* | Guruvenda | Gunchi | Seed | Throughout the forests of Andhra Pradesh |
| 2 | *Achyranthes aspera* | Uttareeni | Chirhitta | Plant | Throughout the forests of Andhra Pradesh |
| 3 | *Adatoda vasika* | Addasaaramu | Arusa | Leaf | Throughout the forests of Andhra Pradesh |
| 4 | *Aegle marmelos* | Bilavamu | Bel | Fruit | Throughout the forests of Andhra Pradesh |
| 5 | *Aloe indica* | Kalabanda | Ghee-kanwar | Plant | Throughout the forests of Andhra Pradesh |
| 6 | *Andrographis paniculata* | Nelavemu | Kariyat | | |
| 7 | *Argyreia speciosa* | Chandrapala | Samundar | | |
| 8 | *Asparagus recemosus* | Pilligeddalu | Satavari | | |
| 9 | *Boerhavia diffusa* | Atikamamidi | Bishakafra | Plant | Throughout the forests of |

| | | | | | |
|---|---|---|---|---|---|
| | | | | | Andhra Pradesh as a weed |
| 10 | *Bombax malabaricum* | Mundlabooruga | Kaantisenbal | | |
| 11 | *Butea superba* | Teegamoduga | Palaslata | Flowar | Throughout the forests of Andhra Pradesh |
| 12 | *Caesalpinia bonduc* | Gachchakaya | Kanja | Nuts | Throughout the forests of AP |
| 13 | *Cassia angustifolia italica* | Sunamukhi | Bhuikhaksa | Leaves | Kurnool district |
| 14 | *Cassia tora* | Tantemu | Chakunda | Seed | Throughout the forests of AP, as a weed |
| 15 | *Catunnaregam spinosa* | Manga | Mainphal | Seed | Throughout the forests of AP, as a weed |
| 16 | *Celeastrus paniculata* | Bavangi | Sankhu | Seed | Throughout the forests of AP, as a weed |
| 17 | *Centella asiatica* | Saraswati | Brahmamanduki | Leaves | In the forest of Vlzag, East Godavari, Krishna, Chittor, Nellore & Warangal districts |
| 18 | *Curculigo orchioides* | Naletadigeddalu | Kalimusli | | |
| 19 | *Decalepis hamiltonii* | Maredugeddalu | Substiture for *Hemidesmus indicus* (S. No. 24) | | |

*Continued*

| 1 | 2 | 3 | 4 | 5 | 6 |
|---|---|---|---|---|---|
| 20 | *Eclipta alba* | Guntagalagara | Bhangra | | |
| 21 | *Gloriosa superba* | Adavinabhi | Karihari | Seed | Throughout the forests of AP |
| 22 | *Gymnema sylvestre* | Podapatri | Merasingi | Leaves | Almost all the forests of AP, as a weed |
| 23 | *Helicteres isora* | Nulitaata | Marorphali | Seed | Throughout the forests of AP |
| 24 | *Hemidesmus indicus* | Sugandhipala | Anantamool | | |
| 25 | *Holarrhena anti dysenterica* | Kodagapala | Kurchi | Seed | Almost all the forests of AP, as a weed |
| 26 | *Holestema adakodien* | Dudipalageddalu | Chirrvel | | |
| 27 | *Ipomoea mauritiana* | Nelagummadi | Bilaikand | | |
| 28 | *Mallotus Philippensis* | Kunkuma | Kamala | | |
| 29 | *Mucuna pruriens* | Dulagondi | Kivach | Seed | Thoughout the forests of AP |
| 30 | *Ocimum basilicum* | Bhootulasi | Banutulasi | Leaves | Throughout the forests of AP, as a weed |
| 31 | *Operculina turpethum* | Tegada | Nisoth | | |
| 32 | *Phyllanthus amarus* | Nelausirika | Bhuinanvalah | Palnt | Throughout the forests of AP |
| 33 | *Plumbago rosea* | Errachitramulamu | Lachitra | | |

| | | | | | |
|---|---|---|---|---|---|
| 34 | *Plumbago zeylanica* | Tellachitraulamu | Chitrak | Leaves | Throughout the forests of AP |
| 35 | *Pueraria tuberose* | Magasirigedda | Patalkunda | Tubers | Forests of Sirikakulam, Visakhapatnam, West Godavari |
| 36 | *Solanum xanthocarpum* | Mullavanga | Kutia | Leaves | Throughout the forests of AP, as a weed |
| 37 | *Syzygium cumini* | Neredu | Jamun | | |
| 38 | *Terminalia arjuna* | Naramamidi | Arjuna | | |
| 39 | *Tinospora cordifolia* | Tippateega | Amrita | Stem | Throughout AP as a weed |
| 40 | *Tribulus terrestris* | Chinnapalleru | Gokhru | Stem | Throughout AP as a weed |
| 41 | *Vernonia cinera* | Sahadevi | Sahadevi | | |
| 42 | *Woodfordia fruiticosa* | Seringi | Dawi | Flowers | Throughout the forests of AP |

*Source:* Records of GCC

## Appendix 6 List of processing units of GCC

| *Sr. No.* | *Processing unit* | *Place* |
|---|---|---|
| 1 | Honey processing units | Rajahmundry, Araku |
| 2 | Sheekakai and soapnut pulverising units | Rajahmundry |
| 3 | Soap making unit | Vizainagaram |
| 4 | Tamarind processing and packing units | V. Madugula (Visakhapatnam), Salur, S. Kota, Kurupam (Vizianagaram) Punganoor (Chittoor), Seethampeta, Pathapatnam (Srikakulam), Narsipatnam, Aganampudi, Pendurthy and Rajulathallavalasa (Visakhapatnam), and Surampalem (East Godavari) |
| 5 | Rajama (red and white), white beans, cutting processing units | Paderu (Visakhapatnam) |

*Source:* Records of GCC

**Appendix 7 Various consumer products of GCC**

| *Sr. No.* | *Product* | *Pack size* |
|---|---|---|
| 1. | 'Girijan' honey | 5 kg./1 kg./500 gms./ 200 gms./50 gms. |
| 2. | 'Ritu' Turmeric soap | 100 gms./75 gms. |
| 3. | 'Ritu' Neem soap | 100 gms/75 gms. |
| 4. | 'Girijan' flower Tamarind | 1 kg./500 gms. |
| 5. | 'Girijan' pulp Tamarind | 1 kg. |
| 6. | 'Girijan' deseeded Tamarind | 5 kgs./1 kg. |
| 7 | 'Girijan' seeded Tamarind | 5 kgs. |
| 8. | 'Girijan' Sheekakai powder | 200 gms. |
| 9. | 'Girijan' Soapnuts | 1 kg./500 gms. |
| 10. | 'Girijan' Soapnut powder | 200 gms. |
| 11. | 'Girijan' Amla powder | 200 gms. |
| 12. | 'Girijan' Hill Brooms (Gr. I & II) | 1 No. |
| 13. | 'Girijan' Rajama (Red) | 500 gms. |
| 14. | 'Girijan' Rajama (White) | 500 gms. |
| 15. | 'Girijan' Rajama (Kashmiri) | 500 gms. |
| 16. | 'Girijan' cuttings | 500 gms. |
| 17. | 'Girijan' White Beans | 500 gms. |
| 18. | 'Girijan' Dry chillies | 500 gms. |

*Source:* Records of GCC

## Appendix 8 Quantities procured, value, and price of gum, and addaleaf, 1973–03

| Sr. No. | Year | Gum | | | Addaleaf | | |
|---|---|---|---|---|---|---|---|
| | | Quantity (quintals) | Value (Rs. lakhs) | Rate (Rs./ quintal) | Quantity (quintals) | Value (Rs. lakhs) | Rate (Rs./ quintal) |
| 1 | 1972–73 | 2704 | 5.34 | 197 | 41994 | 11.35 | 27 |
| 2 | 1973–74 | 6041 | 16.16 | 268 | 32737 | 5.98 | 18 |
| 3 | 1974–75 | 13762 | 42.41 | 308 | 41713 | 12.47 | 30 |
| 4 | 1975–76 | 8767 | 22.80 | 260 | 24380 | 7.66 | 31 |
| 5 | 1976–77 | 6446 | 15.56 | 241 | 45154 | 15.47 | 34 |
| 6 | 1977–78 | 10975 | 45.08 | 411 | 26929 | 7.52 | 28 |
| 7 | 1978–79 | 12411 | 63.63 | 513 | 36448 | 10.36 | 28 |
| 8 | 1979–80 | 26879 | 131.91 | 491 | 34768 | 11.61 | 33 |
| 9 | 1980–81 | 8227 | 30.71 | 373 | 23741 | 9.26 | 39 |
| 10 | 1981–82 | 7464 | 39.19 | 525 | 29566 | 13.71 | 46 |
| 11 | 1982–83 | 9605 | 74.92 | 780 | 42870 | 27.91 | 65 |
| 12 | 1983–84 | 15769 | 143.39 | 909 | 17672 | 7.89 | 44 |
| 13 | 1984–85 | 25676 | 299.28 | 1165 | 32726 | 25.09 | 75 |
| 14 | 1985–86 | 23467 | 290.24 | 1237 | 23287 | 21.01 | 52 |
| 15 | 1986–87 | 8038 | 76.17 | 948 | 36320 | 32.14 | 88 |
| 16 | 1987–88 | 8671 | 106.44 | 1233 | 22687 | 22.41 | 98 |
| 17 | 1988–89 | 16325 | 310.44 | 1902 | 17186 | 18.06 | 105 |
| 18 | 1989–90 | 28507 | 732.05 | 2546 | 18679 | 24.16 | 129 |
| 19 | 1990–91 | 28752 | 692.23 | 2408 | 16666 | 25.60 | 154 |
| 20 | 1991–92 | 22446 | 515.38 | 2296 | 13487 | 16.07 | 119 |
| 21 | 1992–93 | 10916 | 267.21 | 2448 | 21848 | 26.26 | 120 |
| 22 | 1993–94 | 10579 | 396.49 | 3748 | 20948 | 32.56 | 155 |
| 23 | 1994–95 | 6918 | 323.64 | 4678 | 18530 | 35.20 | 190 |
| 24 | 1995–96 | 6633 | 363.58 | 5481 | 26293 | 47.59 | 181 |
| 25 | 1996–97 | 5980 | 364.92 | 6102 | 14764 | 26.88 | 250 |
| 26 | 1997–98 | 6028 | 365.03 | 6056 | 16597 | 48.21 | 290 |
| 27 | 1998–99 | 6254 | 346.2 | 5536 | 10656 | 36.65 | 344 |
| 28 | 1999–00 | 7104 | 478.17 | 6731 | 3521 | 10.99 | 312 |
| 29 | 2000–01 | 8749 | 566.97 | 6480 | 10506 | 46.30 | 441 |
| 30 | 2001–02 | 8948 | 596.99 | 6672 | 3912 | 12.86 | 329 |
| 31 | 2002–03 | 9961 | 647.68 | 6502 | 12625 | 42.50 | 337 |

*Source:* Records of GCC

## Appendix 9 Quantities procured, value, and price of seeded tamarind, and deseeded tamarind, 1973–03

| Sr. No. | Year | Seeded tamarind | | | Deseeded tamarind | | |
|---|---|---|---|---|---|---|---|
| | | Quantity (quintals) | Value (Rs. lakhs) | Rate (Rs./ quintal) | Quantity (quintals) | Value (Rs. lakhs) | Rate (Rs./ quintal) |
| 1 | 1972–73 | 16626 | 6.97 | 42 | 6072 | 4.46 | 73 |
| 2 | 1973–74 | 26397 | 17.71 | 67 | 5556 | 10.74 | 193 |
| 3 | 1974–75 | 12191 | 10.96 | 90 | 5587 | 12.20 | 218 |
| 4 | 1975–76 | 34156 | 20.61 | 60 | 8583 | 10.71 | 125 |
| 5 | 1976–77 | 31169 | 16.04 | 51 | 7668 | 9.06 | 118 |
| 6 | 1977–78 | 59362 | 41.21 | 69 | 15055 | 20.63 | 137 |
| 7 | 1978–79 | 15251 | 13.44 | 88 | 2689 | 5.02 | 187 |
| 8 | 1979–80 | 37156 | 32.12 | 86 | 7072 | 12.17 | 172 |
| 9 | 1980–81 | 11042 | 13.24 | 119 | 400 | 1.01 | 253 |
| 10 | 1981–82 | 17301 | 22.41 | 130 | 3170 | 10.81 | 341 |
| 11 | 1982–83 | 54083 | 72.91 | 135 | 7916 | 21.50 | 272 |
| 12 | 1983–84 | 51525 | 59.52 | 116 | 14702 | 39.59 | 269 |
| 13 | 1984–85 | 25671 | 46.27 | 180 | 1971 | 5.12 | 260 |
| 14 | 1985–86 | 42274 | 74.87 | 171 | 10148 | 38.24 | 376 |
| 15 | 1986–87 | 27431 | 62.73 | 229 | 3189 | 15.28 | 479 |
| 16 | 1987–88 | 45839 | 81.64 | 178 | 8415 | 29.32 | 348 |
| 17 | 1988–89 | 53925 | 114.45 | 212 | 7596 | 31.39 | 413 |
| 18 | 1989–90 | 25556 | 65.03 | 254 | 11233 | 48.03 | 428 |
| 19 | 1990–91 | 38009 | 102.31 | 269 | 6870 | 41.96 | 611 |
| 20 | 1991–92 | 51616 | 124.35 | 241 | 5650 | 29.63 | 524 |
| 21 | 1992–93 | 54795 | 147.03 | 268 | 8356 | 36.47 | 436 |
| 22 | 1993–94 | 56042 | 199.74 | 356 | 5502 | 35.25 | 641 |
| 23 | 1994–95 | 47991 | 191.73 | 400 | 6529 | 46.01 | 705 |
| 24 | 1995–96 | 29991 | 130.14 | 434 | 5988 | 47.78 | 798 |
| 25 | 1996–97 | 56906 | 293.26 | 515 | 4925 | 50.84 | 1032 |
| 26 | 1997–98 | 48743 | 256.26 | 526 | 11546 | 116.61 | 1010 |
| 27 | 1998–99 | 46196 | 309.49 | 670 | 5085 | 60.25 | 1185 |
| 28 | 1999–00 | 61577 | 384.75 | 625 | 7317 | 100.74 | 1377 |
| 29 | 2000–01 | 110573 | 645.51 | 584 | 12168 | 162.99 | 1339 |
| 30 | 2001–02 | 53093 | 296.18 | 558 | 10656 | 94.19 | 884 |
| 31 | 2002–03 | 58846 | 235.17 | 400 | 3506 | 25.86 | 738 |

*Source:* Records of GCC

## Appendix 10 Quantities procured, value and price of tamarind seed, and mohwa seed, 1973–03

| Sr. No. | Year | Tramarind seed | | | Mohwa seed | | |
|---|---|---|---|---|---|---|---|
| | | Quantity (quintals) | Value (Rs. lakhs) | Rate (Rs./ quintal) | Quantity (quintals) | Value (Rs. lakhs) | Rate (Rs./ quintal) |
| 1 | 1972–73 | – | – | – | 2131 | 1.81 | 85 |
| 2 | 1973–74 | – | – | – | 1727 | 1.88 | 109 |
| 3 | 1974–75 | 832 | 0.24 | 29 | 3819 | 5.38 | 141 |
| 4 | 1975–76 | 5940 | 0.80 | 13 | 1965 | 2.90 | 148 |
| 5 | 1976–77 | 8975 | 1.71 | 19 | 3484 | 4.93 | 142 |
| 6 | 1977–78 | 15691 | 3.85 | 25 | 2981 | 5.55 | 186 |
| 7 | 1978–79 | 3957 | 0.90 | 23 | 6801 | 14.28 | 210 |
| 8 | 1979–80 | 9144 | 1.38 | 15 | 2077 | 2.99 | 144 |
| 9 | 1980–81 | 1054 | 0.23 | 22 | 1180 | 2.29 | 194 |
| 10 | 1981–82 | 5057 | 1.65 | 33 | 5820 | 14.48 | 249 |
| 11 | 1982–83 | 9808 | 3.81 | 39 | 3796 | 9.49 | 250 |
| 12 | 1983–84 | 15944 | 5.32 | 33 | 3691 | 10.45 | 284 |
| 13 | 1984–85 | 4584 | 3.42 | 75 | 6503 | 20.73 | 319 |
| 14 | 1985–86 | 11217 | 3.87 | 34 | 3240 | 9.74 | 300 |
| 15 | 1986–87 | 5669 | 2.26 | 40 | 2402 | 7.79 | 324 |
| 16 | 1987–88 | 4430 | 1.25 | 28 | 2217 | 9.97 | 449 |
| 17 | 1988–89 | 4968 | 2.72 | 55 | 3921 | 20.10 | 512 |
| 18 | 1989–90 | 13962 | 7.42 | 53 | 10288 | 51.70 | 503 |
| 19 | 1990–91 | 7633 | 6.12 | 300 | 4129 | 24.77 | 600 |
| 20 | 1991–92 | 11074 | 8.85 | 300 | 12682 | 98.78 | 700 |
| 21 | 1992–93 | 13380 | 11.18 | 300 | 7682 | 53.79 | 700 |
| 22 | 1993–94 | 7358 | 7.10 | 300 | 6790 | 40.99 | 604 |
| 23 | 1994–95 | 8973 | 8.96 | 300 | 3899 | 29.00 | 744 |
| 24 | 1995–96 | 13927 | 23.62 | 300 | 9868 | 69.12 | 700 |
| 25 | 1996–97 | 7101 | 10.64 | 300 | 4071 | 30.46 | 748 |
| 26 | 1997–98 | 4829 | 9.64 | 300 | 11439 | 78.67 | 688 |
| 27 | 1998–99 | 7718 | 15.44 | 200 | 2539 | 25.18 | 992 |
| 28 | 1999–00 | 7586 | 22.83 | 300 | 11934 | 111.41 | 934 |
| 29 | 2000–01 | 14365 | 22.80 | 160 | 9394 | 65.80 | 700 |
| 30 | 2001–02 | 10128 | 18.23 | 180 | 6671 | 40.75 | 611 |
| 31 | 2002–03 | 2765 | 5.53 | 200 | 6252 | 55.07 | 881 |

*Source:* Records of GCC

## Appendix 11 Quantities procured, value and price of mohwa flower, and myrobalans, 1973–03

| *Sr. No.* | *Year* | *Mohwa flower* | | | *Myrobalans* | | |
|---|---|---|---|---|---|---|---|
| | | *Quantity (quintals)* | *Value (Rs. lakhs)* | *Rate (Rs./ quintal)* | *Quantity (quintals)* | *Value (Rs. lakhs)* | *Rate (Rs./ quintal)* |
| 1 | 1972–73 | – | – | – | 20050 | 4.27 | 21 |
| 2 | 1973–74 | 35 | 0.01 | 36 | 12208 | 2.26 | 19 |
| 3 | 1974–75 | 917 | 0.45 | 49 | 6745 | 1.19 | 18 |
| 4 | 1975–76 | 192 | 0.09 | 48 | 8227 | 1.84 | 22 |
| 5 | 1976–77 | 972 | 0.42 | 43 | 8476 | 2.14 | 25 |
| 6 | 1977–78 | 156 | 0.09 | 58 | 11797 | 4.05 | 34 |
| 7 | 1978–79 | 775 | 0.50 | 65 | 13739 | 4.21 | 31 |
| 8 | 1979–80 | 122 | 0.09 | 74 | 9943 | 4.88 | 49 |
| 9 | 1980–81 | 48 | 0.02 | 56 | 13569 | 8.39 | 62 |
| 10 | 1981–82 | 9022 | 9.28 | 103 | 14389 | 10.68 | 74 |
| 11 | 1982–83 | 6636 | 6.61 | 100 | 21010 | 19.81 | 94 |
| 12 | 1983–84 | 11454 | 11.93 | 104 | 15023 | 10.78 | 72 |
| 13 | 1984–85 | 6502 | 20.73 | 319 | 13952 | 9.94 | 71 |
| 14 | 1985–86 | 3240 | 9.74 | 301 | 13165 | 10.46 | 79 |
| 15 | 1986–87 | 6759 | 8.28 | 123 | 12023 | 8.43 | 70 |
| 16 | 1987–88 | 12815 | 18.58 | 145 | 13030 | 8.21 | 62 |
| 17 | 1988–89 | 7462 | 11.14 | 149 | 18447 | 25.06 | 136 |
| 18 | 1989–90 | 13995 | 23.69 | 169 | 17882 | 34.60 | 193 |
| 19 | 1990–91 | 5864 | 11.11 | 189 | 25665 | 62.47 | 243 |
| 20 | 1991–92 | 21263 | 41.60 | 196 | 10291 | 22.53 | 700 |
| 21 | 1992–93 | 9203 | 18.22 | 198 | 5380 | 8.75 | 700 |
| 22 | 1993–94 | 17710 | 42.76 | 241 | 11762 | 24.09 | 700 |
| 23 | 1994–95 | 7024 | 17.14 | 244 | 6775 | 13.70 | 700 |
| 24 | 1995–96 | 13295 | 37.71 | 284 | 16742 | 49.74 | 700 |
| 25 | 1996–97 | 1931 | 5.67 | 294 | 7329 | 23.76 | 700 |
| 26 | 1997–98 | 3474 | 10.16 | 292 | 11812 | 46.80 | 700 |
| 27 | 1998–99 | 364 | 1.37 | 376 | 13664 | 81.03 | 700 |
| 28 | 1999–00 | 12101 | 42.22 | 349 | 18540 | 129.49 | 700 |
| 29 | 2000–01 | 3795 | 17.88 | 471 | 19507 | 100.86 | 517 |
| 30 | 2001–02 | 11360 | 54.37 | 480 | 10685 | 34.80 | 326 |
| 31 | 2002–03 | 10003 | 40.02 | 400 | 12058 | 19.45 | 161 |

*Source:* Records of GCC

## Appendix 12 Quantities procured, value, and price of apiary honey and rock bee honey, 1973–03

| Sr. No. | Year | Apiary honey | | | Rock bee honey | | |
|---|---|---|---|---|---|---|---|
| | | Quantity (quintals) | Value (Rs. lakhs) | Rate (Rs./ quintal) | Quantity (quintals) | Value (Rs. lakhs) | Rate (Rs./ quintal) |
| 1 | 1972–73 | – | – | – | 496 | 1.77 | 357 |
| 2 | 1973–74 | – | – | – | 88 | 0.36 | 409 |
| 3 | 1974–75 | – | – | – | 163 | 0.63 | 387 |
| 4 | 1975–76 | – | – | – | 265 | 1.43 | 540 |
| 5 | 1976–77 | – | – | – | 290 | 1.79 | 617 |
| 6 | 1977–78 | – | – | – | 691 | 5.42 | 784 |
| 7 | 1978–79 | – | – | – | 574 | 3.28 | 571 |
| 8 | 1979–80 | – | – | – | 384 | 2.40 | 625 |
| 9 | 1980–81 | – | – | – | 220 | 1.38 | 627 |
| 10 | 1981–82 | – | – | – | 363 | 3.43 | 945 |
| 11 | 1982–83 | 250 | 2.98 | 1192 | 311 | 3.10 | 997 |
| 12 | 1983–84 | 186 | 2.01 | 1081 | 268 | 2.64 | 985 |
| 13 | 1984–85 | 219 | 2.49 | 1135 | 106 | 1.45 | 874 |
| 14 | 1985–86 | 229 | 2.80 | 1200 | 267 | 2.68 | 1000 |
| 15 | 1986–87 | 527 | 6.68 | 1268 | 228 | 2.14 | 939 |
| 16 | 1987–88 | 433 | 6.82 | 1575 | 334 | 3.43 | 1027 |
| 17 | 1988–89 | 83 | 1.29 | 1554 | 435 | 4.93 | 1133 |
| 18 | 1989–90 | 11 | 0.21 | 1909 | 330 | 4.91 | 1488 |
| 19 | 1990–91 | 38 | 1.04 | 2737 | 488 | 9.80 | 2008 |
| 20 | 1991–92 | 39 | 1.37 | 3513 | 924 | 27.57 | 2984 |
| 21 | 1992–93 | 43 | 1.50 | 3488 | 1428 | 41.93 | 2936 |
| 22 | 1993–94 | 64 | 2.24 | 3500 | 729 | 18.07 | 2479 |
| 23 | 1994–95 | 56 | 2.15 | 3839 | 621 | 18.66 | 3005 |
| 24 | 1995–96 | 69 | 3.53 | 5116 | 1653 | 65.25 | 3947 |
| 25 | 1996–97 | 52 | 2.36 | 4538 | 1557 | 62.53 | 4016 |
| 26 | 1997–98 | 51 | 2.18 | 4275 | 1979 | 77.55 | 3919 |
| 27 | 1998–99 | 11 | 0.47 | 4273 | 973 | 29.77 | 3060 |
| 28 | 1999–00 | 1 | 0.04 | 4000 | 857 | 27.63 | 3224 |
| 29 | 2000–01 | 4 | 0.17 | 4250 | 1991 | 79.61 | 4000 |
| 30 | 2001–02 | 38 | 1.51 | 3974 | 1612 | 66.45 | 4122 |
| 31 | 2002–03 | – | – | – | 2078 | 87.74 | 4222 |

*Source:* Records of GCC

## Appendix 13 Quantities procured, value, and price of soap nuts and pungam seed, 1973–03

| Sr. No. | Year | Soap nuts | | | Pungam seed | | |
|---|---|---|---|---|---|---|---|
| | | *Quantity (quintals)* | *Value (Rs. lakhs)* | *Rate (Rs./ quintal)* | *Quantity (quintals)* | *Value (Rs. lakhs)* | *Rate (Rs./ quintal)* |
| 1 | 1972-73 | 1303 | 1.25 | 96 | 2073 | 1.14 | 55 |
| 2 | 1973-74 | 475 | 0.55 | 116 | 2369 | 1.86 | 79 |
| 3 | 1974-75 | 2152 | 3.71 | 172 | 708 | .73 | 103 |
| 4 | 1975-76 | 827 | 0.71 | 86 | 1414 | 1.31 | 93 |
| 5 | 1976-77 | 310 | 0.28 | 90 | 1304 | 1.00 | 77 |
| 6 | 1977-78 | 1411 | 1.53 | 108 | 1085 | 1.10 | 101 |
| 7 | 1978-79 | 1098 | 1.34 | 122 | 1174 | 1.03 | 88 |
| 8 | 1979-80 | 760 | 1.12 | 147 | 918 | 0.78 | 85 |
| 9 | 1980-81 | 843 | 1.37 | 163 | 674 | 0.72 | 107 |
| 10 | 1981-82 | 669 | 1.03 | 154 | 340 | 0.40 | 118 |
| 11 | 1982-83 | 1550 | 2.32 | 150 | 756 | 1.04 | 137 |
| 12 | 1983-84 | 906 | 1.69 | 187 | 151 | 0.20 | 133 |
| 13 | 1984-85 | 1120 | 2.96 | 264 | 445 | 0.68 | 152 |
| 14 | 1985-86 | 1425 | 5.33 | 374 | 1108 | 1.83 | 165 |
| 15 | 1986-87 | 1821 | 7.32 | 402 | 471 | 0.68 | 144 |
| 16 | 1987-88 | 1288 | 4.52 | 351 | 1610 | 2.86 | 178 |
| 17 | 1988-89 | 2245 | 6.99 | 311 | 606 | 1.29 | 213 |
| 18 | 1989-90 | 3889 | 12.24 | 315 | 1633 | 3.66 | 224 |
| 19 | 1990-91 | 2399 | 9.69 | 404 | 1358 | 4.04 | 297 |
| 20 | 1991-92 | 3566 | 11.84 | 332 | 4454 | 17.33 | 389 |
| 21 | 1992-93 | 3863 | 25.92 | 671 | 1363 | 5.45 | 400 |
| 22 | 1993-94 | 2491 | 17.29 | 694 | 6516 | 24.98 | 383 |
| 23 | 1994-95 | 2783 | 24.55 | 882 | 3121 | 11.08 | 355 |
| 24 | 1995-96 | 1573 | 10.44 | 664 | 6507 | 26.02 | 400 |
| 25 | 1996-97 | 2327 | 17.26 | 742 | 1076 | 4.16 | 387 |
| 26 | 1997-98 | 610 | 4.68 | 767 | 4561 | 16.30 | 357 |
| 27 | 1998-99 | 1054 | 10.13 | 961 | 995 | 3.95 | 397 |
| 28 | 1999-00 | 2185 | 25.69 | 1176 | 3481 | 15.78 | 453 |
| 29 | 2000-01 | 1660 | 20.05 | 1208 | 2607 | 11.72 | 450 |
| 30 | 2001-02 | 2419 | 26.40 | 1091 | 6542 | 29.35 | 450 |
| 31 | 2002-03 | 2564 | 14.62 | 570 | 1946 | 10.17 | 523 |

*Source:* Records of GCC

## Appendix 14 Quantities procured,value, and price of hill brooms and wild brooms, 1973–03

| Sr. No. | Year | Hill brooms | | | Wild brooms | | |
|---|---|---|---|---|---|---|---|
| | | *Quantity (lakhs)* | *Value (Rs. lakhs)* | *Rate (Rs./ 100 pieces)* | *Quantity (lakhs)* | *Value (Rs. lakhs)* | *Rate (Rs./ 100 pieces)* |
| 1 | 1972–73 | 5.04 | 0.87 | 17 | 8.34 | 0.46 | 6 |
| 2 | 1973–74 | 3.85 | 1.06 | 28 | 20.77 | 2.06 | 10 |
| 3 | 1974–75 | 2.42 | 0.68 | 28 | 30.71 | 2.45 | 8 |
| 4 | 1975–76 | 2.09 | 0.84 | 40 | 32.06 | 2.89 | 9 |
| 5 | 1976–77 | 2.30 | 1.37 | 59 | 23.43 | 3.13 | 13 |
| 6 | 1977–78 | 2.73 | 1.65 | 60 | 42.77 | 8.43 | 20 |
| 7 | 1978–79 | 4.62 | 2.22 | 48 | 17.72 | 4.50 | 25 |
| 8 | 1979–80 | 6.25 | 2.52 | 40 | 19.29 | 2.75 | 14 |
| 9 | 1980–81 | 3.16 | 1.38 | 44 | 12.43 | 1.94 | 15 |
| 10 | 1981–82 | 2.95 | 1.24 | 42 | 9.46 | 2.15 | 23 |
| 11 | 1982–83 | 3.82 | 2.10 | 55 | 14.83 | 3.80 | 25 |
| 12 | 1983–84 | 7.02 | 4.48 | 63 | 17.30 | 4.59 | 34 |
| 13 | 1984–85 | 6.01 | 5.64 | 94 | 20.09 | 7.96 | 32 |
| 14 | 1985–86 | 11.54 | 8.76 | 75 | 32.48 | 8.34 | 26 |
| 15 | 1986–87 | 0.86 | 1.94 | 225 | 3.67 | 1.82 | 49 |
| 16 | 1987–88 | 1.81 | 4.83 | 267 | 3.19 | 1.71 | 53 |
| 17 | 1988–89 | 1.01 | 4.91 | 486 | 1.95 | 5.38 | 276 |
| 18 | 1989-90 | 1.41 | 4.54 | 323 | 1.25 | 1.28 | 103 |
| 19 | 1990–91 | 3.01 | 11.18 | 800 | 3.29 | 2.64 | 80 |
| 20 | 1991–92 | 1.85 | 8.36 | 800 | – | – | – |
| 21 | 1992–93 | 0.68 | 2.72 | 800 | – | – | – |
| 22 | 1993–94 | 0.39 | 2.34 | 800 | – | – | – |
| 23 | 1994–95 | 1.23 | 7.19 | 800 | – | – | – |
| 24 | 1995–96 | 2.52 | 19.36 | 800 | 0.02 | 0.19 | 984 |
| 25 | 1996–97 | 3.55 | 27.82 | 800 | 0.01 | 0.15 | 1092 |
| 26 | 1997–98 | 1.15 | 10.10 | 800 | 0.01 | 0.16 | 1046 |
| 27 | 1998–99 | 2.03 | 12.36 | 609 | 0.02 | 0.15 | 925 |
| 28 | 1999–00 | 1.59 | 12.72 | 798 | 0.01 | 0.01 | 1086 |
| 29 | 2000–01 | 1.90 | 16.10 | 848 | 0.00 | 0.04 | 1009 |
| 30 | 2001–02 | 2.43 | 25.15 | 959 | 0.01 | 0.13 | 111 |
| 31 | 2002–03 | 4.37 | 57.82 | 1176 | 0.01 | 0.12 | 1087 |

*Source:* Records of GCC

**Appendix 15 Quantities procured,value, and price of apiary honey and rock bee honey, 1973–03**

| *Sr. No.* | *Year* | *Nuxvomica* | | | *Marking nuts* | | |
|---|---|---|---|---|---|---|---|
| | | *Quantity (quintals)* | *Value (Rs. lakhs)* | *Rate (Rs./ quintal)* | *Quantity (quintals)* | *Value (Rs. lakhs)* | *Rate (Rs./ quintal)* |
| 1 | 1972–73 | 719 | 0.25 | 35 | 751 | 0.06 | 8 |
| 2 | 1973–74 | 1417 | 0.59 | 42 | 309 | 0.02 | 7 |
| 3 | 1974–75 | 3640 | 2.75 | 76 | 320 | 0.03 | 9 |
| 4 | 1975–76 | 3726 | 3.35 | 90 | 41 | 0.01 | 9 |
| 5 | 1976–77 | 2546 | 3.09 | 121 | 271 | 0.03 | 12 |
| 6 | 1977–78 | 4798 | 7.14 | 149 | 154 | 0.02 | 14 |
| 7 | 1978–79 | 1574 | 1.53 | 97 | 154 | 0.02 | 12 |
| 8 | 1979–80 | 3945 | 3.03 | 77 | 41 | 0.01 | 15 |
| 9 | 1980–81 | 1804 | 1.39 | 77 | 150 | 0.02 | 12 |
| 10 | 1981–82 | 7375 | 24.72 | 335 | 155 | 0.01 | 31 |
| 11 | 1982–83 | 2248 | 7.48 | 332 | 149 | 0.06 | 40 |
| 12 | 1983–84 | 708 | 0.74 | 105 | 128 | 0.04 | 31 |
| 13 | 1984–85 | 4588 | 6.65 | 145 | 461 | 0.39 | 85 |
| 14 | 1985–86 | 2057 | 3.08 | 150 | – | – | – |
| 15 | 1986–87 | 1930 | 2.93 | 152 | – | – | – |
| 16 | 1987–88 | 3034 | 5.39 | 178 | – | – | – |
| 17 | 1988–89 | 2769 | 7.44 | 268 | 2134 | 1.91 | 89 |
| 18 | 1989–90 | 6391 | 17.50 | 274 | 4296 | 4.46 | 104 |
| 19 | 1990–91 | 1998 | 3.31 | 166 | 5848 | 5.67 | 97 |
| 20 | 1991–92 | 2452 | 5.92 | 241 | 2295 | 1.83 | 82 |
| 21 | 1992–93 | 5327 | 43.84 | 823 | 878 | 0.63 | 76 |
| 22 | 1993–94 | 5616 | 53.30 | 949 | 1107 | 1.35 | 122 |
| 23 | 1994–95 | 1913 | 9.61 | 502 | 1290 | 1.79 | 139 |
| 24 | 1995–96 | 3443 | 13.73 | 399 | 1779 | 5.08 | 286 |
| 25 | 1996–97 | 1157 | 4.12 | 356 | 8325 | 36.70 | 441 |
| 26 | 1997–98 | 4967 | 18.22 | 367 | 3650 | 9.17 | 251 |
| 27 | 1998–99 | 784 | 2.99 | 381 | 4606 | 13.27 | 288 |
| 28 | 1999–00 | 1312 | 4.53 | 345 | 8379 | 21.64 | 258 |
| 29 | 2000–01 | 1938 | 9.34 | 482 | 7751 | 19.08 | 246 |
| 30 | 2001–02 | 1860 | 10.14 | 545 | 5791 | 11.43 | 200 |
| 31 | 2002–03 | 5399 | 53.35 | 988 | 8108 | 20.05 | 250 |

*Source:* Records of GCC

## Appendix 16 Quantities procured, value, and price of clearing nuts and sheekakai, 1973–03

| Sr. No. | Year | *Cleaning nuts* | | | *Sheekakai* | | |
|---|---|---|---|---|---|---|---|
| | | *Quantity (quintals)* | *Value (Rs. lakhs)* | *Rate (Rs./ quintal)* | *Quantity (quintals)* | *Value (Rs. lakhs)* | *Rate (Rs./ quirtal)* |
| 1 | 1972–73 | 493 | 0.15 | 31 | 553 | 0.43 | 78 |
| 2 | 1973–74 | 378 | 0.11 | 31 | 2012 | 2.27 | 113 |
| 3 | 1974–75 | 125 | 0.04 | 33 | 1468 | 1.13 | 77 |
| 4 | 1975–76 | 58 | 0.02 | 35 | 432 | 0.32 | 74 |
| 5 | 1976–77 | 308 | 0.10 | 35 | 2006 | 1.18 | 59 |
| 6 | 1977–78 | 141 | 0.06 | 46 | 826 | 0.60 | 73 |
| 7 | 1978–79 | 95 | 0.05 | 48 | 2183 | 1.86 | 85 |
| 8 | 1979–80 | 208 | 0.21 | 99 | 232 | 0.31 | 134 |
| 9 | 1980–81 | 677 | 0.73 | 108 | 2810 | 4.27 | 152 |
| 10 | 1981–82 | 417 | 0.51 | 121 | 489 | 0.77 | 157 |
| 11 | 1982–83 | 1173 | 1.76 | 150 | 2028 | 3.98 | 196 |
| 12 | 1983–84 | 545 | 0.86 | 158 | 960 | 1.46 | 152 |
| 13 | 1984–85 | 473 | 0.63 | 133 | 1600 | 3.46 | 216 |
| 14 | 1985–86 | – | – | – | 290 | 1.17 | 390 |
| 15 | 1986–87 | – | – | – | 1825 | 8.25 | 452 |
| 16 | 1987–88 | – | – | – | 276 | 1.04 | 377 |
| 17 | 1988–89 | 764 | 1.54 | 201 | 1888 | 5.19 | 274 |
| 18 | 1989–90 | 1864 | 5.54 | 297 | 1057 | 3.21 | 304 |
| 19 | 1990–91 | 13312 | 59.55 | 400 | 822 | 1.01 | 488 |
| 20 | 1991–92 | 3423 | 19.16 | 400 | 976 | 5.54 | 568 |
| 21 | 1992–93 | 6052 | 47.94 | 400 | 652 | 6.13 | 940 |
| 22 | 1993–94 | 3407 | 28.32 | 400 | 2026 | 29.06 | 1434 |
| 23 | 1994–95 | 353 | 2.36 | 400 | 789 | 10.89 | 1380 |
| 24 | 1995–96 | 1133 | 4.53 | 400 | 673 | 5.38 | 799 |
| 25 | 1996–97 | 496 | 1.99 | 400 | 1299 | 12.21 | 940 |
| 26 | 1997–98 | 254 | 1.01 | 400 | 1149 | 7.95 | 672 |
| 27 | 1998–99 | 153 | 0.61 | 400 | 1843 | 9.08 | 493 |
| 28 | 1999–00 | 1384 | 5.57 | 400 | 1292 | 7.20 | 557 |
| 29 | 2000–01 | 761 | 3.02 | 400 | 1734 | 14.70 | 848 |
| 30 | 2001–02 | 338 | 1.37 | 400 | 2577 | 24.72 | 959 |
| 31 | 2002–03 | 1520 | 12.12 | 800 | 2600 | 30.58 | 1176 |

*Source*: Records of GCC

## Appendix 17

### Quantities procured, value, and price of narmamidi bark and teripods, 1991–03

| Sr. No. | Year | *Narmamidi* | | | *Teripods* | | |
|---|---|---|---|---|---|---|---|
| | | *Quantity (quintals)* | *Value (Rs. lakhs)* | *Rate (Rs./ quintal)* | *Quantity (quintals)* | *Value (Rs. lakhs)* | *Rate (Rs./ quintal)* |
| 1 | 1990–91 | – | – | – | – | – | – |
| 2 | 1991–92 | 5827 | 29.15 | 5 | 50 | 0.25 | 5 |
| 3 | 1992–93 | – | – | – | – | – | – |
| 4 | 1993–94 | 224 | 0.92 | 4.11 | 480 | 4.53 | 9.44 |
| 5 | 1994–95 | 1149 | 6.88 | 5.99 | 202 | 0.91 | 4.50 |
| 6 | 1995–96 | 3158 | 24.40 | 7.73 | 130 | 0.49 | 3.77 |
| 7 | 1996–97 | 7896 | 91.44 | 11.58 | 64 | 0.19 | 2.97 |
| 8 | 1997–98 | 7971 | 93.44 | 11.72 | 63 | 0.13 | 2.06 |
| 9 | 1998–99 | 6022 | 93.49 | 15.52 | 25 | 0.05 | 2.00 |
| 10 | 1999–00 | 6233 | 99.81 | 16.01 | 36 | 0.09 | 2.50 |
| 11 | 2000–01 | 3315 | 62.99 | 19.00 | 87 | 0.19 | 2.18 |
| 12 | 2001–02 | 1079 | 21.58 | 20.00 | 8 | 0.01 | 1.25 |
| 13 | 2002–03 | 8192 | 163.81 | 20.00 | – | – | – |

*Source:* Records of GCC

## Appendix 18

### Quantities procured, value, and price of maredugeddalu and 'others', 1991–03

| *Sr. No.* | *Year* | *Maredugeddalu* | | *Others* | |
|---|---|---|---|---|---|
| | | *Quantity (quintals)* | *Value (Rs. lakhs)* | *Rate (Rs./ quintal)* | *Value (Rs. lakhs)* |
| 1 | 1990–91 | – | – | – | 8.62 |
| 2 | 1991–92 | – | – | – | 42.32 |
| 3 | 1992–93 | – | – | – | 43.70 |
| 4 | 1993–94 | – | – | – | 59.33 |
| 5 | 1994–95 | – | – | – | 54.39 |
| 6 | 1995–96 | – | – | – | 20.64 |
| 7 | 1996–97 | -- | – | – | 29.23 |
| 8 | 1997–98 | 4013 | 57.94 | 14.44 | 16.35 |
| 9 | 1998–99 | 396 | 4.06 | 10.25 | 7.14 |
| 10 | 1999–00 | 378 | 4.48 | – | 43.47 |
| 11 | 2000–01 | 2065 | 28.91 | 14.00 | 70.68 |
| 12 | 2001–02 | 1030 | 15.42 | 14.97 | 96.32 |
| 13 | 2002–03 | 2651 | 44.34 | 16.73 | 78.21 |

*Source:* Records of GCC

## Appendix 19 Trends in total value of agricultural produce procured by GCC, 1991–03

| *Sr. No.* | *Form* | *Intercept* | *Coefficient* | *t-value* | $R^{-2}$ | *F-value* |
|---|---|---|---|---|---|---|
| 1 | Linear | 485.75 | –18.8743 | 1.26 | 0.05 | 1.59 |
| 2 | Semilog | 6.19 | –0.0790 | 1.36 | 0.07 | 1.84 |
| 3 | Double-log | 6.44 | –0.4651 | 1.62 | 0.12 | 2.61 |

*Source:* Estimated

## Appendix 20 Growth in average purchase price of agriculture produce, 1991–03

| *Sr. No.* | *Commodity* | *1990–1991* | *1991–1992* | *1992–1993* | *1993–1994* | *1994–1995* | *1995–1996* | *1996–1997* |
|---|---|---|---|---|---|---|---|---|
| 1 | Cotton | 9.27 | 13.29 | 10.50 | 12.11 | 21.97 | 21.56 | 18.01 |
| 2 | Niger seed | 10.46 | 11.50 | 9.50 | 8.74 | 12.02 | 11.73 | 11.67 |
| 3 | Maize | 1.56 | 3.39 | 3.34 | 2.47 | 3.91 | – | – |
| 4 | Redgram | 8.71 | 9.58 | 8.99 | 8.96 | 12.76 | 15.26 | 11.88 |
| 5 | French beans | 7.78 | 6.05 | 10.38 | 10.92 | 13.71 | 12.37 | 13.27 |
| 6 | Groundnuts | 7.48 | 8.70 | 7.73 | 6.85 | 12.50 | – | – |
| 7 | Jowar | 0.82 | 3.27 | 1.78 | 2.40 | 3.48 | 7.50 | 4.46 |
| 8 | Turmeric | 9.89 | 10.94 | 15.13 | 4.66 | 19.62 | 16.00 | 15.94 |
| 9 | Paddy | 2.03 | 2.91 | 2.75 | 3.68 | 2.77 | – | – |
| 10 | Dry chillies | 8.91 | 19.42 | 8.04 | 12.87 | 21.94 | 31.68 | 27.30 |
| 11 | Cashew nuts | 12.97 | 18.33 | 25.21 | 15.43 | 22.00 | – | 28.18 |
| 12 | Annato seed | 4.85 | 9.96 | 8.00 | – | 10.00 | 36.00 | 27.14 |
| 13 | Others | – | – | – | – | – | – | – |
| 14 | Total | – | – | – | – | – | – | – |

***Contunied Appendix 20***

| *Sr. No.* | *Commodity* | *1997–98* | *1998–99* | *1999–00* | *2000–01* | *2001–02* | *2002–03* |
|---|---|---|---|---|---|---|---|
| 1 | Cotton | 18.39 | 18.82 | 18.20 | 22.30 | – | 16.67 |
| 2 | Niger seed | 11.88 | 12.47 | 16.02 | 15.84 | 12.00 | 14.84 |
| 3 | Maize | – | 3.95 | 4.30 | 3.67 | – | 4.51 |
| 4 | Redgram | 12.26 | 11.01 | 17.14 | 11.63 | 13.82 | 13.02 |
| 5 | French beans | 15.83 | 20.70 | 15.09 | 14.88 | 15.31 | 21.50 |
| 6 | Groundnuts | – | 11.54 | – | – | – | 22.50 |
| 7 | Jowar | 4.17 | 4.57 | 6.09 | 4.34 | 5.00 | 5.00 |
| 8 | Turmeric | 16.67 | 29.22 | – | 21.00 | 34.15 | 30.16 |
| 9 | Paddy | – | 5.00 | 5.84 | 4.87 | 6.15 | 725.11 |
| 10 | Dry chillies | 19.68 | 29.61 | 26.19 | 26.53 | 23.87 | 31.16 |
| 11 | Cashew nuts | – | 0.30 | 40.68 | 38.56 | – | 30.80 |
| 12 | Annato seed | 9.55 | 11.56 | 10.91 | 13.08 | 29.50 | 18.73 |
| 13 | Others | – | – | – | – | – | – |
| 14 | Total | – | – | – | – | – | – |

*Source:* Records of GCC

## Appendix 21 Growth in supply of domestic requirements (Rs. lakhs), 1981–03

| *S. No.* | *Year* | *Rice* | *Sugar* | *Salt* | *Edible oils* | *Kerosene oil* | *Others* | *Total* |
|---|---|---|---|---|---|---|---|---|
| 1 | 1980–81 | | | | | | | 490.45 |
| 2 | 1981–82 | | | | | | | 667.96 |
| 3 | 1982–83 | | | | | | | 704.63 |
| 4 | 1983–84 | | | | | | | 948.12 |
| 5 | 1984–85 | | | | | | | 1206.18 |
| 6 | 1985–86 | | | | | | | 1186.28 |
| 7 | 1986–87 | 1041.15 | 142.76 | 7.21 | 161.39 | 99.04 | 159.32 | 1610.87 |
| 8 | 1987–88 | 1393.00 | 203.28 | 8.77 | 223.99 | 128.60 | 255.83 | 2213.47 |
| 9 | 1988–89 | 1537.84 | 243.70 | 6.61 | 359.08 | 140.72 | 351.83 | 2639.78 |
| 10 | 1989–90 | 1849.02 | 299.94 | 11.66 | 129.73 | 178.77 | 583. 34 | 3052.46 |
| 11 | 1990–91 | 2118.00 | 304.91 | 14.47 | 174.95 | 267.71 | 724.14 | 3604.18 |
| 12 | 1991–92 | 2070.75 | 399.04 | 20.84 | 190.62 | 246.26 | 1109.89 | 4037.40 |
| 13 | 1992–93 | 2545.70 | 465.33 | 12.28 | 159.86 | 256.00 | 851.33 | 4290.50 |
| 14 | 1993–94 | 2774.86 | 459.62 | 10.64 | 104.06 | 293.54 | 1106.88 | 4749.60 |
| 15 | 1994–95 | 2661.92 | 468.50 | 11.76 | 119.55 | 255.16 | 982.91 | 4499.80 |
| 16 | 1995–96 | 2013.90 | 457.21 | 28.15 | 189.90 | 292.55 | 921.90 | 3902.91 |
| 17 | 1996–97 | 2582.97 | 570.32 | 20.36 | 242.56 | 311.07 | 1093.14 | 4820.42 |
| 18 | 1997–98 | 3034.64 | 699.29 | 23.63 | 218.56 | 363.05 | 1164.40 | 5503.44 |
| 19 | 1998–99 | 3405.81 | 709.96 | 26.31 | 334.16 | 390.91 | 1378.79 | 6245.94 |
| 20 | 1999–00 | 3110.22 | 765.41 | 41.05 | 226.03 | 444.96 | 1513.58 | 6101.25 |
| 21 | 2000–01 | 3986.28 | 779.09 | 31.54 | 219.06 | 809.89 | 1927.58 | 7753.43 |
| 22 | 2001–02 | 3535.05 | 567.80 | 48.03 | 257.34 | 910.14 | 1850.02 | 7128.38 |
| 23 | 2002–03 | 3363.47 | 369.93 | 38.87 | 382.14 | 1280.53 | 2570.41 | 8005.35 |

*Source:* Records of GCC

## Appendix 22 Trends in credit operations of GCC, 1991–03

| *S. No.* | *Indicator* | *Intercept* | *Coefficient* | *t-value* | $R^{-2}$ | *F-value* |
|---|---|---|---|---|---|---|
| 1 | Borrowers | | | | | |
| | Linear | 43872.08 | –3126.36* | –2.20 | 0.24 | 4.83 |
| | Semilog | 4.57 | –0.0526* | –2.56 | 0.32 | 6.54 |
| | Double-log | 4.54 | –0.4451 | –1.63 | 0.12 | 2.66 |
| 2 | Amount disbursed | | | | | |
| | Linear | 781.72 | –39.7968 | –1.68 | 0.13 | 2.83 |
| | Semilog | 2.80 | –0.0251 | –1.28 | 0.05 | 1.63 |
| | Double-log | 2.73 | –0.1394 | –0.57 | –0.06 | 0.33 |
| 3 | Recovery | | | | | |
| | Linear | 383.69 | –6.7537 | –0.53 | –0.06 | 0.29 |
| | Semilog | 2.44 | 0.0047 | 0.25 | –0.08 | 0.06 |
| | Double-log | 2.31 | 0.2092 | 0.99 | –0.02 | 0.98 |
| 4 | Loan amount/borower | | | | | |
| | Linear | 1553.08 | 170.9451** | 3.72 | 0.52 | 13.84 |
| | Semilog | 3.23 | 0.0275** | 3.83 | 0.53 | 14.70 |
| | Double-log | 3.19 | 0.3057** | 3.41 | 0.47 | 11.66 |

*Source:* Estimated

## Appendix 23

### Trends in demand, collection and balance of short-term loans (principal and interest) (Rs. lakhs), 1991–03

| *Sr. No.* | *Year* | *Demand* *Arrear* | *Current* | *Total* | *Recovery (collection)* | *Balance* | *% of recovery* |
|---|---|---|---|---|---|---|---|
| 1 | 1990–91 | 0.00 | 160.45 | 160.45 | 75.18 | 85.27 | 46.86 |
| 2 | 1991–92 | 85.27 | 648.45 | 733.72 | 3223.97 | 409.75 | 44.15 |
| 3 | 1992–93 | 409.75 | 1448.58 | 1858.33 | 731.55 | 1126.78 | 39.37 |
| 4 | 1993–94 | 1126.78 | 1148.57 | 2275.35 | 1327.42 | 947.93 | 58.34 |
| 5 | 1994–95 | 947.93 | 757.28 | 1705.21 | 344.77 | 1360.44 | 20.22 |
| 6 | 1995–96 | 1360.44 | 573.00 | 1933.44 | 309.04 | 1624.40 | 15.98 |
| 7 | 1996–97 | 1624.40 | 229.63 | 1854.03 | 201.28 | 1652.75 | 10.86 |
| 8 | 1997–98 | 1652.75 | 287.13 | 1939.88 | 173.66 | 1766.22 | 8.95 |
| 9 | 1998–99 | 1766.22 | 390.31 | 2156.53 | 249.73 | 1906.70 | 11.58 |
| 10 | 1999-00 | 1906.70 | 493.93 | 2400.63 | 190.94 | 2209.69 | 7.95 |
| 11 | 2000–01 | 2209.69 | 502.45 | 2712.14 | 239.25 | 2472.89 | 8.82 |
| 12 | 2001–02 | 2472.89 | 322.88 | 2795.77 | 165.55 | 2630.22 | 5.92 |
| 13 | 2002–03 | 2630.22 | 256.79 | 2887.01 | 57.35 | 2829.66 | 1.99 |

*Source:* Records of GCC

## Appendix 24

### Other loans disbursed by GCC (Rs. lakhs), 1991–03

| *Sr. No.* | *Year* | *Medium term* | *Consumption* | *SHGs* | *Others* |
|---|---|---|---|---|---|
| 1 | 1990–91 | 0.00 | 0.00 | 0.00 | 0.00 |
| 2 | 1991–92 | 66.45 | 102.81 | 6.80 | 0.70 |
| 3 | 1992–93 | 78.95 | 27.47 | 19.34 | 4.65 |
| 4 | 1993–94 | 103.20 | 7.19 | 7.51 | 2.22 |
| 5 | 1994–95 | 19.35 | 0.00 | 0.00 | 1.40 |
| 6 | 1995–96 | 0.00 | 0.00 | 0.00 | 2.70 |
| 7 | 1996–97 | 304.0 | 0.00 | 0.00 | 0.00 |
| 8 | 1997–98 | – | – | – | – |
| 9 | 1998–99 | 76.30 | – | – | – |
| 10 | 1999–00 | – | – | – | – |
| 11 | 2000–01 | – | – | – | – |
| 12 | 2001–02 | – | – | – | – |
| 13 | 2002–03 | 1.76 | – | – | – |

*Source:* Records of GCC

## Appendix 25 Sanctioned and existing staff in the division and GPCMSs of Bhadrachalam division as on 30.11.03

| *Sr. No.* | *Post* | *Society* | | | | | | | |
|---|---|---|---|---|---|---|---|---|---|
| | | *Divisional office* | | *Bhadrachalam* | | *Chintur* | | *Venkatapuram* | |
| | | *Sanctioned* | *Existing* | *Sanctioned* | *Existing* | *Sanctioned* | *Existing* | *Sanctioned* | *Existing* |
| 1 | Divisional manager | 1 | 1 | – | – | – | – | – | – |
| 2 | Senior manager | – | 1 | 1 | 1 | – | 1 | 1 | – |
| 3 | Junior manager | 2 | – | 1 | – | 1 | – | 1 | 1 |
| 4 | Senior assistant | 2 | 3 | 4 | 3 | 4 | 2 | 4 | 2 |
| 5 | Junior assistant | 2 | 4 | 2 | 1 | 1 | 2 | 2 | 1 |
| 6 | CCPAs | – | – | 6 | 3 | 6 | 4 | 7 | 5 |
| 7 | Jr. Acct./DEO | 1 | 1 | 1 | – | 1 | 1 | 1 | – |
| 8 | Jr. typist | 1 | – | – | – | – | – | – | – |
| 9 | H.V. driver | – | – | 1 | 1 | 1 | 1 | 1 | 1 |
| 10 | L.V. driver | 1 | 1 | 1 | – | 1 | – | 1 | 1 |
| 11 | Lory cleaner | – | – | 1 | 1 | 1 | – | 1 | – |
| 12 | Attenders | 1 | 1 | 1 | – | 1 | – | 1 | 1 |
| 13 | Salesman | – | 2 | 11 | 9 | 14 | 9 | 21 | 14 |
| 14 | MCWs | – | 3 | 11 | 9 | 13 | 8 | 21 | 6 |
| | Total | 11 | 17 | | 25 | | 27 | | 32 |

***Continued Appendix 25***

| Sr. No. | Post | Society | | | | | |
|---|---|---|---|---|---|---|---|
| | | Palwancha | | Yellandu | | Dammapeta | |
| | | Sanction-ed | Exist-ing | Sanction-ed | Exist-ing | Sanction-ed | Exist-ing |
| 1 | Divisional manager | – | – | – | – | – | – |
| 2 | Senior manager | 1 | 1 | 1 | – | 1 | 1 |
| 3 | Junior manager | 1 | – | 1 | 1 | 1 | – |
| 4 | Senior assistant | 4 | 3 | 4 | 4 | 4 | 1 |
| 5 | Junior assistant | 2 | 2 | 2 | 1 | 2 | 2 |
| 6 | CCPAs | 7 | 3 | 5 | 3 | 6 | 3 |
| 7 | Jr. Acct./DEO | 1 | 1 | 1 | – | 1 | 1 |
| 8 | Jr. typist | – | – | – | – | – | – |
| 9 | H.V. driver | 1 | 2 | 1 | 2 | 1 | 1 |
| 10 | L.V. driver | 1 | 1 | 1 | 1 | 1 | 1 |
| 11 | Lorry cleaner | 1 | 2 | 1 | – | 1 | – |
| 12 | Attenders | 1 | 1 | 1 | – | 1 | – |
| 13 | Salesman | 19 | 16 | 33 | 28 | 29 | 26 |
| 14 | MCWs | 19 | 12 | 33 | 11 | 29 | 10 |
| | Total | | 41 | | 48 | | 44 |

***Continued Appendix 25***

| Sr. No. | Post | Society | | | | | |
|---|---|---|---|---|---|---|---|
| | | Manuguru | | Kukunoor | | Total | |
| | | Sanction-ed | Exist-ing | Sanction-ed | Exist-ing | Sanction-ed | Exist-ing |
| 1 | Divisional manager | – | – | – | – | 1 | 1 |
| 2 | Senior manager | – | – | – | – | 5 | 4 |
| 3 | Junior manager | 1 | 1 | 1 | – | 10 | 4 |
| 4 | Senior assistant | 4 | 2 | 4 | 1 | 34 | 18 |
| 5 | Junior assistant | 1 | 2 | 1 | 1 | 15 | 15 |
| 6 | CCPAs | 4 | 3 | 4 | 1 | 46 | 25 |
| 7 | Jr. Acct./DEO | 1 | 1 | 1 | 1 | 9 | 1 |
| 8 | Jr. typist | – | – | – | – | 1 | – |
| 9 | H.V. driver | 1 | 1 | 1 | 1 | 8 | 5 |
| 10 | L.V. driver | 1 | – | 1 | – | 9 | 5 |
| 11 | Lorry cleaner | 1 | – | 1 | – | 8 | 3 |
| 12 | Attenders | – | 1 | 1 | – | 9 | 4 |
| 13 | Salesman | 12 | 12 | 9 | 8 | 147 | 124 |
| 14 | MCWs | 12 | 7 | 9 | 2 | 147 | 65 |
| | Total | | 26 | | 16 | 347 | 274 |

*Source:* Records of the division

# Appendix 26 Scheme of establishment of grain banks in tribal villages

## Introduction

Indebtedness among tribals is a common phenomenon, which arises from the fact that most tribals live at the level of bare subsistence and own very few assets. Any outward situation resulting from crop failure or other natural calamities or events like illness, death, marriage, etc. adversely affects economic position of tribals leading to an unending debt trap. Because of poor cushioning, any interruption in the day-to-day wage earning situation immediately affects nutritional status of tribal families and fall in nutritional standards affects the most vulnerable sections (children, especially infants, and pregnant and lactating mothers). This lowers their resistance to disease, and infection. Besides tribals, SCs, and others living below the poverty line in remote and backward tribal areas also fall prey to this situation. By the time information reaches administration, it is often too late for these vulnerable sections. As a result, these have been reports, from time to time, about deaths of tribals in general and children of poor tribal families in particular.

The central planning committee for preventive measures against deaths of children in remote and backward areas has found May to September as the lean agricultural period which happens to be monsoon season. During this period, daily wage earners in tribal areas often fall ill or otherwise unable to go out for work. Supply of essential commodities to the remote areas has a tendency to fall during heavy rains. Left with no choice tribals dependent on minor forest produce. Thus, it is necessary to have un-interrupted availability of food grains to these families throughout the year. The concept of grain golas (banks) is 'contribution of entire community from which a needy family can draw grains in need'.

## Objective and coverage

The main objective of the scheme is to provide a safeguard against fall in nutritional standards of STs living in remote rural areas. It also seeks to inculcate amongst STs habit of self help with a view to take care of their basic requirements. A grain bank can be established in any village having over 50% tribal population. To begin with, 13 states (Andhra Pradesh, Bihar, Gujarat, Kerla, Madhya Pradesh, Manipur, Orissa, Rajasthan, Tamil Nadu, Uttar Pradesh, West Bengal, Tripura, and Maharashtra) are identified for this purpose. As per the circular, village will be identified by the concerned states according to maximum and acute poverty of ST population.

Grain banks will primarily be meant for STs families. However, SC families living in these villages could also be made members, if they wish. One quintal of local grain/member family will be contributed to the grain bank by the central government through TRIFED. The scheme would be implemented by a working committee consisting to traditional tribal head man of each village. BDO of concerned block, project officer (ITDP), and District Magistrate of the concerned district. The scheme may also be implemented through NGOs of repute working in tribal areas. Ministry of Tribal Affairs of the Government of India will be the nodal agency at the central and would be implemented through TRIFED.

### Implementation of the scheme

Identification of village, formation of working committees, and organising meetings with ST population to participate in the scheme form part of implementation. Working committee may have upto 7 members depending upon the strength of membership of grain bank. In case there is no traditional village head man, chairman of the village committee will be elected by the members of the working committee. Other members of the committee will be elected by entire tribal population of the village. Atleast 2 seats of the membership shall be reserved for women. If SC families are also participating, one member of the working committee may be an SC. The village committee will be given Rs. 2000 for purchasing weights and balance, and another Rs. 2000 will be for arranging storage facilities. Grant of grains at the rate of one quintal of grian/member family will be made available by state TDCCs/ Corporations.

Member-families of the grain bank will be entitled to take loans of food grians in four installments upto 25 kgs each during rainy season or in other period of scarcity. The loans will be repaid with interest at the time of next harvest, thereby recouping the stock. The type of grain to be repaid would be the same as the type of grain loaned. There will be an interest to the maximum of 10% of the loan taken. If the stock is repaid within three months, interest will be 5% and for period beyond three months and upto six months, interest will be 10%. If no repayment in made within six months, membership of the individual or family would lapse, but it can be revived if repayment is made subsequently.

## Supervision

The project officer (ITDP) with the help of BDO of concerned block will not only take initiative in setting up the grain banks but also monitor, and supervise the progress. After village committee have been set up, project officer will arrange purchase of food grains from the nearest public distribution system to the tune of one quintal/member family for every grain bank and its transportation to the concerned village within the allocated financial ceiling. It was proposed to start the scheme from 1996–97 @ Rs. 61,000/grain bank. The scheme would be launched in 703 villages in the first year. The entire cost/grain bank would be one-time grant, with no recurring expenditure. Unit cost of setting up a grain bank is given below.

## Grain banks in Andhra Pradesh

Government of Andhra Pradesh has sanctioned 56 grain banks for benefit of 2181 tribal families with an amount of Rs. 14.56 lakhs in Paderu ITDA. Villages have already been identified in 11 mandals of agency in July 2002, and the work of constituting working committee and establishment of grain banks is in progress.

## Appendix 26 Unit cost of grain bank recurring

| *Sr. No.* | *Particulars* | *Amount Rs.* |
|---|---|---|
| 1 | Cost of 100 quintal of food grains @ Rs. 6/kg. | 60000.00 |
| 2 | Grant for purchase of weights and banace | 2000.00 |
| 3 | Grant for storage facilities | 2000.00 |
| | Total | 64000.00 |

*Source:* Department of budgets (2002)

## Appendix 27 Growth in membership, share capital, and turnover of Chintapalli GPCMS, 1991–03

| *Sr. No.* | *Year* | *Membership* | *Share capital (Rs. lakhs)* | *Turnover (Rs. lakhs)* |
|---|---|---|---|---|
| 1 | 1990-91 | 10210 | 0.44 | 142.25 |
| 2 | 1991-92 | 10850 | 0.67 | 157.88 |
| 3 | 1992-93 | 11340 | 0.84 | 102.83 |
| 4 | 1993-94 | 11540 | 1.68 | 124.72 |
| 5 | 1994-95 | 11964 | 1.74 | 122.25 |
| 6 | 1995-96 | 12012 | 1.87 | 119.8 |
| 7 | 1996-97 | 12012 | 1.87 | 151.56 |
| 8 | 1997-98 | 12012 | 1.99 | 173.28 |
| 9 | 1998-99 | 12013 | 1.99 | 174.5 |
| 10 | 1999-00 | 12013 | 2.00 | 201.16 |
| 11 | 2000-01 | 12013 | 2.00 | 272.32 |
| 12 | 2001-02 | 12013 | 2.01 | 209.68 |
| 13 | 2002-03 | 12013 | 2.61 | 253.12 |

*Source:* Records of GPCMS

## Appendix 28 Sources of income for GPCMS

| *Sr. No.* | *Item* | *Percentage or Rs./quintal* |
|---|---|---|
| 1 | Commission on procurement of MFP (%) | 3.0 |
| 2 | Commission on procurement of agricultural produce (%) | 2.0 |
| 3 | Mandal level stockiest commission (Rs./quintal ) | |
| | a. Rice | 5.90 |
| | b. Sugar | 5.15 |
| 4 | Mandal level stockiest transport charges | |
| | a. Upto first 8 kms. (Rs./quintal) | 5.05 |
| | b. Beyond 8 kms. (Rs./quintal) | 0.19 |
| 5 | Margin on essential commodities | |
| | a. Rice (Rs./quintal) | 12.92 |
| | b. Sugar (Rs./quintal) | 15.53 |
| | c. Kerosene (Rs./litre) | 0.12 |
| 6 | Commission on food for work scheme (Rs./quintal) | 7.00 |
| 7 | Transport charges on food for work scheme | |
| | a. Upto first 8 kms. (Rs./quintal) | 5.05 |
| | b. Beyond 8 kms. (Rs./quintal) | 0.19 |
| 8 | Margin on sale of other daily requirements (%) | 5 |
| 9 | Margin on rice supplied to hostels (Rs./quintal) | 14.38 |
| 10 | Sale of empty gunny bags (Rs./bag) | 4.00 |
| 11 | Commission on loans recovered (%) | 2 |
| 12 | Grant towards salaries | 60%* |

*Currently all the societies are given upto 60% of wage bill by GCC
*Source:* Records of GPCMS

## Appendix 29 Availability of rice on various cards/family

| *Sr. No.* | *Type* | *Rice* | |
|---|---|---|---|
| | | *Quantity (kgs.)* | *Price (Rs./kg)* |
| 1 | Pink | 4 kgs./member (subject to maximum of 20 kgs./family) | 9.00 |
| 2 | White | 4 kgs./member (subject to maximum of 20 kgs./family) | 5.25 |
| 3 | Antyodaya | 35 | 3.00 |

*Source:* Records of GPCMS

## Appendix 30 Probable difficulties in the management of GPCMs

| *Activity* 1 | *Existing system* 2 | *Possibilities* 3 | *Outcome* 4 | *Remarks* 5 |
|---|---|---|---|---|
| **1 Procurement** | | | | |
| Over-billing | Tribals bring their items to shadies to sell them to GPCMS. They are to be paid price as per the grade or quality and quantity. For example<br>Grade Price<br>G1 120<br>G2 100<br>G3 80 | It is possible that an item of higher grade is accounted at a lower grade and paid accordingly. However, actual billing is done for higher grade. For example, the item brought to GCC may be grade 1 but the tribal is paid only Rs. 100/unit as against actual of Rs. 120 and the bill may be prepared as for grade 1 | Tribal is paid less, without benefiting GCC, and difference is retained by concerned | This occurs due to lack of awareness on the part of tribal as he/she is illiterate. In order to overcome this flaw, general awareness has to improve. We can also tackle this by suitably introducing a system by which some sort of colour coding may be given for the bills issued for respective grades, where tribal understands rate at which he/she is to be paid. The tribal may also be asked to sign/put his thumb impression on counter foil |

| *1* | *2* | *3* | *4* | *5* |
|---|---|---|---|---|
| Weighment | There are instances of under weighment upto 5–10% | The tribal is paid less amount but GCC is billed for higher amount | While the tribal gets lower compensation, GCC pays higher amount | It is generally found that in majority of items handled by GCC, quantity can be ascertained by volume, and rates fixed accordingly. As for other items, like addaleaves and tamarind, appropriate weighing methods are to be adopted |
| Range of price | In case of agricultural produce, GCC declares a range of price for procurement to compete with private traders. This is supposed to give CCPAs some flexibility to meet the market rates | Since price has a range, it is possible that trible is paid minimum price of the range whereas GCC is billed for higher price from the range | While tribal gets lower compensation, GCC pays higher amount | |
| Encouraging private traders | In each society there are points/shandies | Instead of visiting the shandies, it is possible that | Tribal gets lower compensation where- | 10–15 society members to form a group and monitor |

| 1 | 2 | 3 | 4 | 5 |
|---|---|---|---|---|
| | for procurement of MFP/AP | at the end of the month procurement is done from private traders to meet target at rates less than the declared prices | as GCC pays a much higher amount. Difference gets pocketed by private parties and CCPAs. In the ultimate analysis, tribal has no direct interaction with GCC. Possibility is much higher where the procurement is done exclusively by private traders | society's activities in their area, and if necessary leader of the group brings to notice of the manager |
| **2 DR depots** Purchasing other DRs | Based on the indents raised by DR depots, other DRs are being purchased every month by respective divisional managers | Having some sort of understanding with supplies of other DR items, DRs are supplied at a price higher than actual price or poor quality items are accepted | GCC again is paying higher than the actual market price, and accepting supply of poor quality items | Requirements by depots can be ascertained well in advance and purchasing can be done in bulk by calling tenders at the head office for supply of DR items to divisions/societies. For the |

| 1 | 2 | 3 | 4 | 5 |
|---|---|---|---|---|
| | | | | transportation of these items, either the supplier can be asked or may be transported by vehicles available at divisional office |
| Sale point | Sale of essential and other DR items are being done as per the needs of tribals | Weighment of rice, kerosene, etc. are not being done properly. There is around 3–5% variation being noticed but collection is being done for full. Essential commodities may be diverted into the outside market | Reducing sales turnover, loosing confidence on GCC, etc. | Supervision is required on salesmen's activities |
| Depots timings | Depots are expected to be kept open as per predetermined schedule decided by the manager | Some of the depots are not opened for days together and sometimes not being opened at all during a week | Decrease in sales turnover | Sudden visits to depots |

*Continued*

| 1 | 2 | 3 | 4 | 5 |
|---|---|---|---|---|
| **3 Credit** | | | | |
| Selection of loanees and loan disbursed | Selection of loanees is being done by CCPA by visiting villages under his jurisdiction. While selecting loanees, past record of loanees and their repayment ability are considered and loan is given as per GCC rules | Some of the beneficiaries are non-existent, and loans are given on by namee names | Real beneficiaries are not able to avail credit facilities due to this practice. Loans are not recovered resulting in a loss of capital | Suggested to maintain case history of individual and counsel them from time to time |
| Loan recovery | GCC officials are expected to visit villages for recovery of loan. Invariably they do not visit villages | The records are not updated resulting in default. At times, receipts are not issued for amounts received, resulting in a loss to GCC | Beneficiaries are losing confidence on GCC, and shown as defaulters | Manager has to review weekly schedule of all society staff and also collect feedback from tribals |
| **4 Godowns** | | | | |
| | MFP/AP, ECs, and | While receiving stocks a | CCPAs have to | While bringing awareness on |

| 1 | 2 | 3 | 4 | 5 |
|---|---|---|---|---|
| | DR items are being stored in godowns which are located at society/divisional office | high quantity is being compensated towards dryage resulting in 1 to 2% loss to GCC. Similarly, in dispatches of ECs quantity being dispatched is less than the actuals. Difference is being sold to outsiders which is around 2% | make up for these differences by other means resulting in bad practices. As a result, salesman is delivered less quantity forcing him too to adopt poor weighment practices | allowances for dryage, it is also suggested that standards for individual items may be evolved and applied accordingly |
| **5 Check post** | | | | |
| | GCC is having monopoly rights on procurement of 25 MFPs. To avoid smuggl-ingGCC has check points at various key positions within their society's jurisdiction. Check post employee is to check all the vehicles which are passing through check post | Vehicles are allowed to go through check posts without verification. Possibilities of ceased items not being reported to GCC also exist | GCC is loosing heavy amount at this point. It will be around one lakh particularly add-aleafs, hill brooms, tamarind, amla etc. | At present measurers are looking check posts. It is suggested to keep salesman cadre employees to avoid pressure from outsiders. It is suggested to keep check point at sales depot or near to the society whichever is convenient |

*Source*: Ramanan (2003)

## Appendix 31 Various stages in procurement and marketing of MFPs

| *Sr. No.* | *Commodity* | *Stages* |
|---|---|---|
| 1 | Addaleaf | Leaf cutting, gathering of leaves from ground, bundling leaves, drying, storing, cutting of stem, storing, bundling, and marketing. |
| 2 | Gum karaya | Blazing, gathering, cleaning, drying, grading, storing, and marketing. |
| 3 | Cleaning nuts | Shaking the branches/felling, gathering fruits from ground, washing and pounding, drying, storing, and marketing. |
| 4 | Rock bee honey | Locating honey combs in the forest, emitting smoke, gathering, cleaning/cutting wax, boiling honey, storing honey, and marketing. |
| 5 | Myrobalans | Shaking branches/felling, gathering fruits from ground, drying, storing, and marketing. |
| 6 | Mohwa flower | Felling/shaking branches, gathering flowers from ground, drying, storing, and marketing. |
| 7 | Mohwa seed | Searching tree and shaking branches, gathering, drying, cleaning skull, storing, cleaning after drying, drying, storing, and marketing. |
| 8 | Narmamidi bark | Cutting bark, gathering bark, drying, storing, and marketing. |
| 9 | Nuxvomica | Shaking branches, gathering fruits from ground, separating seeds from the fruit, rubbing seeds with dust, washing seeds with water, drying, storing, and marketing. |
| 10 | Seeded tamarind | Shaking branches/felling, gathering fruits from ground, drying, removing shell, rubbing with water, storing, and marketing. |

| | | |
|---|---|---|
| 11 | Hill brooms | Cutting grass, gathering grass, drying, cleaning, broom making, storing, and marketing. |
| 12 | Wild brooms | Cutting sticks, gathering sticks, drying, cleaning, broom making, storing and marketing. |
| 13 | Gum olibanum | Blazing, gathering, cleaning, drying, grading, storing, and marketing. |
| 14 | Sheekakai | Searching trees and plucking fruits, gathering and putting into bag or baskets, drying in front of house, storing, cleaning fruit, and marketing. |
| 15 | Marking nuts | Felling fruits, gathering, sorting out seeds, drying, storing, and marketing. |
| 16 | Pungam seed | Felling, gathering, drying, storing, cleaning shells, and marketing. |
| 17 | Rauwolfia serpentina | Digging the roots, gathering, drying, storing, and marketing. |
| 18 | Soapnuts | Felling fruits/shaking branches, gathering, drying, storing, and marketing. |

*Source:* Field visits

# Index

Table 4 Growth (Rs. lakhs) in procurement of agricultural produce in Chintapalli GPCMS: 1991–[illegible]

| Sl. No. | Year | [illegible] seed | [illegible] seed | [illegible] beans | [illegible] | [illegible] | Total |
|---|---|---|---|---|---|---|---|
| [illegible] | [illegible] | [illegible] | [illegible] | [illegible] | [illegible] | [illegible] | [illegible] |

Source: Records of the GPCMS